European
Vacation

AVALON
TRAVEL

European Vacation Rentals
First Edition
Steenie Harvey

Published by Avalon Travel Publishing
1400 65th Street, Suite 250, Emeryville, CA 94608, USA

Text © 2003 by Steenie Harvey.
Maps © 2003 by Avalon Travel Publishing, Inc.
   All rights reserved.
Some photos and illustrations are used by permission
   and are the property of the original copyright owners.

Printed in China through Colorcraft Ltd., Hong Kong

ISSN 1536-2736
ISBN 1-56691-567-8

Please send all
comments, corrections, additions,
amendments, and critiques to:

European Vacation Rentals
Avalon Travel Publishing
1400 65th Street, Suite 250
Emeryville, CA 94608, USA
email: info@travelmatters.com
website: www.travelmatters.com

Printing History
1st edition—January 2003
5 4 3 2 1

Editor: Kate Willis
Copy Editor: Leslie Miller
Graphics: Melissa Sherowski
Design & Production: Amber Pirker
Map Editors: Mike Balsbaugh, Naomi Adler Dancis, Olivia Solís
Cartographers: Kat Kalamaras, Mike Morgenfeld
Index: Leslie Miller

Front cover photo: © Nik Wheeler
Back cover photos: © Steenie Harvey

Photo on page 1: Steenie Harvey; photo on page 5: Wonderful Copenhagen; photo on page 17: Steenie Harvey; photo on page 19: Steenie Harvey; photo on page 39: Steenie Harvey; photo on page 59: Steenie Harvey; photo on page 61: Steenie Harvey; photo on page 81: Steenie Harvey; photo on page 127: Steenie Harvey; photo on page 140: Steenie Harvey; photo on page 149: Steenie Harvey; photo on page 151: Steenie Harvey; photo on page 169: Steenie Harvey; photo on page 189: Steenie Harvey; photo on page 191: Steenie Harvey; photo on page 211: Steenie Harvey; photo on page 229: Wonderful Copenhagen; photo on page 231: Wonderful Copenhagen; photo on page 255: Steenie Harvey

Distributed by Publishers Group West

Contents

GERMANY, AUSTRIA, AND SWITZERLAND

ITALY, GREECE, CYPRUS, AND MALTA

SPAIN AND PORTUGAL

Acknowledgments

For my ever-patient husband Michael who endures my black moods and tantrums when the words look like gobbledygook. For my darlin' daughter Maggie for the endless tea and chit-chat. For my editor at Avalon, Kate Willis, who keeps me afloat with all her good cheer and encouragement. A heartfelt thanks to you all.

And a dedication to my grandchildren whose happy little faces make me remember that there's more to life than work. Thomas, twins Harry and Paddy, Cassie, Tara and Jack—bless you.

PART I

Introduction

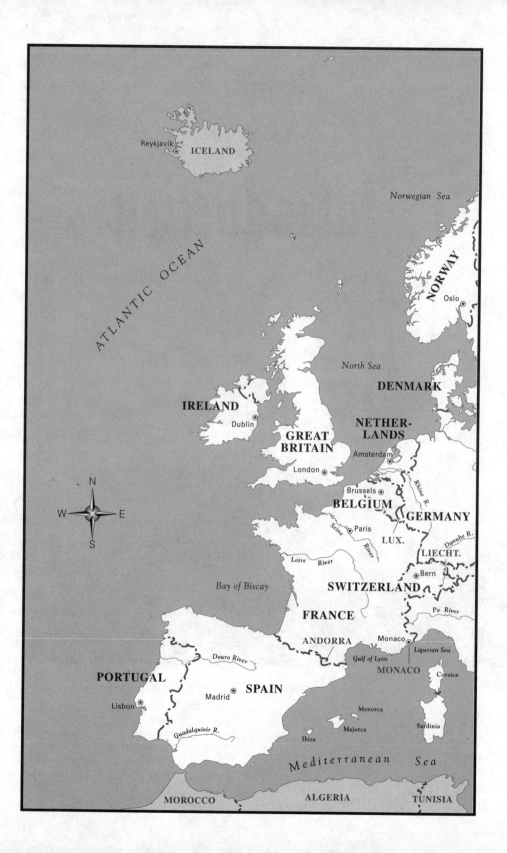

1 Renting in Europe

Most travelers are curious about the way other people live, but here's the thing—you'll get few insights if you always stay in hotels. Even if it's only for a short while, wouldn't you like to feel as if you belong to one of Europe's great cities? Or to be on first-name terms with the locals in a medieval village where the tourist coaches never go?

If so, you should do what many Europeans do—rent your way around this fascinating continent. For those of you who value your freedom, there's simply no better way to go. Yes, you need to be an independent spirit with a sense of adventure, but I would guess that probably describes you. Why else are you reading this book?

Maybe you're looking for the perfect place to spend your vacation, or thinking about moving to Europe for work purposes? Or maybe you're an active retiree with time on your hands? Maybe you simply want to try something different. Whatever the reason, there's something immensely satisfying about getting hold of a proper front door key and living in a real neighborhood. There are financial benefits too—renting a house or an apartment almost always works out cheaper than a hotel stay.

Why Rent?

To cite one example: a springtime trip to the trapped-in-a-time-warp Belgian city of Bruges. I rented a small apartment in the very center of town, next to the medieval marketplace. The total cost for a four-night stay for two of us was $134. Those same four nights in any medium-class hotel would have set us back at least $240.

Whether it's for a short three days, a leisurely three months, or even a "let's see how we like it" prelude to buying property, the options of where to lay your head are tremendous. You could be unlocking the door to a stylish Portuguese villa, a flat in bohemian Berlin, or a quintessential English country cottage with a thatched roof and roses clambering around the porch. How do you fancy a studio in Paris or a houseboat in Amsterdam? A "little gray home" in Ireland's wildly romantic west, an apartment in a centuries-old Italian palazzo, or even a log cabin in Scandinavia? The choice is yours. And if you've ever wondered about the joys of the troglodyte lifestyle, you could even try renting a cave home near the Spanish city of Granada.

I've been spending time in other people's homes for decades—when I was growing up in England, my family always spent our summer vacations in rental properties. Sometimes we stayed in small cottages lost in Devon's and Cornwall's flowery lanes, other times we traveled into the wild Welsh mountains of Snowdonia. One summer we rented a house on Scotland's Isle of Skye, where a friendly farming neighbor taught me how to milk goats. It was a wonderful way of discovering some of the most beautiful parts of Britain. Those early years left me with a wealth of happy memories as well as a huge appetite for travel.

The Beauty of Renting

I lived in London for a while, renting a flat in Tufnell Park, but always seized every opportunity to indulge my wanderlust. Being contrary-minded, I soon realized that you didn't have to spend vacations where the mainstream tour companies wanted you to go. While my workmates baked on the crowded beaches of Spain's Costa Brava, I was drifting around Italy, renting an apartment in Rome and then a stone-built *trulli* home in Apulia, Italy's deep south. The beauty of renting is that you can choose just about anywhere you want to go—returning to favorite places, or discovering brand-new corners of the map.

Of course, holidays aren't the only reason to journey down the European rental route. For instance, you or your partner might be sent to Europe on a work assignment. Many multinationals have a European base. If the company is sending you abroad, why not negotiate a deal whereby **you** rather than the company chooses the neighborhood where you'll be living? After all, what suits the young and fancy-free may not hold the same appeal to an executive relocating with a young family. Or perhaps you're a freelancer—assignments often go to those who are prepared to travel on short notice. When accommodation isn't part of the deal, you'll save by renting an apartment rather than spending huge chunks of your hard-earned fee on pricey hotel rooms.

Maybe you're a retiree with plenty of time to travel. Haven't you found that the typical hotel-based touring holiday always seems far too short to fully savor a country's lifestyle? Just when you've discovered that idyllic Portuguese harbor town, or figured out how to use the Paris Métro, it's time to go home. Well, there's nothing to stop you from spending a summer drifting through the Greek archipelago, stopping off at whatever island takes your fancy. Or staying put for a while, stepping back into another century and discovering the luscious landscapes of *la France profonde* (France's rural heartland).

Live Like a Local

Leaf through the brochures and you'll see that most touring holidays don't even scratch the surface of great art-house cities like Paris, Rome, and Florence.

Instead of taking the "if it's Tuesday, it must be Belgium" touring option, why not live like a local for a month or two? And you don't have to be a student looking for a year abroad to consider one of the great university cities as a place to further your education. It's never too late to study French in Provence, or German in Vienna.

The grand facade of Zürich's Bahnhof, the railway station. This is the starting point of Bahnhofstrasse, the Swiss city's premier shopping street.

© Steenie Harvey

For me, there's no question about where to stay when I travel. Whether it's for business or pleasure, renting apartments and cottages has always seemed the most appealing way of discovering Europe's most exciting cities and holiday regions. For starters, you're getting an insider's look at different styles of architecture and how people's homes are furnished. And some of the best pleasures are downright simple, especially if you love shopping in markets and cooking with local ingredients.

Small hotels and pensions usually have a rigid timetable: you get fed when **they** decide. That kind of arrangement doesn't suit me—when I'm on a working assignment, I often have to start at an unearthly hour to meet a schedule. Having my own kitchen facilities means I can eat breakfast at 6 A.M. if necessary. And that's the time you'll need to be up if you ever want to photograph an authentic North Sea fish market—by the time normal people crawl out of their beds, the action is all over. Tough luck on the tourists who wonder where all the stalls and fishmongers have disappeared to when they emerge from their hotels at 10 A.M.

Taking it from the vacation viewpoint, I usually like my mornings to be leisurely affairs, not a helter-skelter rush to get dressed, made up, and down to the hotel dining room before they clear the breakfast tables. I don't like maids banging on the door when I'm in the bathroom, I don't like tripping over piles of dirty laundry, and I thoroughly resent paying hefty room service charges for the likes of a curled-up sandwich and the pots of dishwater that foreign hotels pass off as tea. Though I admire much about Continental Europeans, they simply don't know how to make a proper brew of industrial-strength, English-style tea. Or a bacon *butty* (sandwich), come to think of it.

The Drawbacks of Renting

Any disadvantages? Well, you may find something to gripe about if you look hard enough. As with any type of transaction, you pay a premium for quality. The furnishings in some cheaper rental properties aren't exactly state of the art, kitchens can sometimes be rather basic, and the showers in Greek bathrooms never seem to work properly. In some out-of-the-way places, the available rental stock may be extremely limited and not quite what you're used to.

A few years ago, I went traveling through the east of the newly reunified Germany with my husband. We spent two strange nights in Quedlinburg, staying in what appeared to be a converted garden shed in the landlord's backyard. Live just like a Saxon? I couldn't get that old Tom Petty number out of my head, *You Don't Have To Live Like A Refugee*. However, we suffered no ill-effects, and the rest of eastern Germany was fine. To be honest, I've never had a really rotten rental experience anywhere.

Where to go? When to go? For how long? How much do you want to spend? Once you've sorted out those questions, finding a rental property that's right for you doesn't require a degree in rocket science. The most important step is to get in touch with local sources—and this book aims to give you plenty of ideas. Although you can certainly rent European properties through home-based agencies, you'll be paying a hefty premium, far more than if you make local arrangements.

Vacation Rental Criteria

You may be wondering what criteria I used to select the places mentioned in this book. Wherever possible, I've chosen establishments where I've stayed myself, or that friends, family, and work acquaintances have recommended. (In the case of long-term rentals, and again wherever feasible, I've selected agencies belonging to a professional real estate association such as FNAIM in France.) Most of the time I tend to make my own holiday arrangements direct with owners, but I've also used vacation rental agencies such as Gîtes de France and Mackay's in Scotland.

At the beginning of each chapter, you'll see contacts for each country's national tourist office in the United States and Canada. They'll give you overviews of location options and self-catering accommodation agencies. If the tourist office lists a vacation rental agency, you can be sure it's legitimate. However, be prepared to do some spadework to find your ideal vacation rental from home. Think regional! Those who do their digging on a more localized basis will uncover the widest array of rental options. Regional tourist offices will also send you booklets of privately owned vacation rentals—these too are bona fide. If you can access the Internet, much of the same information can be gleaned from databases on each tourist board's official website.

If time is short, email has made it a lot simpler to make bookings and get

Punting is a popular pastime in Cambridge, England.

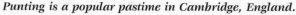

© Steenie Harvey

VACATION RENTALS—THE FAQS

Q: How far in advance should I book?

A: If you're planning your visit for July or August, book as far in advance as possible. In fact, if you can start making inquiries shortly after New Year is out of the way, do so. High summer is Europe's main holiday season and the choicest properties are booked up months in advance. Some families have standing bookings, returning to the same seaside villa or rural cottage year after year. All the Mediterranean seaside resorts and the most delicious parts of the French and Italian countryside are full to bursting point at this time of year. That's not to say that it's impossible to find something in July or August if you leave it to a couple of months before—or simply turn up on spec. Just that your options will be extremely limited.

Easter, Whitsun (late May/early June), and the period around May Day are also fairly hectic if you're considering the French Riviera, southern Spain, or Portugal's Algarve. And to book a chalet in Austria and Switzerland's main skiing resorts over Christmas and New Year's, or an apartment in Venice for Carnival time, you should start making inquiries in summer. Outside of those periods, between one and two months should be more than adequate to put plans into place.

And if you have a sudden impulse to get away from it all, use the Internet. The choice of properties might not be as great as you'd like, but available accommodation is only a mouse click away.

Q: Is there a seasonal variation in rental prices?

A: Yes. In most places you'll pay a hefty premium to rent in the main July and August holiday period (see above). Due to supply and demand, rents can be more than triple what you would pay in the off-season. Except for ski resorts and over the Christmas/New Year's/Easter period, rents are at their lowest from October through April. May, June, and September are considered to be the shoulder season—rents are likely to be higher than in gloomy January, but not as high as in July and August.

Q: Will I be charged a deposit—and how much?

A: Normally, yes, though I've booked apartments in Amsterdam, Spain, and Germany where the owners have simply taken my word that I'll turn up. There is no standard practice. Some agencies and owners ask you to pay a 30 percent deposit when booking and the remainder within six or eight weeks of your arrival. Others request a deposit, with the balance to be paid on arrival. And some owners simply ask you for your credit card number as a guarantee—if you fail to show, you'll be charged one or two nights.

Q: How do I pay the deposit?

A: If an agency or privately owned establishment is geared up to take credit cards, you can normally pay the deposit by this method. Visa is the most widely used card in Europe. I'm reluctant to send my own credit card details by email, so once I've been offered accommodation, I usually phone with the information.

The other main method of making payment is to go to your own hometown bank and obtain a foreign currency draft for the required amount against a recognized bank in whatever European country you're planning to visit. (For example, a check in British pounds sterling drawn against Barclays Bank in London. Or, if it's France, Germany, or one of the other countries in the Euro-zone, a check in euros drawn against one of their main banks such as Deutsche Bank, Credit Lyonnaise, etc.) You then send this draft to your chosen agency or individual to be cashed—for peace of mind, send it by registered or certified mail.

Personal checks in dollars are not a good idea. Sure, foreign banks take them—I often pay U.S. dollar checks into my own bank in Ireland—but they take a devil of a long time to clear.

Q: Is there a minimum rental period?

A: There is flexibility, but agencies usually look for a minimum one-week stay. Outside of July and August, I've found that individual owners are usually happy to accommodate you for less time, though they generally look for a minimum stay of three days. Places need to be cleaned between guests so single night bookings aren't really cost-effective for apartment and cottage owners.

Q: What happens on arrival—and how do I find my cottage/apartment/villa?

A: If you've booked through an agency, they'll invariably send out maps pinpointing the property's location, a designated time of arrival, and owner contact details. Individuals who don't live on the property also usually supply all the relevant information—how to get there, what time you should arrive, etc.

However, it must be said that there's no exact blueprint detailing what's likely to happen. Always expect the unexpected. Last month I took a trip to Tenerife in the Spanish Canary Islands. I arranged to stay in an apartment owned by a German couple in Puerto de la Cruz for three days. A couple of days before leaving home, I got an email: "Dear Steenie, we won't be here at the weekend. We'll leave your keys around the corner at Bar Pepito." Although I'm used to quirky German apartment-owners, I had a few panic-stricken moments imagining all the things that could go wrong. Where was Bar Pepito and what corner did they mean? What if the bartender wouldn't give me the key? I know enough Spanish to get around, book a room, and order a meal, but it's not exactly up to full-scale problem-solving. Needless to say, it all worked out fine—I didn't end up sleeping on the beach.

Q: Will I have to pay a security deposit—and how much?

A: Many agencies and a few individual property owners do ask for one. For the average home, it's likely to be around $50 to $250. For something really palatial and movie-star standard, undoubtedly a lot more. You can pay in cash, by credit card, or in traveler's checks. If you haven't decided to emulate Conan the Barbarian and trash the property, the security deposit will either be returned at the end of your stay or posted home to you. There is nothing dubious about this practice if you're using a reputable agency—and paying a security deposit for vacation cottages is the norm in Scandinavia.

Q: Will a three-room apartment be big enough for two couples?

A: Unless you're very good friends, probably not. Before you book, check how many bedrooms a property has. A "room" is not a bedroom. This sounds idiotically simplistic, but listings can often be confusing. Switzerland in particular is full of contradictions. The country is divided into cantons, and each canton has its own way of doing things. For example, in Geneva canton the kitchen is counted as a room, whereas in other cantons it is not. Thus Geneva listings translate as follows:

Studio: One room with kitchenette and bathroom.

Two-room apartment: One large room, kitchen, and bathroom.

Three-room apartment: A living room, kitchen, one bedroom, and bathroom.

Four-room apartment: A living room, kitchen, two bedrooms, and bathroom.

In some other cantons, a "three-room apartment" would net you two bedrooms plus kitchen and bathroom. It's all very strange, and not what you'd expect from the oh-so-precise Swiss. (Obviously something went wrong in the translation, but I've even heard of one family who rented an apartment in Zurich that was described as "three-bedroom." To their dismay, it only had one.) When booking in Switzerland, perhaps the best thing to do is to explain how many people are in your party and how many bedrooms are needed.

Happily the rest of Europe isn't quite so intent on baffling its overseas visitors. When a

continued on next page

VACATION RENTALS—THE FAQS (continued)

property is described as having two bedrooms, that's exactly what it turns out to have. But to be certain, check with the agency or owner before making a definite booking.

Q: Do vacation rental properties come furnished?

A: Yes. Wherever you go, you will not be sleeping on the floorboards of a totally bare room. What the furnishings and cooking facilities are like is a bit harder to answer. In general, properties come with everything you're likely to need, but you have to be realistic. A $20 per night holiday apartment is not going to have king-size beds covered in goosedown quilts, antique furniture, and a hot tub. Nor will it have every single bit of kitchen equipment that has ever been invented. The more you pay, the better things are likely to be. From my own experiences, Greece has the most sparsely equipped properties—on many of its islands, studio apartments at the cheaper end of the price scale can be very spartan indeed.

Q: Self-catering, or serviced, apartments— what do these terms mean?

A: Especially in Britain and Ireland, you'll often hear vacation rentals described as "self-catering properties." I use this term myself a few times throughout the book. A self-catering property is a holiday cottage or vacation rental with kitchen facilities, so you are required to shop, cook, and clean up. No maid is going to come along and clean up your clutter—by opting for "self-catering," you are quite literally catering for yourself.

"Serviced" apartments are usually found in big cities, often attached to a hotel with its own business center where you can use a fax and have access to the Internet.

Although they have kitchen facilities and all the other "self-catering" facilities of a vacation rental, you can usually avail of extra services if you wish. For example, taking breakfast in the adjoining hotel, or asking a maid to clean your apartment on a daily basis. Serviced apartments are particularly popular with business people who want hotel facilities combined with home comforts.

Q: Do I need to rent a car?

A: That depends on where you're going and what you plan to do. For a property buried in the silent, green heart of the countryside, I'd say "yes." Especially in France and Italy, some of the nicest rural cottages and villas are often found three miles or so down a lane, a lengthy walk away from the nearest village or bus stop.

On the other hand, driving around a city you don't know can be a real headache. If I

information from many other sources within European countries. Ah, but is it safe? Well, although I've never experienced a suspicious outfit, everybody knows that there are a few sharks circling through cyberspace. **Use your common sense.** If you've found the perfect chalet listed on the Austrian tourist board's database, or through one of the major agencies I've given throughout the book, go for it. Everything will be fine—you can make your booking, send your deposit by money order, or telephone your credit card details to Herr Schmidt (or whatever the owner's name is). No problems, no sleepless nights, and no doubt a wonderful vacation waiting for you in the Tyrolean Mountains. On the other hand, you may chance upon a Web page giving details and pictures of a fantastic-looking villa in Spain. Five bedrooms, swimming pool, huge gardens, the works. A steal at $500 for two weeks in July. But why doesn't the site carry a phone number or address that can be checked out? Why does the contact email end in .ru, which indicates your reply is going to be winging its was planning to spend most of my time in a capital like London, Berlin, or Paris, I'd use public transportation. As for driving in Rome—that's my idea of a short cut to a nervous breakdown.

Q: I don't speak any foreign languages— is this a problem?
A: It shouldn't be, but do invest in a good phrase book. After all, if a family from Lisbon rented a property from you, they wouldn't be expecting you to speak Portuguese, would they?

Honestly, though, I've never found language to be a stumbling block. Although I speak adequate German, that's about it. For everywhere else, I rely on phrase books— and phrase book Spanish, French, Greek, and Italian has always been good enough for me. Portugal? I left it all to my husband who took a six-week "learn the basics" course before we went exploring the green and relatively undiscovered north. (Unlike the Algarve and Lisbon, they're not really used to tourists in that part of the country.)

In the majority of countries, you'll find most people in the service industries know a smattering of English. Plus tourist offices and large rental agencies regularly make bookings for overseas vacationers.

Wherever you are, why should day-to-day activities like shopping be problematic? You'll not get fobbed off with a pile of ghastly looking fish heads—not unless you actually point to them! Europe has supermarkets, you know. Just pile whatever you want into a basket, and look at the total on the register.

Obviously North Americans won't encounter a language barrier in Britain and Ireland, but they're not your only options if you quail at the thought of foreign tongues. Just about everybody in Switzerland, the Netherlands, and Scandinavia speaks impeccably correct English. Malta, Cyprus, Portugal's Algarve, and the islands and coastal resorts of southern Spain are all good bets for the linguistically challenged, too.

Although this book primarily cites agencies and other places where you can make bookings in English, this isn't always possible in "off-the-beaten-track" destinations. In northwest Spain, northern Portugal, many parts of Italy, and what was the former East Germany, English speakers are rare. Yes, lots of establishments will answer queries in English, but don't be surprised if you discover that the property owner doesn't speak it—there's at least one 12-year-old Italian girl sending out emails for her non-English-speaking parents! Outside of central Paris and along the Riviera, the French also expect visitors to converse in their language.

way to Russia? And why do you have to send off all the rental money in advance to a post office box in Cyprus? If I saw something like that, I wouldn't touch it with the proverbial bargepole. And neither should you.

It must be said, though, that email and the Internet are useful tools. In the past, it took weeks instead of minutes to book a holiday in Italy. We've already made plans (through email) to return to one of our favorite Italian haunts this summer. Tuscany's rural Renaissance heartland of sunflowers, olive groves, and cypress trees really is ravishing. It has barely changed since the 14th century, and every single hilltop seems to be crowned with a castle or a higgledy-piggledy hill town. We're renting an *agriturismo* apartment in a gorgeous stone farmhouse near San Gimignano, a jewel-box town whose medieval towers rise above a landscape that time forgot. We spent two days here last summer—this time we intend to treat ourselves to two weeks. The view is pure 14th century, but farmhouse guests can also enjoy the more modern bliss of a swimming pool—perfect for a lazy day break from exploring the city streets of Siena and Florence. Roll on June ... I can already hear the crickets calling.

Long-Term Rentals

Vacation rentals are easily arranged, but there's nothing scary about renting for the longer term either. Affordable options can be found in most European countries, though rents are always higher in sought-after cities rather than at the back of the rural beyond. Of course, as you might expect, long-term rentals are a bit more bound up in red tape and bureaucracy than holiday homes. Without a residency permit, most European countries only allow you to stay put for a three-month period. However, we live in a global marketplace and your company may decide that you're the person to run their London or Zürich office. Obviously if your job takes you to Europe, your company will obtain the necessary work permit. Once that has been approved, getting hold of a residency permit will be a mere formality.

Students are also treated favorably. So long as you're accredited to a bona fide university, language school, or study institution, you can obtain a temporary resident permit. In most cases this is usually issued for a year initially, and can be renewed depending on how long the course lasts.

In some countries, longer-term stays are also an option for those who have left the workplace and the nine-to-five grind. Providing you have the means to support yourself, retirees and other people of independent means shouldn't encounter any problems in negotiating an extended stay in countries such as France, Italy, Spain, and Ireland.

For country-specific visa information, go to the relevant chapter in this book.

Converting Prices—Dollars to Euros

Europe's big news in 2002 was its adoption of the euro currency. Twelve European Union (EU) countries—Austria, Belgium, Finland, France, Germany, Greece, Ireland, Italy, Luxembourg, the Netherlands, Portugal, and Spain—now use the euro as their currency. In January 2002, the first euro bills and coins appeared. (The symbol of the euro resembles an "E" or a rather shallow "C" with two horizontal bars through the middle, €.) (For more information on the euro, go to the European Union's Website at http://europa.eu.int/euro.)

For the purpose of this book, I've listed all prices in U.S. dollars. Be aware that these prices are approximate, since exchange rates fluctuate. At the time of publication, one euro equaled about $0.95.

Bear in mind as you travel around that not all European countries are switching to euros. As of now, Britain, Denmark, and Sweden are holding out. Switzerland and Norway, which are not EU members, continue to use their own currencies. For those countries not converting to the euro, you should check exchange rates before you travel, to give you an idea of how much you are getting for your dollar.

Medical Insurance

But no matter how long you plan on being away from home, one vital topic that needs addressing is medical insurance. Yes, some European countries do offer free or reduced-rate medical care, but it's not for the likes of the average North American traveler. In general, only a country's own nationals

EUROPE WITH KIDS

A European self-catering holiday isn't out of the question just because you have young children. Years ago, we took our five-year-old daughter to Spain, and traveled there and back from London entirely by boat and train.

The journey home was a two-night marathon, punctuated by card-playing nuns and generous mamas who stuffed the poor underfed wench with bread and salami. Our daughter loved every minute of it. The only occasion for tears and tantrums before bedtime was when we refused to indulge her appetite for yet another ice-cream!

Wherever you choose to go, one of the great things about a self-catering property is that it allows families of all ages the freedom to holiday at their own pace. Staying in cramped hotel rooms with a couple of toddlers certainly wouldn't be **my** idea of fun, and renting a proper home gives everyone lots more space to spread out. Another big plus is that there are far more opportunities

for kids to make new friends if you stay in a community with real next-door neighbors.

Nobody wants to be chained to the kitchen stove, but having cooking facilities means you'll be able to cater for any fussy eaters as well as cutting down on the costs of restaurant bills. Most youngsters turn into real little Moaning Minnies when presented with spinach, stuffed pigeons, and other strange and unrecognizable foodstuffs. (And so do husbands ...) Mine would happily eat steak every day, but if you have non-meat eaters in the family, be warned that most restaurants in German-speaking countries seem to operate as vegetarian-free zones.

Where are the best places for family vacations? Well, much depends on the age groups. Not everywhere is really suitable for toddlers, so do some homework on local weather conditions and discover what facilities are likely to be available. For example, many Greek islands aren't overly blessed with sandy

continued on next page

EUROPE WITH KIDS (continued)

beaches and the eastern Mediterranean can often be dangerously hot in July and August. Wafted by cooling Atlantic breezes, Portugal's seaside villages are far more suitable for the bucket-and-spade brigade—and the country has excellent beaches.

Not that it has to be a beach holiday. If you're traveling with youngsters, take a closer look at Northern Europe. Along with its ancient history and chocolate box villages, Britain has lots of exciting theme parks and child-friendly attractions. In the cyclist-friendly Netherlands, you can bike for miles along quiet, specially designated cycle paths and in high summer it's warm enough to go swimming and sailing at the North Sea coastal resorts. And the great Scandinavian outdoors was made for activities—everything from white-water rafting to gentle pony-trekking. Most kids would be thrilled at the prospect of paddling a canoe home to a lake-side log cabin or little red cottage with meals grilled outside on a campfire.

If your tastes run to *Sound of Music* scenery and flowery meadows, then the Swiss, Austrian, and Bavarian Alps of south-ern Germany should also be a wow with all ages. Most Alpine ski centers have thrown off their snowy duvet covers by late April, emerging into the sunshine as summertime resorts. They offer a wide range of sports, and the cable cars continue to whizz up and down the mountains. You might have to put long hikes on hold, but even with little ones, you can still enjoy some memorable picnics amongst the glittery splendor of the peaks.

Families with older teenagers really should wait until they've left home before renting anywhere that describes itself as "a rural retreat." Going by my own experience with a teenage terror, these guys and gals crave places to hang out as well as bags of action. Their idea of fun usually revolves around heart-in-your-mouth water sports, throbbing discos, and cafés where they can eyeball the local talent. Sad though it seems, those idyllic hideaways where the only sounds are the whirr of cicadas and the mut-terings of gnarled old grandpas engaged in a card game are wasted on most adolescents.

Southern Spain has long been a huge favorite with teenagers of all nationalities. Even if beach life bores you rigid and the kids detest tramping around museums and art galleries, you could always compromise. Why not dangle the promise of a Costa del Sol villa to follow a city stay? Lively but not loud, the northern half of the Spanish island of Mallorca is also likely to prove a winner with sporty teenagers. So too is the French Riviera—how many sulky 15-year-olds would turn up their noses at the prospect of strutting their stuff along the seriously cool promenades of Nice, Cannes, or St. Tropez?

Or consider Venice coupled with the Ital-ian lakes: Lake Garda is within easy reach of Verona and Padova, and the lake itself offers water sports aplenty. Indeed, many of its stylish waterfront towns have their own lidos and stretches of beach below the lemon groves. The entire region resonates with history and culture and here's an added bonus—you can feast your eyes on a mountain backdrop whilst sipping a glass of wine and listening to a string quartet.

and those foreign citizens who hold long-term residency permits (and thus pay into the tax and social security systems) can avail of any health care benefits. Europeans need medical insurance when traveling in the United States and Canada and North Americans are treated likewise by European governments. So, whether it's for a short trip or an extended stay, make sure your private health insurance covers you.

In the meantime, close your eyes and picture yourself relaxing in a sun-dappled garden or on a shady terrace, planning the next day's adven-tures, and enjoying your own European home-away-from-home.

PART II

Great Britain and Ireland

2 Great Britain

Back in the late 1990s, *Newsweek* magazine coined the phrase "Cool Britannia." Britain—the coolest place on the planet? A tremendous amount of hype was generated on both sides of the Atlantic, and it became thoroughly unfashionable to show an interest in anything that wasn't on the cutting edge of art, music, and fashion.

Yet despite the media's attempts to rebrand Britain, people still come to marvel at the country's past—Stonehenge, Hadrian's Wall, the soaring cathedrals of Viking York and Salisbury, and the Cotswolds with their thatched-roof cottages, village antique shops, and riverbank tearooms.

Being a deeply uncool person myself, I'm pleased to tell you that "highbrow" culture has not been swept away entirely. Go look at a display of pre-Raphaelite paintings, enjoy Shakespearean theater, and listen to wonderful classical music such as Elgar's cello concerto. Culture that dates from a time when the catch phrase was Rule Britannia, rather than Cool Britannia.

Where to stay? For sheer excitement, London is unbeatable but it isn't the only choice. Britain spreads out an intricate patchwork of contrasts, both in its landscapes and its towns and villages. And, of course, in its people too. The further north or west you travel, the less likely you are to encounter those infamously frosty characters who sniff at Johnny Foreigner and his peculiar ways. Being a Brit myself, I can tell you it's a fallacy that everybody is standoffish. I'm biased, but one of Britain's friendliest counties is the one where I was born—Derbyshire. I urge you to discover this unsung region of craggy hills and dales, even if it's only for a short vacation. If you're academically inclined, consider one of the great university cities like Cambridge, or Oxford of the dreaming spires. And, like Wales, Scotland's heather-clad Highlands are gorgeous.

Attempting to cram Britain's potential for holidays and longer stays into a single chapter is a mission impossible. For alternatives, start by contacting the British tourist offices.

British Tourist Authority, 551 5th Ave., Ste. 701, New York, NY 10176-0799, 800/462-2748, www.visitbritain.com.

British Tourist Authority, Suite 120, 5915 Airport Road, Mississauga, Ontario, L4V 1T1, tel. 888/847-4885, fax 905/405-1835.

Legalities

Although North American tourists don't need visas or prior entry clearance, admission is for a maximum of six months in any one year. Extended stays are tricky to negotiate unless you're coming with a work permit or for bona fide study purposes.

To be granted "right of abode," you'll either need at least $1,110,000 (£750,000) to invest, be an entrepreneur with $296,000 (£200,000) minimum to start a business, or be a "retiree of independent means." Qualifying in this latter category means being at least 60 years of age. You'll also need an annual income of at least $37,000 (£25,000) that can be freely

Scotland's Cawdor Castle, near Inverness, is said to be haunted by a lovesick "Green Lady" who leapt from the battlements.

© Steenie Harvey

transferred to the United Kingdom. In addition to regulations on age and finances, you'll also need to show a "close connection" with the U.K. Ways to meet this requirement include having close relatives settled in the U.K., having lived there at any time previously, having been employed by a British company, or having long-estab-lished business contacts. If entry clear-ance is granted, a four-year residency permit is given.

Those hoping to emulate the American author Bill Bryson (*Notes From a Small Island*) in becoming a U.K.-based writer must prove they can support themselves and any depend-ents. If granted entry clearance, you won't be able to take up any other work apart from that relating to self-employment as a writer. The same goes for artists and other creative types too. For more information contact:

British Embassy, 3100 Massachusetts Ave. NW, Washington, DC 20008, 202/588-7800, www.britainusa.com.

British High Commission, 80 Elgin St., Ottawa, Ontario K1P 5K7, 613/237-2008.

The Language

Bliss—no wretched phrase books to pack. You already know Brits say "lift" instead of elevator and "pavement" instead of sidewalk, but isn't it great that you don't need to learn another language? Don't kid yourself! Not everybody speaks with the cut-glass accents of BBC newsreaders. I'm mar-ried to a Scotsman whose baffling vocabulary includes *simmits* (vests), *neeps* (turnips), and *greetin weans* (crying children). These aren't obscure words from the Outer Hebrides—you'll hear them in Edinburgh, Glasgow, and every other Scottish town.

If you've ever wondered what a glottal stop is, now's your chance to find out. To mangle the English language like a native Londoner, don't pronounce the letters h and t, and turn every sentence into a question. "He came from outer space" translates as: "'e came from ou'er space, din 'e?" You'll also encounter impenetrable accents in Yorkshire, Birming-ham, Liverpool, and many other places besides. In my own native county, Derbyshire, the usual greeting is "Ay up, me duck" rather than a simple "Hello."

Wales is officially bilingual and has its own "foreign" language—*Gymraeg* or Welsh. Although everybody can speak English, Welsh is the language of choice for 19 percent of the Principality's inhabitants. If you're in Wales for an extended period, the Welsh Language Board has information on adult language classes.

Welsh Language Board, Market Chambers, 5-7 Mary St., Cardiff CF10 1AT, Wales, tel. 44/0-29-2087-8000, fax 44/0-29-2087-8001, email: ymholiadau@bwrdd-yr-iaith.org.uk.

Vacation Rentals

The great British holiday is extremely popular with locals as well as visitors. The same "when should I book?" rules are much the same as almost everywhere else in Europe. Needless to say, London is popular year-round, so don't leave making arrangements until the very last minute.

If you are planning to stay in the British countryside or at the seaside in July or August, make your booking as far in advance as possible. That dear little cottage—thatched roof, roses around the door—certainly won't be available if you wait until June to inquire. Many British families start making summer vacation plans as soon as Christmas dinner is out of the way.

Incidentally, bookings for rural and seaside properties are generally for a week in high summer, Easter, and Whitsun (early May). It might be Friday to Friday, or Saturday to Saturday. Outside of those high-season periods, it is usually possible to rent for a long weekend or a midweek break of three to four days. There are exceptions, though. Scotland's National Trust only accepts bookings of less than a week for its holiday properties during winter.

A couple of things to watch out for in Scotland. *Hogmanay* (New Year) may be memorable, but it's not the most cost-effective time to visit Edinburgh, where the country's most riotous celebrations take place. Just as with hotels, the price of rental accommodations in the city increases dramatically at this time of year—and rentals are hard to come by. Also, if you are planning a trip to the Highlands in August or early September, ask the tourist office for a list of when and where local Highland Games are scheduled. A few years ago, we wanted to see the Highland Gathering at Braemar in Aberdeenshire. We saw the spectacle—but the nearest place we could find accommodation was in a village 40 miles away!

Many companies and private individuals facilitate stays in holiday

USEFUL HOUSING TERMS

To let—to rent
Letting agency—real estate agency
Flat—apartment
Self-catering—rental property with kitchen facilities

Bedsit—room to rent in a house
Mews house—row house
Building society—savings and loans bank or credit union
First floor—second floor in the United States

accommodations. The Tourist Authority website also has a searchable database of officially approved accommodations. Check it out at www. travelbritain.org. Hundreds of country cottages are available through companies like Rural Retreats, Classic Cottages, and English Country Cottages who (despite the name) also have properties in Wales and Scotland. One of my own favorite places is Cornwall, a county of toy-town fishing ports, smuggler's coves, and empty moorlands. It's a great place to walk and cycle, following fingerpost signs to places like seaside Mousehole and St.-Just-in-Roseland. Most villages are as pretty as they sound, buried amongst a maze of lanes where honeysuckle and dog-roses grow wild. If you enjoy folklore, Cornwall is rich in legends about *piskies* (fairies) and King Arthur too. Avoid the crowds at Tintagel and hike the moors to Dozmary Pool, legendary burial place of King Arthur's sword, Excalibur. Available through Classic Cottages, the Old Post Office is a 16th-century thatched cottage in North Cornwall, a mile from the coast and St. Agnes village. Sleeping six, it rents for between $372 and $697 weekly, depending on the season.

English Country Cottages has a U.S. outlet through British Travel International, an easy way to book in advance. Ask for the full brochure as the website only gives a sample of the 2,500-plus cottages available. If you like the idea of the West Country, featured properties include a 600-year-old thatched Devon cottage. Sleeping four, this rents from $395 to $790 weekly, depending on the season. Three hundred yards from a village inn, Plum Tree Cottage in the Dorset hamlet of West Lulworth sleeps four and rents for between $430 and $965 per week. Find out more by going to www. britishtravel.com.

Classic Cottages, Leslie House, Lady St., Helston, Cornwall TR13 8NA, tel. 44/0-1326-555555, email: enquiries@classic.co.uk.

Rural Retreats, Station Rd, Blockley, Moreton-in-the-Marsh, Gloucestershire GL56 9D2, England, tel. 44/0-1386-701177, fax 44/0-1386-701178, email: info@ruralretreats.co.uk.

English Country Cottages/British Travel International, P.O. Box 299, Elkton, VA 22827, 800/327-6097.

VACATION RENTAL AGREEMENTS

Electricity and heating are almost always included in rental prices. Sometimes you have to rent bed linens and towels—usually in the region of $10 per person, weekly. You'll be asked for a deposit when booking—how much depends on who you book through. It may be $150, it may be 50 percent of the cost, it may be the total holiday price. If booking through a company, the balance is usually due six or eight weeks before your holiday. Freelance owners may allow you to pay the balance on arrival, but not every individual is geared for credit card payments.

Long-Term Rentals

Every town's main street has realtors' offices, though in Britain they're called estate agents. Some are individuals, others are part of countrywide chains. Although their main business is selling homes (around 67 percent of Britain's housing is owner-occupied), most offices usually have rental departments too. To find agents in your chosen area, just walk down the main street. Or contact the head offices of some larger groups.

Your Move, Victoria House, Hampshire Court, Newcastle-upon-Tyne, Tyne & Wear NE4 7YJ, tel. 44/0-845-8456151.

Strutt & Parker, 13 Hill St., Berkeley Square, London W1X 8DL, tel. 44/0-20-7629-7282, fax 44/0-20-7629-0387, email: marketing@struttandparker.com.

Halifax Property Services, Halifax plc Head Office, Trinity Rd., Halifax, Yorkshire HX1 2RG, tel. 44/0-1422-333333. The company has numerous local offices. Find agents through the website www.halifax.co.uk.

Residential agencies are also found in most towns—leaf through the telephone directory's yellow pages. Like with private rentals, their "To let" (lease) listings are generally advertised in local rather than national newspapers. There's a vast choice of both furnished and unfurnished properties. If you can access the Internet, a foray into these sites produces dozens of contact names and lists what's currently available: www.propertyfinder.co.uk, or www.findaproperty.com

As there's no real language barrier, you may think it's simple to avoid agency fees and find apartments through newspapers' classified ads or

Perthshire, Scotland

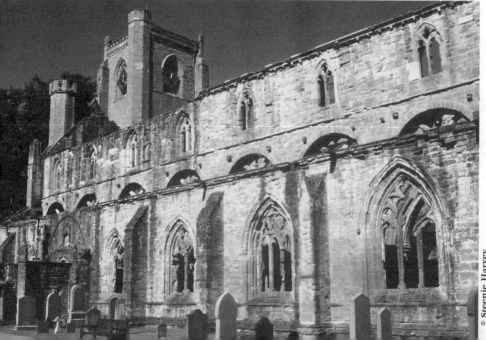

© Steenie Harvey

magazines like *Loot*. Certainly try it, but you'll need to be fast off the mark. In London, reasonably priced rentals are invariably snapped up before the *Evening Standard* even hits the newsstands.

LONG-TERM AGREEMENTS

Leases generally run for either six months or a year, and you'll need to provide one or two months' rent as a deposit. There's no hard and fast rule regarding agency fees. Some, such as the Streatham Accommodation Bureau, charge one week's rent. The Cambridge Accommodation Bureau and Oxford's Finders Keepers charge an application fee of $222.

Rents are usually payable by direct debit through a U.K. bank account. You can also use this facility to pay utility bills, which aren't generally included. However, in rental properties at the lower end of the market (e.g., student bedsits/efficiencies), you may have to feed coins into an electricity meter.

Owners are generally liable for insuring the property and its contents, but you should arrange your own insurance policy to cover personal possessions. Agents will be able to recommend a broker.

Once You're There

As far as health care issues, while good medical services are widely available, free treatment under Britain's National Health Service is only available to U.K. and EU residents. Tourists and short-term visitors needing treatment have to pay; charges are similar to those assessed in the United States. The embassy keeps lists of doctors, but if you have a minor ailment, simply contact any general practitioner throughout the country for an appointment as a private patient. You may have to sit in a crowded waiting room for hours, but you will be seen eventually.

Some Costs: 250 g (8.75 oz) cheddar cheese $2.22, 1 kg (2.2 lb) chicken breasts $9.73, 100 g (3.5 oz) coffee $2.45, loaf of sliced bread $0.87, 1 liter (1.76 pt) milk $0.87, 500 g (17.5 oz) bacon $3.87, six eggs $1.15, 1 kg (2.2 lb) potatoes $1.11. Food bills won't be as expensive if you shop in large supermarket chains rather than convenience stores. Names to watch for are Tesco, Sainsbury, Asda, and Safeway. A week's car rental, economy model, from $190 to $287. Train ticket, London to Edinburgh, $121 single, $140 return. Average household costs for utilities per annum amount to $1,500 for heating, electricity, water, and telecoms.

The retail banking sector offers numerous options. Major players in the banking field include Barclays, HSBC, Lloyds TSB, and Royal Bank of Scotland. All have a wide range of personal banking services. You can link up to these and many smaller banks and building societies (savings and loan institutions) from www.moneyweb.co.uk.

London

"When a man is tired of London, he is tired of life; for there is in London all that life can afford." That quote is still as true today as when Samuel Johnson voiced it in 1777. But there's lots more to Britain's capital than just history and tradition. Spending all your time within a couple of miles of Piccadilly Circus won't give you an inkling of the city's true character.

Multicultural London is essentially made up of little villages, each with their own identity. Look at a map of the Tube, (the underground rail system), and all those myriad stations. Aren't you curious about places like Shepherds Bush, Wood Green, or Holloway Road? It isn't a case of "here be dragons"; these are neighborhoods where Londoners of a myriad ethnic backgrounds live, work, and go to school. Don't write them off simply because they're not known as tourist hangouts.

In central London, Underground stops like Knightsbridge, South Kensington, and Sloane Square seem comfortably familiar. Some Americans don't consider staying anywhere else. Well, unless you're fabulously wealthy, you'll probably choke on your cup of Earl Grey tea when you discover what long-term rents are. It costs an absolute minimum of $1,700 per month for cramped studios in choice districts such as Westminster, Kensington, or Holland Park. A one-bedroom apartment (sleeping two) is likely to rent for $2,300 minimum monthly. Multinational corporations often point their expatriate workers towards the leafy outer suburbs (places like Wimbledon, Richmond, and Twickenham, home of English rugby) but rentals there are equally outrageous.

Most Londoners don't pay these nightmare prices. In the early 1970s, a Greek landlord rented me a furnished bedsit in north London's Tufnell Park, a working-class district where monthly rents for one-bedroom properties average $1,045. Fairly affordable, but still light years distant from the £40 ($60) it cost me! I really enjoyed living there and made many Irish and Greek friends. In today's world, for $1,103 monthly, a studio apartment was being offered in the heart of Hampstead village, a little further up the road. Also north of the Thames, in the Abbey Road–St. John's Wood area, $1,100 per month is typical for a furnished studio with separate kitchen and bathroom.

Although nowhere is inexpensive, affordable options exist south of the Thames too. Areas worth considering include Vauxhall, Balham, Clapham, Lambeth, and Brixton. Brixton? Ill-informed foreigners usually raise their eyebrows and shudder in remembrance of the riots of the 1980s. But times have changed—Brixton's reputation for being an inner-city problem area vanished a long time ago. It's now a fashionable neighborhood—London's African and Caribbean community comprise around 40 percent of the ethnic mix, with the other 60 percent being Britons, Cypriots, Vietnamese, Chileans, and Maltese.

Whatever your own ethnic background, I think you'll be enthralled by the different types of music, aromas, and languages that makes Brixton one of south London's most exciting areas. Even if you decide to live elsewhere, visit the Electric Avenue market (Monday to Saturday). Locals shop to the sound of gospel choirs and reggae music, students sell copies of the *Socialist Worker*, and harmless eccentrics stand on soapboxes proclaiming the end of the world. You'll find yams, breadfruit, mangoes, and other unusual fruit and vegetables from all over the world; fishmongers selling flying fish and shark; stalls swathed in colorful African textiles; and Jamaican fast-food outlets tempting you to step inside for spicy meat and vegetable patties.

The typical monthly rent in Brixton is $820 for a one-bedroom furnished flat; $1,280 for a two-bedroom flat; $1,770 for a three-bedroom flat. Furnished studios here and in other south London enclaves start at around $700. In west London, a furnished single studio could be rented for $505 monthly; a two-bedroom flat near Shepherd's Bush tube station for $1,420. If you insist on a more upmarket address, $2,220 was being asked for a furnished three-bedroom flat with views of Hyde Park, in W2's Sussex Gardens. Pricey, but not quite as pricey as a two-bedroom apartment in Chelsea's Ratcliffe Gardens, quoted at $3,100. Although it's expensive, you do get a furnished kitchen and marble bathroom with power shower.

Abbey Lettings, 350 South Lambeth Rd., London SW8 1UQ, tel. 44/020-7498-0888.

Admiral Properties, 88 Belsize Lane, Hampstead, London NW3 5 BE, tel. 44/020-7431-1133.

Tauntons, 95 Uxbridge Rd., London W12 8NR, tel. 44/020-8740-6666.

Haywards, 31 Plympton Street, London NW8 8AB, tel. 44/020-7723-2666, fax 44/020-7723-9548, email: residential@haywards-surveyors.co.uk.

Streatham Accommodation Bureau, 159 Streatham High Rd., London SW16 6EG, tel. 44/020-8677-9089.

These are only a tiny sample of London agents offering long-term rentals. If you can access the Internet, an excellent site with links to more than 50 London rental agencies is www.net-lettings.co.uk. Rents are often quoted by the week rather than the month, and you'll have to budget for the agency fee. A week's rent is the typical fee.

Like in most European cities, agents charge hefty premiums for short-term rentals. Although you won't have the same extensive choice of neighborhoods as with long-term rentals, you don't have to live cheek by jowl with all the other tourists in expensive central London. Harrods isn't where ordinary mortals shop for day-to-day groceries!

Price Apartments started renting to American academics in 1955, but you don't have to be a professor to use their services. Near Regent's Park, Madame Tussaud's, and the Royal Academy of Music, their Balcombe Street

CLERKENWELL—LONDON'S "SECRET VILLAGE"

Take a Circle or Central Line underground to Farringdon, last stop before Central London merges into the financial district of the city. Here you're in the ancient neighborhood of Clerkenwell, once a byword for radicalism and subversion. Wat Tyler, leader of the Peasants' Revolt, set up camp on Clerkenwell Green in the 14th century. Over the ensuing centuries, the Green also served as a rallying place for Welsh dissenters, Irish Fenians, and supporters of the Paris commune. Lenin found his way here too, editing the Bolshevik underground newspaper *Iskra* from a house on the Green—now the Marx Memorial Library. In later years, Farringdon Road was the site of offices of the Communist newspaper, *The Morning Star*.

When I lived in London, Clerkenwell was a fairly run-down district, home to squatting bands of drippy hippies. Now it has become thoroughly gentrified: City professionals pay a fortune for loft apartments, and streets overflow with new bars, cafés, and restaurants. Yet the dark deeds of history refuse to fade from Clerkenwell's backstreets—the House of Detention on Clerkenwell Close housed jailbirds in the early 17th century up until Victorian times. If you're interested in poking around the cells and examining instruments of torture, this former prison is open to visitors. Across Clerkenwell Road lies the glitter of Hatton Gardens, center of London's diamond trade. The street was named after Elizabeth Hatton, victim of a grisly murder in 1646. The murderer ripped out Elizabeth's heart in a nearby dark alley, which then became known as Bleeding Heart Yard. According to local lore, the heart was still pumping out blood when Elizabeth's body was found the next day.

studios sleeping one or two people rent from $694 to $777 weekly. If you like the idea of being at the heart of the West End and the theater district, a Covent Garden apartment sleeping between two and five rents for $1,450 weekly. Other properties include a garden flat beside the river Thames in Putney. This rents for $911 weekly.

Lero Properties is an estate agent but they also have a portfolio of short- and long-term accommodations. Five minutes from Oxford Street, in a tree-lined Victorian square, you could opt for a short-term rental in Craven Gardens Lodge. Studios from $480 weekly; one-bedroom apartments from $740; two-bedroom apartments from $1,180.

Price Apartments, 33 Balcombe St., London NW1 6HH, tel./fax 44/020-88709234, email: nprice@priceapts.co.uk.

Lero Properties, 24 Leinster Terrace, London W2 3ET, tel. 44/020-7402-7768, email: lero@cravenlodge.swinternet.co.uk.

Derbyshire

I know few North Americans have heard of Derbyshire, but be adventurous. Head "up north"—it isn't all smokescapes, metal-bashing factories, and dark satanic mills. I grew up in these parts and if you insist on Blakeian imagery, go for "clouded hills." They're here, fastening the moorland tapestry of south Yorkshire to Derbyshire's Peakland villages and craggy green dales.

An hour's journey from Derby or Manchester, 30 minutes from Sheffield, Castleton is a mecca for ramblers, rock hounds, and cavers. The village perches atop a spectacular limestone underworld and four cavern systems have been opened up as show caves to the public. Down labyrinthine passageways, lamps reveal Tolkien-like fantasies: bristling stalagmites, fossil-encrusted walls, showers of stalactites glittering as wickedly as elvish swords.

Peak Cavern is the largest, and it's hard to imagine a more cold and eerie workplace. Eighteenth-century rope makers used it to ply their trade, walking backwards, twisting lengths of twine as they went. Speedwell Cavern is reached by boat. Like an illuminated ribbon, the underground canal arrows past old lead-mine workings to a Bottomless Pit that once gobbled 40,000 tons of rubble without any effect on the water level. These caverns hoard dozens of secrets—water entering the pit vanishes for 22 hours before reappearing at Russet Well, less than a mile away.

Castleton's most important mineral wealth is Blue John, a semi-precious fluorspar with colors varying from blues to roseates. Miners have delved for it since Roman times and village shops brim with Blue John jewelry and ornaments. Try to be here on Oak Apple Day (May 29th) when Castleton continues to celebrate Charles II's Restoration. Festooned in garlands, a horsebacked "king" leads a dancing procession to all six village inns. The most atmospheric is the 17th-century Cheshire Cheese Inn with beamed ceilings and log fires. Stop in for a pint of Tetley's Bitter before climbing to Sir Walter Scott's "Peveril of the Peak," a ruined Norman castle.

North sweeps the Dark Peak wilderness of towering gritstone crags and plunging precipices. You can wear your walking boots out reaching beauty spots like Axe Edge, Alport Castles, or the waterfalls cascading from Miry Clough to Grains in the Water. Serious hikers make for the Hope Valley and Edale village, the start of the Pennine Way's 250 foot-slogging miles to the Scottish border.

South of the Hope Valley, Dark Peak changes to White Peak, boggy moors to farming country, where sheepdog trials and agricultural shows abound. An excellent base for discovering White Peak villages and dales is spa town Buxton. Its mineral waters reputedly cure a variety of ills so join the locals collecting the free supply bubbling from St. Ann's Well or swim in the spa pool. You'll be in good company: as the Earl of Shrewsbury's captive guest, Mary Queen of Scots came here to relieve her rheumatism.

Renowned for antiques and craft fairs, Buxton possesses a spilt personality. The graciousness of its classical Georgian Crescent, Pavilion Gardens, and ornately marbled Opera House contrast vividly with the down-to-earth Market Square. It's the highest in England, bordered with fish-and-chip shops, higgledy-piggledy pubs, and canopied arcades. Tuesdays and Saturdays are the days for market bargains and if you fancy putting together a picnic, nose out Pugson's on Terrace Road, the self-styled "best cheese shop in the north."

Bound for outlying Peak villages, Buxton's buses pass near many of the Dales, glittering with trout streams and completely traffic-free. For an energetic day's rambling through wooded gorges, over stiles, and across stepping stones, catch the Buxton-Bakewell bus as far as Topley Pike. From here you can follow the Monsal Trail's fingerpost signs to Wyedale, Cheedale, and into Miller's Dale. Gorgeous though the setting is, there are no jolly corn millers in this particular dale. Past the raging millrace, past the pinched cottages of Apprentice Row, Litton Mill is a grim relic of the days when cotton was king and even children slaved over the looms in appalling conditions. By all accounts, these really were dark satanic mills.

Other Peakland villages worth visiting include Hathersage, where the 10-foot-long grave of Robin Hood's companion, Little John, lies in the churchyard. Eyam (pronounced Eem) is the plague village—back in 1665 it placed its homesteads in voluntary isolation to prevent the disease from spreading further. The village stocks and sundial date from that period and the 250 inhabitants who died are commemorated on Plague Sunday, the last Sunday in August. Picture-postcard Tissington, complete with village green and duck pond, is famous for its Ascension Day *well-dressings*. Decorating the village wells, these are vibrant pictures of Biblical scenes, colorfully created from flower petals, leaves, and bark.

Old stone churches such as this one in Iona Scotland can be found throughout the British Isles.

© Steenie Harvey

HOLIDAY IN WALES

Snowdonia, historic castles like Conwy and Caernarfon, and the Swallow Falls at Betws-y-Coed—that's North Wales, but there are some gorgeous spots in South Wales too. Some of Britain's best coastal walks are in Pembrokeshire's National Park—you can tramp for 180 miles along the coastal path.

Below Mount Snowdon, Bedgellert is a picture-book North Wales village with two rivers and a humpbacked bridge. Riverside Cottage, a little stone-built cottage for two, rents for between $244 and $526. A larger property (sleeping up to six) in the Conwy Valley near Betws-y-Coed rents for between $177 to $510 weekly. For a North Wales cottages brochure contact:

Sea & Mountain Cottages, Snowdon Tourist Services, High St., Porthmadog, Gwynedd LL49 9PG, tel. 44/0-1766-513829.

Quality Cottages' properties include a stone-built farmhouse on St. David's Peninsula. Part of Pembrokeshire's jagged coastline of cliffs, caves, and rock pools, this is a perfect place to fish, paint, and pony-trek. You can take boat trips to offshore islands to watch puffins, kittiwakes, and other seabirds. Dolphins, seals, and porpoises often surface in these waters too. Sleeping seven, the farmhouse has beamed ceilings, log burning fires, and a traditional Welsh dresser in the kitchen. Weekly rent is $421 low season, $1,124 high.

Quality Cottages, Cerbid, Solva, Haverfordwest, Pembrokeshire SA62 6YE, tel. 44/0-1348-837874, email: enquiries@qualitycottages.co.uk.

The Rees family has a number of cottages on their small holding near Pembrokeshire's St. Brides Bay. Sleeping between two and six people, rents are between $240 to $890 weekly. Children (and adults) can help feed the Jersey cows and collect eggs from the hens and ducks. Unfortunately, the farm isn't served by public transportation. John Rees told me that guests would probably need a car—or enjoy doing lots of walking.

Mr and Mrs Rees, Rogeston Cottages, Portfield Gate, Haverfordwest, Pembrokeshire SA62 3LH, tel. 44/(0)1437-781373, email: john@pembrokeshire-cottage-holidays.co.uk.

To glimpse how the other half lives, visit Chatsworth House. Near Bakewell, this stately home is open between Easter and October. Built in 1555, it contains room after room of treasures from a bygone age. Chatsworth's 1,000 acres of parkland were landscaped by Capability Brown, and the formal gardens showcase a maze, fountains, classical statuary, and a number of those odd little buildings known as architectural *follies* that Britain seems to specialize in.

The widest choice of holiday rentals is on the official Derbyshire Peak District website at www.peakdistrict-tourism.gov.uk. Sykes Cottages' portfolio of northern England holiday homes also includes some enticing cottages. Sleeping four, stone-built cottages at Edale rent from $236 to $435, depending on the season. Four miles from spa town Buxton, surrounded by great walking country, Dale Grange Cottage adjoins a farmhouse in Chelmorton village, which has an inn and a medieval church. The cottage, sleeping up to six people, rents for between $236 and $464 weekly.

Sykes Holiday Cottages, York House, York St., Chester CH1 3LR, tel. 44/0-1244-345700, fax 44/0-1244-321442, email: info@sykescottages.co.uk.

Near the village of Bakewell, and sleeping two, Henry's Haunt is a small cottage on the Harthill Hall estate, at the heart of the National Park. Henry VIII (the one with the six wives) is believed to have stayed at the Hall and the cottage's furnishings include a Victorian barrel stove and a four-poster bed. Depending on time of year, this rents for between $444 and $621 weekly. Properties on the estate also include a converted chapel that dates back to 1296. Accommodating six, this rents from $917 to $1,154 weekly.

Harthill Hall Cottages, Harthill Hall, Alport, Bakewell, Derbyshire DE45 1LH, tel. 44/0-1629-636190, email: harthillhall@tesco.net, www.harthillhall.co.uk.

For longer stays (six month minimum lease), Marshall's Agency has a Peak District office in Buxton. Sample rentals include a two-bedroom furnished house in Buxton for $962 per month and a stone-built converted barn overlooking fields for $1,028 per month. Six miles from Buxton, an apartment in Lognor village rents for $592 monthly. Usual terms are a month's rent in advance plus a deposit equivalent to a month's rent.

Frank Marshall & Co., 8 The Quadrant, Buxton, Derbyshire SK17 6AW, tel. 44/0-1298-23038, fax 44/0-1298-77291.

Oxbridge

Oxbridge isn't really a place at all. It's the nickname given to the venerable university cities of Oxford and Cambridge. Each is home to a number of famous colleges, which are entirely separate from one another. Not realizing this, foreigners often ask directions for "the university," which doesn't get them very far.

Oxford sits on the doorstep of the Cotswolds. (Incidentally, the Cotswolds isn't a county, but the collective name given to the ancient wool towns and honey-colored villages of three of the wealthiest counties in Middle England: Gloucestershire, Warwickshire, and Oxfordshire.) The city's largest college is Christ Church and day-trippers from around the world come to peek through the main gate below Tom Tower and admire the famous quad with its Mercury statue and lily pond. Sadly, the visitors are usually on a breakneck itinerary and have no time to enjoy any leisurely pleasures. So why not stay awhile?

Wouldn't you like to punt along the River Cherwell to a riverside pub in the evenings, listen to the cathedral choir at Evensong, or read in the garden where the original Alice in Wonderland played? (Lewis Carroll—real name Charles Dodgson—was a mathematics fellow at Christ Church.) The Ashmolean Museum is a treasure-house and you can easily spend an entire day in the weird and wonderful Pitt Rivers Museum. It's a memorial to those batty Victorian explorers who traveled the globe on anthropological expeditions, collecting everything from Pacific Island fertility pendants to gruesome shrunken heads.

Interestingly, Oxford wasn't built around its colleges. Well before medieval scholars arrived, the 11th-century Domesday Book of Norman Times mentions a city of over a thousand buildings. For non-university students, the true heart of the city beats around Carfax crossroads, at High Street's western end. There has never been much love lost between "Town and Gown," and previous centuries saw students and the general townsfolk engaging in running street battles. In 1355, a riot ensued after some students visited a Carfax tavern and refused to pay for what they claimed was "filthy wine." Townsfolk waded in on the side of the innkeeper, students poured out the halls. They battled for three days, joined by an eager crowd from the countryside who broke through the city walls to join the fray. It's said that more than 100 corpses littered the streets. As a punishment, Oxford's *hoi polloi* were forbidden to receive the sacraments and the mayor himself was ordered to make an annual penance at the high altar of St. Mary's Church. As the students got off scot-free, this led to much ill-feeling between the two communities. The rivalry between Town and Gown has often been dubbed the Seven Hundred Years' War. However, things have gotten a tad more civilized; although there are still some rough-and-ready Carfax pubs, you're extremely unlikely to encounter an Oxford mob baying for blood and threatening to string you up by your college scarf. Well, not unless you insult a tavern-owner!

Cambridge—one of Britain's great university cities

© Steenie Harvey

Throughout Oxford, long-term rentals are fairly steep. One- and two-bedroom furnished apartments in the Jericho quarter, often featured in the famous Inspector Morse novels, rent for between $1,000 and $1,258 monthly. Three-bedroom houses can fetch rents of $1,332 to $1,924; four-bedroom properties from $2,110 to $2,804. Rental agencies include:

Elwood & Co, 214 Banbury Rd., Summertown, Oxford OX2 7BY, tel. 44/0-1865-426410, fax 44/0-1865-426411.

Finders Keepers, 226 Banbury Rd., Summertown, Oxford OX2 7BY, tel. 44/0-1865-311011, fax 44/0-1865-556993.

STUDY FOR LEISURE

What's a *wodewose*? And what did Roman soldiers do for evening entertainment? Spend time in Britain and you could discover the answers to these questions and much else besides: how to spot valuable antiques, become an expert on Victorian children's literature, or even learn to make medieval stringed instruments such as the lute, psaltery, or bardic harp. Whether your fascination is with the arts, nature, or history, you're sure to find the perfect study program. No formal qualifications are necessary and not all courses take place in the summer. Most towns offer regular evening "adult education" classes and options range from archaeology to opera for beginners. Local libraries are good places to find out what's being offered.

For weekend and weeklong courses on natural history and heritage, contact the Field Study Council (FSC). Throughout the year, 11 residential centers in England and Wales run courses on topics such as heraldry, wildlife wood carving, bat detection, badger-watching, fungus forays, and painting in Constable country. Weeklong courses average about $444, including room, board, and tuition; weekend courses average $178.

Field Study Council Central Services, Preston Montford, Montford Bridge, Shrewsbury, Shropshire SY4 1HW, England, tel. 44/0-1743-852100.

Cambridge has weekend, weekly, and monthlong courses throughout the year. Recent study options have included the Falklands War, medieval book production, Beowulf, and "Sutton Hoo and the Anglo-Saxon Kingdom." Most courses last three days, and typical fees are $220 including accommodation, $127 if making your own arrangements.

Board of Continuing Education, Madingley Hall, Cambridge CB3 8AQ, tel. 44/0-1954-280238/280208.

Oxford is always popular, so book early for summer study courses. Students can access the excellent libraries and there are plenty of opportunities to visit museums, art galleries, and theaters. Recent courses have included royal palaces, pre-Raphaelite painters, and British myths and legends. (That wodewose? He's a hairy, club-carrying wild man said to lurk in the English Greenwood. Sometimes known as the Green Man, he can occasionally be spotted as a pagan-type carving in medieval churches.)

In addition to summer study programs, a range of one-day and weekend study breaks take place throughout the year. Whether you're interested in the rise of monasticism or Thomas Hardy's novels, it's a wonderful opportunity to enjoy Oxford as a bona fide student.

Department of Continuing Education, 1 Wellington Square, Oxford OX1 2JA, England, tel. 44/0-1865-270360, email: enquiries@conted.ac.ox.uk.

The Summer Academy links 13 British universities and provides another chance to gain an insight into everything from obscure Arthurian legends to Jane Austen's genteel world. There are almost 100 weeklong residential summer courses; locations include Stirling in central Scotland, Swansea and Aberystwyth in Wales, and York and Sheffield in northern England. Held between early June and late August, most courses cost $710 to $866 and include full board, accommodation, and related excursions.

Summer Academy, Keynes College, the University, Canterbury, Kent CT2 7NP, England, tel. 44/0-1227-470402, fax 44/0-1227-784338, email: summeracademy@ukc.ac.uk.

QB Management, 114 London Rd., Headington, Oxford OX3 9AX, tel. 44/0-1865-764533, fax 44/0-1865-764777.

Cambridge lies in East Anglia's fenlands, a flat landscape of prairie-like fields, and huge skies made famous by the artist John Constable. Its magnificent colleges include Peterhouse (founded in 1284) and King's, whose chapel is the grandest building in the city and home to Rubens's *Adoration of the Magi*. Harvard students may want to peek inside Emmanuel College's chapel—it contains a plaque to former student John Harvard who sailed on the Mayflower in 1636 and gave his name to the U.S. university. But this is more than just a city of dogleg shopping lanes and student cyclists. Its Science Park is Britain's answer to Silicon Valley and the city and surrounding villages are home to many computer and biotech boffins. Here you can expect to pay between $880 and $1,330 monthly for a two-bedroom furnished property. Long-term monthly rents for three- and four-bedroom homes are somewhere between $1,260 for unfurnished to $2,000 furnished. Rental agencies include:

Spires International, 185 East Rd., Cambridge CB1 1BG, tel. 44/0-1223-300903, fax 44/0-1223-358903, email: head-office@spires.co.uk.

Eurolet, 69a Regent St., Cambridge CB2 1AB, tel. 44/0-1223-462007.

For vacation rentals within either city, check the British Tourist Authority's database or the www.holiday-rentals.net site. Addresses to put in your notebook are:

Clarence House, 13 Clarendon St., Cambridge CB1 1JU, tel./fax 44/0-1223-841294. Holiday flats sleeping two to four from $510 to $658 weekly.

Home From Home, 78 Milton Rd., Cambridge CB4 1LA, tel. 44/0-1223-323555. Holiday flats sleeping two to four from $480 to $725 weekly.

Oxmoor Holiday Cottages, Lower Farm, Noke, Oxford OX3 9TX, tel. 44/0-1865-373766. Cottages from $440 weekly.

Just 25 minutes from Oxford, Rural Retreats can rent you the Old School Cottage at Asthall, a hamlet in the Windrush Valley with its own manor house, parish church, and a village inn called the Maytime. Sleeping four, this rents for $950 weekly during early summer. You'll also find properties on www.oxfordcity.co.uk.

Scotland

Spangled lochs, storybook mountains, and some of the world's best salmon fishing. Great golf, gluggable whiskey, and the grand old city of Edinburgh. *Ceilidhs* (a traditional Scottish party featuring Gaelic music, dancing, and poetry), caber-tossing, and rumors of a monster of the deep—there's no place quite like Scotland. The grandeur of the landscape appeals to all romantics and Queen Victoria's purchase of Balmoral Castle in 1855 definitely started a vacation trend. Senior members of the British royal family still spend their summer holidays in the Highlands.

Although you can't rent royal castles like Balmoral or magnificently spooky Glamis, many other exciting possibilities exist. For instance, the National Trust for Scotland (NTS) has vacation apartments in Culzean Castle, on the cliff tops of west coast Ayrshire. This castle was built in the 1770s and it has an interesting American connection. The Marquess of Alba donated it to the National Trust in 1945—and in return he asked that part of the castle be given to General Eisenhower for his lifetime, as a "thank you" for commanding Scottish soldiers during World War II. One of the rental properties available is Royal Artillery Cottage in the castle's Clock Tower courtyard. Sleeping four, this rents for $392 weekly during winter, $592 in high summer.

The National Trust for Scotland is a conservation charity, the official guardian of Scotland's natural and cultural heritage. Their holiday properties come in all shapes and sizes: snug stone cottages, farmhouses (called *crofts* in Scotland), and Victorian town houses with pepperpot turrets and crenellated battlements. For brochures, contact:

National Trust for Scotland, 28 Charlotte Square, Edinburgh, Scotland EH2 4ET, tel. 44/0-131-243-9300, email: holidays@nts.org.uk.

A rural retreat within easy reach of Edinburgh? On Scotland's sunnier east coast, Fife is a pastoral county of farmers and fishermen whose best-known settlement is the university and golfing town of St. Andrews. Quiet lanes meander through barley fields to the East Neuk ("neuk" is a Scottish word for corner). Here you'll come across attractive fishing villages like St. Monans and Pittenweem. Houses with crow-stepped gables cluster around harbors where the herring fleet anchors. Pittenweem has a sleepy feel, but it gained notoriety in 1704 when it was the site of a mass witchcraft trial, similar to the happenings in Salem, Massachusetts.

The Royal Highland Gathering takes place in early September at Braemar in the Scottish Highlands.

In Falkland, a pretty Fife village not far from St. Andrews's famous golf course, the National Trust has a two-bedroom apartment in St. Andrews House. Built for a 17th-century courtier, it overlooks the orchard and garden of Falkland Palace. Rents are $392 weekly in winter, $592 in July and August.

If you want to stay in one of Fife's East Neuk fishing villages, Mackay's has an 18th-century fisherman's cottage in Lower Largo. Sleeping five, it rents for $370 weekly low-season, $414 in September, and $518 in July and August.

Mackay's Agency, 30 Frederick St., Edinburgh, Scotland, tel. 44/0-131-225-3539.

Mackay's has more than 2,000 Scottish holiday properties. I've used them to rent a holiday property for a ski trip to the winter sports resort of Aviemore in Inverness-shire's Cairngorm Mountains. Sleeping five, bungalows similar to the one we rented cost $325 weekly in January; $673 in July and August. If you enjoy hill-walking and pony-trekking, Aviemore also makes an excellent summer retreat.

Inverness-shire is associated with Bonnie Prince Charlie's doomed attempt to restore the Stuart dynasty to the throne. In its deep glens and brooding moors, you can almost hear the clashing broadswords and battle cries of the old Highland clans—Culloden Moor is where many gallant Bravehearts perished in the last land battle fought on British soil. Wild legends go hand-in-hand with wild scenery and Inverness (the Highland "capital") is a handy base to go monster-hunting on Loch Ness.

Sir Walter Scott described Perthshire as Scotland's "most beautiful and varied county" and it's one of my favorite parts of the Highlands too. An hour from Edinburgh, it mixes sensational scenery with a turbulent and often bloody history. Loch Leven was the lonely island prison of Mary Queen of Scots, and Pitlochry was where the Old Pretender's forces fired the first shots in the Jacobite cause. Here too is Scone, the crowning place of Scotland's ancient kings. If you know your Shakespeare, you may want to follow in the steps of Macbeth, the "fiend of Scotland." Birnam Wood, the wood that went walkabout, borders Dunkeld village and the river Tay.

With their steep, slated roofs, cottages in Perthshire's Highland villages are mostly built from sparkling silver-gray granite. Balqquidder village is where the infamous outlaw Rob Roy MacGregor lived and died. Mackay's Agency has an 1840s farmhand's cottage here that sleeps four. Rents (inclusive of a bag of coal!) start at $190 weekly during winter, reaching $606 weekly during high summer.

Near the Perthshire town of Kirkmichael, Bakehouse Cottage is a cozy cottage for two that rents for between $266 and $410 weekly depending on the season. With a car, it makes a good base for day trips to Loch Ness, Glencoe, St. Andrews, and Edinburgh. For this and other Highland homes for both short- and long-term rental contact:

CKD Finlayson Hughes, 45 Church St., Inverness IV1 1DR, tel. 44/0-1463-226990.

For a long-term stay, you may want to consider Edinburgh. Even in winter, the Scottish capital is never short of visitors, so there's always a buzz (as well as a nip) in the frosty northern air. The city's internationally renowned events include the Fringe, now as famous as the more staid Edinburgh Festival. Thousands more visitors hit town to see the Military Tattoo or to join in the Hogmanay (New Year) festivities.

The downside is that it's a fairly expensive city for accommodations. Monthly rents in good suburban locations range from $750 to $1,030 for two-bedroom apartments, $790 to $1,700 for three-bedroom properties, and $1,220 to $1,855 for four-bedroom homes. That's suburbia and tenants are paying a minimum of $1,200 monthly for two-bedroom flats in the atmospheric old town of *wynds* and *closes*, and also posh Morningside, the Georgian new town. If you're puzzling over what *wynds* and *closes* are, remember that I did warn you that British English is not quite the same as American English ... you are going to return home armed with all kinds of weird and wonderful expressions. A "wynd" is a common Scottish term for an alley, and a "close" is an even narrower passageway, usually leading nowhere, that runs up between the side of houses. However, in northern England, a close is confusingly called an entry. **Edinburgh Solicitors Property Centre,** 85 George St., Edinburgh, tel. 44/0-131-624-8000, email: espc@espc.co.uk.

Edinburgh vacation rentals start at around $355 weekly for one-bedroom apartments sleeping two, $673 for four-bedroom apartments sleeping eight. In the Georgian quarter, weekly rents can reach $2,072 for large luxury apartments. What's even more enticing for landlords (but not vacationers), is that such rents often double during the Festival and New Year periods. However, both Mackay's and Scotland's National Trust have some reasonably priced vacation rentals. The curiously named Gladstone's Land is an NTS property on Lawnmarket, close to the Royal Mile and Edinburgh Castle. Originally the home of a prosperous 17th-century merchant, the property has been furnished to give an authentic glimpse of life in Edinburgh's old town some 300 years ago. Sleeping two, a bijou flat in Gladstone's Land rents for $450 low season, $590 in high summer.

3 Ireland

The friendliness of the Irish people is legendary. In fact, they make you feel so welcome, you'll find it hard to say goodbye. The Emerald Isle has been my home for 12 years now, and although the weather isn't perfect, I've never regretted moving here.

Dublin, the capital, is a center of activity, but don't let it dominate your entire stay. Ireland's gorgeous scenery is unmatched—every visitor has their own dream location. For some, it's county Kerry's Lakes of Killarney; for others it's the wild seascapes of Donegal. There's so much to keep on coming back for: county Cork's crescent moon coves and picturesque harbor towns, the moonscaped Burren region where rare wildflowers bloom every spring, the fairy-tale lands of Connemara in county Galway, and Kilkenny where time-toppled monasteries lie lost in verdant fields.

If you have children, Ireland is marvelous for old-fashioned family holidays. Outside the cities there's hardly any traffic, and kids can cycle to the village shop to buy provisions. They'll be perfectly safe, so let them go and play in the woods, fish in rock pools, and hang out with local youngsters. During school summer holidays, most Irish parents certainly don't worry that they don't see their offspring from dawn until dusk.

What I especially love about Ireland is its sense of history, its colorful folklore, and the distinct feeling that you can step back into what storytellers call "the time long ago." Every landmark, every place-name seems to tell a story. With its tales of heroic deeds and supernatural forces, the Celtic

Age continues to cast mesmeric shadows across a landscape that abounds in mysterious stone circles, standing pillars, and curious earthen mounds that were once believed to be an abode of the fairy folk.

Tourism Information, Bord Fáilte, 345 Park Ave., New York, NY 10154, 212/418-0800, www.irelandvacations.com.

Ireland Tourist Office, 2, Bloor St. West, Suite 1501, Toronto M4W 3E2, tel. 800/223-6470.

Legalities

North American citizens don't need visas for tourist or business stays up to 90 days. Providing you can support yourself, staying on longer shouldn't be difficult. There's little red tape involved in gaining residency. Permission to stay is renewed on an annual basis. After five years you don't need to continue re-registering—you're now classed as a permanent resident.

If you decide to remain in Ireland, once your three months' stay is coming to an end you must register with the police. (In Ireland they're titled the Garda Síochána, which everybody abbreviates to "the Guards.") Except for in Dublin, registration formalities are handled by local police stations. Within the capital, apply to the Aliens Registration Office at Harcourt Street. Detailed information is available from Irish embassies.

Embassy of Ireland, 2234 Massachusetts Ave. NW, Washington, DC 20008, 202/462-3939.

The Lake Isle of Inisfree: Through dark enchantments, the Children of Lir were turned into swans in a famous Irish legend.

© Steenie Harvey

Embassy of Ireland, 130 Albert St., Ottawa, Ontario K1P 5G4, 613/233-6281.

Aliens Registration Office, Garda Síochána, Harcourt St., Dublin 2, tel. 353/0-1-475-5555.

The Language

Gaeilge a fhoghlaim nó a fheabhsú. That translates as "learn and improve your Irish." However, although Irish Gaelic is Ireland's first official language and is taught in schools, it's only used in a few far-flung pockets known as *Gaeltacht* areas. English is the day-to-day language, but learning some Irish words will add to your enjoyment. Throughout the country, age-old Irish language names are commemorated in an almost endless litany of colorful place-names: *Inisbofin*—the island of the white cow; *Slievenamuck*—the mountain of pigs; *Cluain-tarbh*—the meadow of the bull.

The Bord na Gaeilge website at www.bnag.ie has extensive links. Principal course providers for adults wishing to learn Irish include Gael Linn and Oideas Gael. The latter run holiday courses in county Donegal—some are intensive language study, but other courses allow you to combine Irish with activities such as hill-walking, Irish dancing, and learning to play the bodhran drum. A week's language course (45 hours) costs about $152.

Gael Linn, 26-27 Merrion Square, Dublin 2, tel. 353/1-6767283, email: gaellin@eircom.net.

Oideas Gael, Gleann Cholmcille, co Donegal, tel. 353/73-30248, email: oifig@oideas-gael.com.

Vacation Rentals

Winter and summer alike, Dublin attracts a horde of visitors. For many, especially those from Britain, it's a kind of last minute idea—"hey, let's go and check out Dublin's pubs this weekend." Although you certainly don't have to book months in advance for a stay in Ireland's capital city, I'd advise North Americans to allow a six-week time frame to make sure of getting somewhere nice and centrally located. Leave it until the last minute and you'll be hard pressed to find even a shabby hotel room on a Friday or Saturday night. (And some hotels are very insalubrious indeed—caught out with a late plane back from Malta, I recently had to pay almost $60 for an overnight stay in a dump.)

July and August are the peak months in rural Ireland. For cottages in the most popular counties—Cork and Kerry—the rule for advance booking is the same as always: book as far ahead as you can. Donegal is also chock-ablock these months with many Irish families (and many more from across the border in Northern Ireland) on vacation in the Republic's wildest and northernmost county. At this time of year, you'll invariably need to book for a week. It's generally Saturday to Saturday, though there are exceptions. At other times of year, you can usually opt for long weekends or three- or four-day midweek stays.

Where to go for the best holiday? Kerry has Ireland's highest mountains, the looking-glass lakes of Killarney, and the Dingle Peninsula. Galway has the Irish-speaking Aran Islands and the fairylands of the Connemara region. I love both these counties but Cork is equally splendid with its colorful villages and small harbor towns.

If you can't access the holiday accommodations database on the tourist board's website, the same information is contained in the *Self-Catering Guide*, which has more than 3,000 officially approved private listings. Issued annually, and obtainable through tourist board offices, it gives property descriptions, owners' addresses, and phone numbers. This is the cheapest way to find vacation homes in Ireland and most Irish people use it for home-based holidays. To give you a sample of what's available, one Galway listing I liked the look of is Clifden's old coastguard's station (Sky Rd., Clifden, Connemara, Co Galway, tel. 353/0-95-21311.) Fabulous views of the Connemara coast and islands—an apartment sleeping four costs between $285 to $418 weekly.

There are agencies too. The Rent-an-Irish-Cottage company has small cottage complexes in Cork, Kerry, and many other scenic locations. Most cottages are thatched and all have open peat fires. Prices from $242 for long weekends and $1,090 weekly, depending on cottage size and time of year. At Durrus in Ireland's scenic southwest, a cottage sleeping four rents for $304 weekly between September and October. Trident Holiday Homes have a wide selection of properties throughout Ireland, from country cottages to apartments and family houses in Dublin. Prices for one-bedroom apartments in the capital start at around $360 weekly. Also try Irish Cottage Holiday Homes, which acts as a central booking point for numerous small, privately owned cottage complexes.

Rent-an-Irish-Cottage, 51 O'Connell St., Limerick, tel. 353/0-61-411109, email: info@rentacottage.ie.

Trident Holiday Homes, 15 Irishtown Rd., Irishtown, Dublin 4, tel. 353/0-1-6683534, www.thh.ie.

Irish Cottage Holiday Homes, 4 Whitefriars, Aungier St., Dublin 2, tel. 353/0-1-4757596, www.ichh.ie.

VACATION RENTAL AGREEMENTS

Each owner and rental company has their own arrangements, but in a lot of cases the procedure is to pay around 30 percent of the rental price when you place a booking. The balance may be due four to six weeks before the start of the hire date, or on arrival. Electricity, heating, and bed linen is often included in the rental price, though in some homes you may have to feed coins into a meter for electricity. You may also have to pay extra ($12–24) to rent bed linens and towels. Some property owners also request damage deposits of $80–115.

Long-Term Rentals

Unlike many European countries, Ireland is a nation of homeowners rather than tenants. This effectively means there isn't any huge glut of private rental accommodations available at any one time. Although some Irish buyers have bought investment homes for capital appreciation plus rental income, these properties are invariably in apartment buildings. Particularly if you want to base yourself in Dublin, you may have to settle for a rented apartment rather than a house.

There are various ways to find long-term rental properties. Many landlords rent privately, so it's always worth checking the "Accommodation to Let" advertisements in local newspapers. Each county has its own newspaper—weeklies such as the *Sligo Champion*, *Roscommon Herald*, *Longford*

Holy Ireland: the Marian Shrine at Knock

Leader, etc. If you're considering a home in Dublin, the property sections of national dailies like the *Irish Times* and *Irish Independent* list private rentals as well as lots of agencies within the capital. Specific home-rental agencies are found in Cork and sizeable provincial towns such as Sligo and Wexford as well as in the capital. In addition, larger Dublin estate agencies (realtors) such as Lisneys, Sherry Fitzgerald, and Hooke & Macdonald have their own separate rental offices.

One Internet site that is useful for tracking down rental properties is www.irishpropertynews.ie. For example, a three-bedroom furnished house, near Kinsale, County Cork was recently advertised for $665 per month. Within Cork city itself, a four-bedroom house was available for long-term rental at a rent of $1,045 per month.

Provincial auctioneers and estate agents handle most rural rentals. As their main business is the buying and selling of houses, some will only have one or two rentals on their books, though others may be able to offer you a dozen or so choices. Auctioneers almost always have their offices on a town's main street. You can find listings of members through professional bodies such as the IAVI (Irish Auctioneers and Valuers Institute) and IPAV (Institute of Professional Auctioneers and Valuers).

IAVI, 38 Merrion Square, Dublin 2, tel. 353/1-6611794, fax 353/1-6611797, www.iavi.ie.

IPAV, 129 Lower Baggot St., Dublin 2, tel. 353/1-6785685, fax 353/1-6762890, www.ipav.ie.

LONG-TERM RENTAL AGREEMENTS

When renting property, you'll almost certainly be asked to sign a lease. A lease usually runs for a year, but you can occasionally make other arrangements for shorter periods. There's usually the opportunity to renew, though a handful of properties may be rented solely for six months over the winter. A lease is a legally binding document and if you leave before the agreed rental term is up, the landlord is entitled to demand payment for any outstanding amounts owed. While this may not happen, (few landlords are likely to come chasing you across the Atlantic), you can effectively wave farewell to the deposit you will have had to provide. Of course, tenants are protected too and the landlord cannot throw you out on a whim. You're only likely to encounter trouble if you neglect to pay the rent or somehow damage the property.

Rents are paid monthly in advance. Most landlords and rental agents seek a security deposit too—this is usually equivalent to a month's rent, though it may sometimes be a little more. Providing you haven't damaged the property or its contents, this sum will be returned to you once the lease is up and you vacate the premises.

Once You're There

If you need to visit a doctor for a minor ailment, most general practitioners charge a consultation fee of around $35. Although you'll need private medical insurance if you're vacationing in Ireland, all residents, irrespective of nationality, are entitled to free hospital care. Treatment isn't dependent upon income and more than half of Ireland's residents don't have any private health insurance at all. Unfortunately free medical care isn't quite as enticing as it first sounds. Unless you were being rushed to the hospital for emergency treatment, you're likely to find yourself at the end of a lengthy waiting list. Having private health insurance allows people to jump the queue when they need more routine treatment.

Some Costs: 1 liter (1.76 pt) milk $0.86, bread $1.14, 100 g (3.5 oz) Nescafé coffee $2.82, 250 g (8.75 oz) sausages $0.86, 1 kg (2.2 lb) pears $2.00, 1 liter (1.76 pt) orange juice $1.08, large chicken $6.00, bale of peat briquettes $2.23 (one bale should keep a fire blazing all night). A week's car rental, economy model, from $140 low season to around $240 in high summer. Rail fare, Dublin-Cork return (round-trip), $42.

Even small towns have branches of Bank of Ireland or Allied Irish Banks, the country's two main retail banks. Nonresidents can open accounts—and if you can prove you have a permanent address in North America, you'll get a far better rate of savings than residents do. The most commonly accepted credit cards are Visa, MasterCard, and American Express.

Dublin

Dublin, Ireland's capital, was once a Viking settlement. Its turbulent tale began in the 9th century when Norse ships breached the river Liffey and established a trading post of wattle houses. Eventually falling to the Anglo-Normans, *Dubh Linn* (the Dark Pool) rapidly developed into an important medieval city, minting its own silver and with a flourishing merchants' guild. It was to be the hub of English rule in Ireland for more than seven centuries.

An active commercial seaport, full of raffish Georgian charm, this gap-toothed braggart of a city offers a real curiosity shop of experiences. It's home to a third of the population and with half of them under 25, it's a young-hearted city with a thriving club scene as well as a reputation for being pub capital of the world. Yet there's a lot more to Dublin than just bricks, books, and booze—the kaleidoscope flicks from Croke Park and an All-Ireland hurling final, to antique dealers in the ramshackle Liberties quarter, to equine spectacle at the annual Horse Show. Above all, Dublin cherishes individualism and the city often seems to be bursting at its creative seams with writers, artists, film directors, actors, musicians, and fashion designers.

You never quite know how a visit is going to be rewarded. Take one blustery April morning—within 30 minutes I found a bookstore offering impromptu Gaelic lessons, an eccentric bearing messages from extra-terrestrials, and in Trinity College there were two Tibetan monks creating a sand mandala, a complex and delicately colored geometric mosaic.

Central Dublin straddles the murky river Liffey. The picturesque way of crossing between the quays is over the wrought-iron Halfpenny Bridge, named after a former toll charge. The city's northside includes O'Connell Street, where the marble-halled General Post Office still bears bullet damage from 1916's Easter Rising. Here too is Moore Street Market, where latter-day Molly Malones flog everything from strawberries to cigarette lighters, "five for a pound."

South of the river, don't miss the chance to see Dublin's most precious literary relic, the 8th-century Book of Kells. A fabulously illuminated gospel text, it's housed in Trinity College, the country's most prestigious university. Founded in 1592 for "the reformation of the barbarism of this rude people," Trinity allows visitors to wander through its campus of rain-polished cobblestones, where courtyards are lined with bicycles.

Flower sellers on Dublin's Grafton Street

© Steenie Harvey

In tourism's poker game, southside Dublin holds the picture cards. Along with a plethora of museums, galleries, and libraries, here are all the handsome Georgian doors that you see on postcards; Dublin Castle and ministerial limousines en route to Ireland's parliament, Dáil Eireann; and the two great cathedrals— Christchurch and St. Patrick's. The latter is best known as the place where Jonathan Swift of *Gulliver's Travels* fame lies buried, rather than as the place where Cromwell's troopers stabled their horses in 1643. This part of the city is also home to St. Stephen's Green, a spacious park laid out by the Guinness family in the 1880s. Only a stone's throw away from the park, dedicated shoppers should make for Grafton Street.

An amble west along the Quays reveals a more chaotic world. Merchant's Arch is the gateway to Temple Bar, an atmospheric warren of 18th-century lanes and cobbled alleyways that have been given the renaissance treatment. Tagged as "Dublin's Left Bank," its psychedelic murals and mendicant Hare Krishnas are doing their valiant best to recapture the Summer of Love. Among bijou restaurants and specialist bookstores, cramped shops carry all the essentials—that's if your idea of essentials includes sharks' teeth, platform shoes, incense sticks, chunks of crystal, and the sounds of Joni Mitchell!

Whether you're here for a holiday or a longer stay, Dublin rental accommodations are far more expensive than in provincial towns and rural areas. Vacation rentals through Trident Holiday Homes (address above in Vacation Rentals) start at $360 weekly for one-bedroom apartments, $584, $720, and $830 for two-, three-, and four-bedroom homes, respectively. They're all in nice areas such as Donnybrook and Ballsbridge.

For long-term rentals, much depends on whereabouts in the city you plan to base yourself. According to the IAVI (Irish Auctioneers and Valuers Institute), the bottom line for rental accommodations in the capital is $722 per month. This rents a one-bedroom studio, though these small furnished units more typically range from $760 to $925 in expanding outer suburbs such as Lucan and Blanchardstown. In sought-after southside districts like Ballsbridge and Temple Bar, the city's refurbished medieval quarter, the figure is more like $1,025. Outside the city center, the DART light railway commutes to swish pockets of beside-the-sea suburbia where homes have recently traded hands for one million dollars and more. Rental prices in areas such as Howth and Killiney are sky-high.

More spacious apartments typically range from $900 to $1,446 monthly. For example, a two-bedroom apartment in the swanky seaside suburb of Dalkey rents for $1,130. Town houses in good neighborhoods like Ballsbridge and Sandymount rent for approximately $2,375, though the corporate sector willingly pays up to $5,320 monthly for quality properties. In traditional residential districts like Rathgar and Terenure, three- and four-bedroom family homes rent for between $1,415 and $1,805, with similar homes in Lucan and the newer suburbs fetching around $950. Dublin's larger agents also usually have homes in rural county Dublin as well as in Wicklow, Meath, and Kildare—satellite counties within commuting distance of the capital.

Sherry Fitzgerald Residential Lettings, 12 Merrion Row, Dublin 2, tel. 353/1-6399290, fax 353/1-6399295, email: info@sheehyres.ie.

Hooke & Macdonald, 52 Merrion Square, Dublin 2, tel. 353/1-6610100, fax 353/1-6766340, www.hookemacdonald.ie.

Lisney, 24 St. Stephen's Green, Dublin 2, tel. 353/1-6382700, email: dublin@lisney.com.

Cork City and County

Bridges, waterways, and convivial pubs characterize salty old Cork. The Republic of Ireland's second largest city, this ancient settlement takes its name from the Irish word *Corcaigh* meaning "a marshy place." Although it's called a city, and has its own university, it's small by American reckonings—just 180,000 inhabitants. Founded as a monastic settlement by St. Finbarre in the 7th century, the city once clustered on 13 separate islands reclaimed from the estuary of the river Lee.

Cork's skyline is one of steeples and chimney pots rather than highrise developments. Although the Vikings razed the original settlement, the picture hasn't changed much since the 18th century, when the city began spreading outwards and upwards. Higgledy-piggledy streets and terraced houses were laid out along the hillsides, and clipper ships came to unload their cargoes of West Indies rum and sugarcane along the Leeside Quays. Although today's container ships now dock downriver in Cork Harbour, Cork still considers itself a seaport city—on some sidewalks you still see the bollards where vessels were tied up and moored. The Latin motto on the city's coat-of-arms is *Statio bene fida carinis*: "a safe haven for ships."

Nowadays most of the old waterways have become stone thoroughfares and the city's center has effectively been turned into a single island by the twists of the river Lee. Here you'll find a mix of wide Georgian malls and backways just begging to be explored. All the tantalizing places are within walking distance of Patrick Street, the city's main shopping street.

Cork city rentals start at around $510 for furnished studios. The *Irish Examiner* covers the Cork area in its classified ads or try Absolute Property Management. Their rental portfolio recently included a two-bedroom city center apartment for $820 monthly. They also have properties throughout the east of the county. Cobh (pronounced Cove), a small town with a strong seafaring history, is only a short distance from Cork city. Two-bedroom apartments here go for around $680 monthly. Within walking distance of the beaches at Inch, and five miles from Midleton, home of Jameson whiskey distillery, the agency had family houses between $790 and $1,360 monthly.

A bus ride from Cork city, and with the West Cork wilderness on the doorstep, Kinsale is county Cork's prettiest harbor town. It's a lovely place to rent a property: the town's ancient buildings are painted in a rainbow palette and festooned with hanging wooden signs. In summer, the atmosphere is almost Mediterranean. Steep cobblestone alleyways are ablaze with floral decorations, while down in the marina a fleet of fishing boats bobs alongside smart white yachts. And everywhere you turn, there are restaurants—Kinsale is known as Ireland's "gourmet capital." Although the average cost of a three-course meal in a top-class establishment weighs in at a hefty $28–35 per head (wine extra), the food is sublime: delights such black sole, red mullet, and seared scallops on a bed of wild samphire.

Two old military forts, the star-shaped Charles Fort and James Fort, guard the harbor entrance, a three-mile walk from Kinsale town center. Within the town, the lanes around Market Square are chock full of craft shops, galleries, and specialty food stores. On Market Square itself, take a peek inside the Old Courthouse—it contains a small museum with an eclectic mix of weird objects: deck chairs from the *Lusitania,* which was

THE RUB OF THE GREEN

Ireland's great appeal for visiting golfers is the extraordinary diversity of its 350-plus courses. One day you can be at the seaside, battling against the westerly winds and giant sand hills of fearsome Atlantic links such as Sligo, Enniscrone, or Connemara where "the Hazards" include drystone walls and the occasional sheep who has decided to go walkabout.

The next you can be relaxing on a glorious parkland course like Glasson near Athlone. Here you can really arrive in style as Glasson has its own jetty for Shannon River cruisers. Or maybe you fancy stepping back in time to the Ascendancy Era? Then visit Adare, a village full of thatched cottages in county Limerick. The golf course here is in the grounds of a Gothic manor house.

Dublin's residents have a tremendous choice: more than 50 venues within an hour's drive. Along with venerable clubs such as The Island at Malahide, where golfers once required a boat to reach the greens, Powerscourt, Druid's Glen, and Portmarnock are all names to make golfers salivate.

From north Donegal's Ballyliffen to the cliff tops at Bantry Bay, there are few courses where the scenery isn't a bewitching distraction. Beside Clew Bay in Mayo, Westport GC huddles below the holy mountain of Croagh Patrick. Kerry is a golfer's heaven and the legendary courses don't just include Waterville, Dooks, and Ballybunion—at Killarney you'll need to keep your eye on the ball and not the visual delights of MacGillicuddy's Reeks. Cork offers up Fota Island and the Old Head of Kinsale.

Greens fees cost from as little as $28 at small Midlands clubs to $237—the cost of a round at Cork's prestigious Old Head of Kinsale. Most courses welcome visitors, but phone the club secretary beforehand to get tee times and check restrictions. There's little point in arriving at a top course and expecting to wield a *niblick* (type of golf club) if your vacation coincides with a tournament event.

Packed with information, the Golfers Guide to Ireland is available from tourist offices. A list of affiliated clubs can also be obtained from the Golfing Union of Ireland, 81 Eglinton Rd., Dublin 4, tel. 353/0-1-269-4111, www.gui.ie.

torpedoed offshore in 1915; transportation orders consigning convicts to Australia; cannonballs from the Battle of Kinsale when the town fell to the English in 1601. I was astounded by a court report from 1714, when two harbor porters were sentenced to be flogged, then hanged on Kinsale's Garrow Green. Their crime? Demanding to work two hours less in their 74-hour week.

According to local agents Sheehy Brothers, 47 percent of properties in Kinsale are bought for investment purposes, and there's a lively rental market. Sample properties for long-term rental include a three-bedroom town center apartment for $964 monthly and a three-bedroom penthouse with spectacular views for $1,092. If you're seeking a vacation rental, Sheehy's also rents properties by the week. Small apartments rent for around $542 weekly in high season and a three-bedroom house with harbor views rents for $422 weekly in April, $482 in May and October, $663 in June and September, and $784 in July and August. Home-from-Home Holidays also has town houses here—weekly rent for a house sleeping five is $241–603.

Absolute Property Management, 81/82 S. Main St., Cork, tel. 353/0-21-4251288, fax 353/0-21-4251315, email: absolute@apartments.ie.

Sheehy Brothers, 10 Short Quay, Kinsale Co. Cork, tel. 353/0-21-4772338, fax 353/0-21-4772472.

Home-from-Home Holidays, 26/27 West Cork Technology Park, Clonakilty, West Cork, tel. 353/0-23-33110.

The Kingdom of Kerry

A land of shimmering lakes and mist-wreathed mountains, Kerry is a deservedly popular holiday destination. County Cork's next-door neighbor, Kerry's rocky peninsulas dip into the Atlantic like a witch's bony fingers and the silver beaches stretch for miles. For scenery to make your spine tingle, travel the famous Ring of Kerry. Encircling a mountain chain called MacGillicuddy's Reeks, this 80-mile circuit around the Iveragh Peninsula is laden with stunning pictures of bays and islands and secret coves. But don't spend all your time in the car—Rossbeigh has an idyllic beach and all around you lies classic countryside for pony-trekking and family rambles.

Pull on your walking boots and tackle Carrauntoohill, at 3,414 feet Ireland's highest peak. Or meander the Kerry Way's network of old drovers' tracks and coastal paths. Littered with archaeological treasures, part of the Way links the pretty villages of Caherdaniel and Sneem. Along this section you'll come across Staigue Fort, a Neolithic ringfort with 13-feet-thick walls and an elaborate system of stairways.

Crammed with holiday homes and pubs galore, Killarney town is the main center for exploring the Ring of Kerry. Horse-drawn jaunting cars trip out to beauty spots like the Torc Falls, the Meeting of the Waters, and 13th-century Ross Castle. Water coaches journey across Lough Leane, the largest of Killarney's Lakes. As you putter along you're treated to some tall tales—O'Sullivan's Cascade supposedly once bubbled with whiskey!

West of the Ring of Kerry, the wild Dingle Peninsula deserves more than a fleeting visit. Rich in Celtic remains, its most famous relic is the Gallarus Oratory—an early church built entirely of unmortared stone and still watertight after more than a thousand years of Irish weather. All roads on this peninsula lead to Dingle town with its gaily painted shop fronts and 52 pubs to serve a resident population of around 1,500. Dingle is bilingual—the people here speak both English and Irish Gaelic—and its eccentric streets are a joy to explore. From Dingle harbor, the lobster fishermen ferry visitors out to see Funghi—a bottlenose dolphin who has made a permanent home in these waters. Offshore lie the Blasket Islands—and it's beyond these uninhabited islets that you'll find Tir na n'Og, the Land of Everlasting Youth. Well, at least that's what Kerryfolk say...

Kerry has an immense choice of holiday properties. Killorglin Golf Club, three miles from Caragh Village, cottages all have three bedrooms and rent for between $338 and $627 weekly, depending on the season. Book well in advance for August 10–12. This is when Killorglin hosts the

St. Patrick and the Snakes: According to folklore, St. Patrick stood on the summit of County Mayo's Croagh Patrick mountain and banished the snakes and other venomous creatures into nearby Lough na Corra. A former pagan sun sanctuary that went by the name of Cruachan Aigle, the mountain remains a pilgrimage site to this day.

© Steenie Harvey

Puck Fair, one of Ireland's biggest livestock markets. A goat is crowned "king" for three days and horses are traded on a spit and a handshake.

Twelve miles south of Kenmare town and the Ring of Kerry, Kenmare River Cottages sleep between six and eight. Weekly costs range from $265 off-peak to $796 high season. Beside Wine Strand Beach, at the heart of Dingle Peninsula's *Gaeltacht* area, Wine Strand Cottages sleep up to eight and rent from $171 weekly low season to $665 in high summer.

North's usually has a good selection of long-term rental properties in the Tralee area in the $400 to $680 per month range. Ideal for a family, a five-bedroom bungalow near Abbeydorney village rents for $572 monthly.

Caragh Village Holiday Homes, Caragh Lake, Co. Kerry, tel. 353/0-66-9769200.

Dream Ireland Holiday Rentals, Lodgewood, Kenmare, Co. Kerry, tel. 353/0-64-41170.

Wine Strand Cottages, Ballyferriter, Dingle, Co. Kerry, tel. 353/0-66-9156044.

James North, Denny St., Tralee, Co. Kerry, tel. 353/0-66-7122699.

The Northwest

Mass tourism hasn't discovered the spectacularly rugged checkerboard of Ireland's northwestern counties. Visit Sligo and Donegal and you enter a secret land that seems to lie at the very ends of the earth. Edged by miles of dramatic Atlantic coastline, it's a region of waterscaped wilderness where traditional values and the Gaelic language are still going strong.

All the way to Malin Head, Ireland's most northerly point, hospitable little towns and villages stand on the threshold of glorious scenery. If you're here on vacation, why not combine your stay with some outdoor activities? You can play golf against blue-penciled mountain backdrops, sail the wide sweep of Donegal Bay, hike or pony-trek through twilight glens. For fisherfolk, there's shore and deep-sea angling as well as scores of loughs (lakes) shimmering away in dragonfly colors.

Bridging the Garavogue River, the spires of Sligo town are overshadowed by Benbulben, a tabletop mountain where the mythical hero Diarmuid met a grisly end on the tusks of a magical, green-eared boar. The town center is jammed with old-fashioned tearooms and small shops where you can buy anything from edible seaweed to tweed capes and tin whistles. Quirke's Butchers is a source of mythological wooden carvings; Mullaney's Drapery keeps archaic shipping registers listing passengers on 19th-century emigrant ships. Pubs? Sligo has dozens, and many hold lively music sessions. And then there's Hargadons ... Modestly describing itself as "a pearl, a gem, a jewel in the crown of Mother Ireland," this peculiar drinking-den is on O'Connell

Street. It's a warren of smoky brown snugs where shelves sag under the weight of whiskey jars and even the atmosphere is intoxicating. Needless to say Hargadons serves a great pint of Guinness but just look around you—there's a potbellied stove, huge glittering mirrors, open turf fires, and customers who can talk the hind leg off the proverbial donkey. Don't miss it.

The poet William Butler Yeats was inspired by the Sligo countryside, his "land of heart's desire." Local beauty spots include Lough Arrow, Glencar Waterfall, Ladies Brae, and Lough Gill with its enchanted Isle of Inisfree. On Lough Gill's southern shore is the holy well of Tobernalt, whose crystal waters are reputed to have healing powers. It's surrounded by a woodland grove where sacred statues are bedecked in flowers, and trees are garlanded with rosary beads and other votive offerings.

Six miles from Sligo town, Knocknarea is another of the county's miniature mountains. At 1,083 feet high, it's topped by a cairn known locally as Maeve's Grave and it gives you a fantastic lookout over the domain of Ireland's legendary warrior queen. Down below, Carrowmore has a pony-trekking center as well as the largest megalithic necropolis in Europe.

When the tide is right, you can walk across from seaside Strandhill to the original Coney Island. Way back when, a Sligo ship's captain was amazed to find his port of call hopping with exactly the same kind of inhabitants as back home—rabbits (*Coinin* in Gaelic). This, apparently, is how New York's Coney Island got its name.

Into the west: Friendly people, traditional ways, and bewitching scenery

Other Sligo seaside villages include Rosses Point—along with a championship golf course it has golden beaches, caves, cliff-top walks, and keening seabird colonies, noisy as a convention of banshees. More golf and beaches at Enniscrone, which still has its Edwardian seaweed baths where you can discover the benefits of thalassotherapy. Three-bedroom holiday homes rent for between $300 and $710 weekly here.

Before heading into Donegal, walk the coast at Streedagh, where three of the Spanish

© Steenie Harvey

Armada's fleet were shipwrecked in 1588. It's a lovely spot for collecting shells or simply poking about in tidepools. Who knows—you may even turn up Spanish treasure.

The Blue Stack Mountains and all the wild highlands of Donegal loom straight ahead. Meaning "fort of the foreigner," you need a car to appreciate this county fully—public transport is very limited. If you're following the coastline, one of the first settlements you'll come to is Killybegs: the "town of the little churches" and Donegal's main fishing port. From here a twisty road smothered in wandering sheep brings you to Slieve League, Ireland's highest sea cliffs. Carry a good map—you're now in one of the *Gaeltacht* areas where the signposts are in Irish, not English.

With its thatched and whitewashed cottages, Glencolmcille is one of Donegal's prettiest communities. Tempting tracks dip into tranquil glens, past rocky hillside farms and down to the sea. A "folk village" represents different country lifestyles and the whole area teems with prehistoric monuments. St. Colmcille had a retreat here and anyone with the pilgrimage bug should come for the saint's feast day, June 9th.

Late July has Marys from here, there, and everywhere heading towards Dungloe. The town hosts the northwest's biggest event, the "Mary from Dungloe" festival. Whatever your name, you'll get caught up in street theater, face-painting competitions, and a torrent of Irish music and dance. Dungloe makes a great base for exploring Donegal's high western corner. You can visit islands like Tory and Aranmore, or take a panoramic coastal drive to the Bloody Foreland, named after its flaming sunsets. But don't neglect the hinterland, which guards much of the county's most breathtaking scenery.

A quartz-tipped beacon, Mount Errigal towers 2,466 feet above everything. Spreading below is Glenveagh National Park—10,000 mountainous hectares of loughs and forests and waterfalls. Deep in the heart of this wilderness is Lough Beagh and its romantic castle, whose gardens are a picture of exotic blooms and classical statuary.

Where to stay? Well, you can choose from an array of options through the tourist office brochure or website. If your requirements are an island setting and a traditional thatched-roof cottage where you can have a peat fire blazing in the hearth, Donegal Thatched Cottages are near Dungloe on Cruit Island, which is linked by a road bridge to the mainland. Prices for three-bedroom cottages start at $213 in January, rising to $755 weekly in July and August. The Rectory Cottages are in the seaside village of Maghery, four miles from Dungloe town. These cost from $180 to $580 per week.

For long-term rentals in the northwest, contact local realtors' offices. A furnished apartment in Sligo or a little country bungalow will cost you $570–680 per month. Sligo town is your best bet for the widest choice of accommodations—agents with rental properties here include H&H and Sligo Estates.

Cahermore Holiday Homes, Enniscrone, Co. Sligo, tel. 353/0-96-36996.

Donegal Thatched Cottages, Conor & Mary Ward, Upper Rosses, Rosses Point, Co. Sligo, tel. 353/0-71-77197.

The Rectory Cottages, Denis & Nuala Hanlon, Crucknagera, Dungloe, Co. Donegal, tel. 353/0-75-21286.

H&H Property Center, Savoy Buildings, Market St., Sligo Town, Co. Sligo, tel. 353/0-71-41250/47013.

Sligo Estates, Quay St., Sligo Town, Sligo, tel. 353/0-71-43425.

Shannon Adventures

The Shannon is Ireland's longest river—220 miles from its source in county Cavan down to the Atlantic. Vikings and Irish chieftains once struggled for control of this mighty water highway and it still bristles with reminders of long ago: castles, round towers, and a wealth of early Christian settlements.

Apparently the Shannon was formed due to the antics of a pagan goddess, Sinainn. She annoyed the guardian spirit of a magic well—its waters rose up and chased her westwards to the Atlantic where she drowned. Sinainn belonged to the *Tuatha de Danaan*, the light-loving gods of prehistory who were eventually driven underground. They dwelt in caves, earthen raths, and hollow hills and mortals knew them as fairies or "the Good People." In this land of strange enchantments it's still considered unlucky to build a new house across a "fairy path" or cut down thorn trees—magic trees protected by spirits called *lughnantisidhe*.

If you yearn to get even further away from it all, you could spend a vacation afloat, chugging along Ireland's waters at a stately six miles an hour. The Shannon opens up into a number of loughs (lakes) and you don't have to be an expert to take to the water. River cruisers are easy to handle, friendly lock-keepers help you through any tricky stretches, and—best of all—no commercial traffic disturbs the Shannon's serenity. Plenty of taverns line the riverbanks and after soaking up the sights, the perfect way to end the day is with a glass of Guinness in a cozy waterfront pub. You can start your odyssey at any number of Shannon towns and villages, all with a good choice of cruiser rental companies.

One of the lower Shannon's main marinas is Killaloe in county Clare. Linked to Ballina village in county Tipperary by a 13-arch stone bridge, Killaloe is the main settlement on Lough Derg. The Shannon's largest lake, its name comes from the Irish word *dergherc*, meaning "lake of the bloody eye." The one-eyed King Euchy mistakenly told a malicious poet named Ahirney to take whatever he so wanted as a gift. Ahirney demanded the king's remaining eye and the blood from Euchy's empty socket turned the entire lake red. Killaloe was once Ireland's ancient capital, and Brian Boru had his 11th-century palace here. Vikings visited too—Thorgrim's stone cross in the cathedral is inscribed in Norse runic script.

Many unspoiled villages with mooring facilities string Lough Derg's shores. Along with two excellent music pubs, Paddy's and the Derg Inn, Terryglass village also has two holy wells, one reputedly holding the cure for hangovers! With a high round tower, the remains of six churches and monastic cells, Lough Derg's most historic islet is the holy island of Iniscealtra. According to ancient annals, it once boasted a tree that distilled "juice tasting of honey with the headiness of wine." In 1609, 15,000 pilgrims gathered here but the church eventually suppressed the annual festivities, which seem to have been more bacchanalian drink-fest than pious pilgrimage.

If you enjoy exploring twisty, old-fashioned streets, stop at Athlone, the main town on the Shannon's middle stretch. Its Norman castle was rebuilt because the original structure was targeted by an estimated 21,000 cannonballs, courtesy of William of Orange's invading army in 1691. Dating from 1630, Sean's Bar on West Quay is popular with boaters. A short distance from Athlone, Clonmacnoise was Ireland's greatest monastic city and an important center for learning. Founded by St. Ciaran in A.D. 545, its churches and round towers survived Viking attacks but not the attentions of the English garrison from Athlone who ransacked the saint's two round towers and eight churches in 1552. The surrounding water meadows are home to one of the country's rarest birds, the corncrake.

North of Athlone is Lough Ree, the Lake of Kings. Although not so famous as Scotland's Loch Ness, this is also reputedly the haunt of a water monster. In 1960, three Dublin clergymen described seeing *something* with a serpentlike head and a knobby body. Sightings go back centuries and the *Life of St Mochua* actually maintains the monster devoured a hapless villager. Lough Ree may also hide a supernatural city within its depths. Legend tells that mortals often visited this city, and a Clonmacnoise monk named Cormac decided to check the story for himself. Blame the fairies, blame the monster, but Cormac was never seen in this world again.

For more saintly legends on the Upper Shannon, moor at Tarmonberry and walk up the hill to Whitehall Church. The churchyard contains a "stone boat," apparently used by St. Barry for Shannon crossings. Local lore says villagers also used it until "they lost their innocence." St. Barry's Holy Well sprang from the site where the saint apparently battled with yet another water monster.

Upriver is Carrick-on-Shannon, a neat little town with some good waterfront pubs. Try Cryan's for traditional Irish music or Glancy's if you hanker for foot-stomping country and western. If you fancy catching your own supper, shops stock fishing tackle and live bait. Complete with riverside walk, one of the northern Shannon's prettiest tributaries is the Boyle River, which leads into Lough Key.

Lough Key is named after *Cé*, the druid of King Nuadha of the Silver Arm. The lake's wooded islets include Castle Island where the lovesick princess Una Bhan was imprisoned. Una pined for her lowborn lover who attempted to swim the lake on a chilly winter's night. Needless to say he drowned and Una died of grief—two intertwined trees on the island are said to mark the lovers' graves. Lough Key is surrounded by a Forest Park where I've often spotted gray herons in the reedbeds, tiny goldcrests flitting through the treetops, and deer and foxes along the trails. In springtime, the woods burst with bluebells: one walk takes you across a Fairy Bridge to the Bog Gardens; other tracks lead to ring forts, a *souterrain* (underground burial chamber), and a "Wishing Chair."

Cabin cruisers are fully equipped so all you need is food supplies. Companies ask for a deposit of around $450, which is returnable—providing you don't sink the boat! Don't worry—you're given all necessary navigation instruction beforehand. Rental costs vary, and a lot depends on boat size as well as the season. July and August are the expensive times. Small two- or three-berth cruisers start at around $515 per week, but you could pay $2,415 for an eight-berth cruiser in peak season.

Emerald Star, 47 Carrick-on-Shannon, Co. Leitrim, tel. 353/0-78-20234, www.emeraldstar.ie.

Athlone Cruisers, Jolly Mariner Marina, Athlone, Co. Westmeath, tel. 353/0-902-72892.

Carrick Craft, The Marina, Carrick-on-Shannon, Co. Leitrim, tel. 353/0-78-20236.

Waveline Cruisers, Killinure Point, Glasson, Co. Westmeath, tel. 353/0-902-85711.

PART III
France and the Low Countries

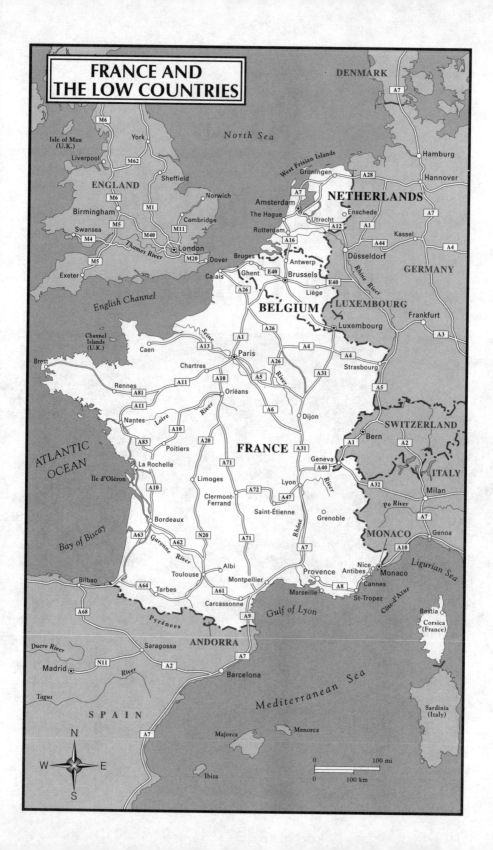

FRANCE AND THE LOW COUNTRIES

DENMARK

North Sea

Isle of Man (U.K.)
York
Liverpool
ENGLAND
Sheffield
Norwich
Birmingham
Cambridge
Swansea
London
Dover
Exeter
Calais

West Frisian Islands
Groningen
NETHERLANDS
Hamburg
Hannover
Amsterdam
The Hague
Enschede
Utrecht
Rotterdam
Kassel
Düsseldorf
GERMANY
Bruges
Antwerp
Ghent
Brussels
Calais
Liège
BELGIUM
LUXEMBOURG
Frankfurt
Luxembourg

Thames River

English Channel

Channel Islands (U.K.)

Brest
Caen
Chartres
Paris
Seine
Strasbourg
Rennes
Orléans
Bern
SWITZERLAND
Nantes
Loire
River
Dijon
Poitiers
FRANCE
Geneva
La Rochelle
Île d'Oléron
ITALY
Milan
Limoges
Lyon
Clermont-Ferrand
River
Po River
Bordeaux
Saint-Étienne
Grenoble
Genoa
MONACO
Garonne River
Albi
Provence
Nice
Monaco
ATLANTIC OCEAN
Toulouse
Montpellier
Antibes
Cannes
Bay of Biscay
Bilbao
Tarbes
Marseille
St-Tropez
Côte-d'Azur
Ligurian Sea
Carcassonne
Gulf of Lyon
Bastia
Pyrénées
Corsica (France)
ANDORRA
Duero River
Saragossa
Madrid
River
Barcelona
Mediterranean Sea
SPAIN
Sardinia (Italy)
Tagus
Majorca
Menorca
Ibiza

N
W   E
S

0   100 mi
0   100 km

4 France

Great wines, great art and architecture, and style with a capital S. La Belle France is one of Europe's most seductive countries. Some people come for a month and stay for a lifetime so be careful—you might never find your way home again. Not only do the French have cities that are real *grandes dames*, they also possess a sun-kissed coastline and a golden countryside marbled with bewitching seams of tradition. This is a place where gourmet meals last for three hours at a stretch, and the clothing stores really are to die for.

Whether you're seeking a short- or long-term rental, the thorniest question is deciding where to lay your head. Paris or the provinces? The medieval wine villages of Alsace or the wild Celtic fringe of Brittany? The lavender fields of rural Provence, the walled towns and mystic castles of the Languedoc, or the moonlit bays and palm-lined promenades of the glamorous Riviera? The capital, Paris, is synonymous with romance, elegance, and heavenly food, but a country of 60 million people has lots to offer. For an overview of possibilities, contact the French tourist office.

French Government Tourist Office, 444 Madison Ave., New York, NY 10022-6903, 410/286-8310, fax 212/838-7855, www.francetourism.com.

French Government Tourist Office, 30 St. Patrick St., Suite 700, Toronto, Ontario M5T 3A3, 416/593-4723, fax 416/979-7587.

Legalities

North American citizens staying in France for up to 90 days don't need visas. Extended stays mean obtaining a long-stay visa (*Visa de Séjour long*) from the French consulate. It isn't possible to arrive as a tourist and then change status to that of a resident. The authorities require you to return home to apply for the appropriate visa. You'll also need documentation for

the red tape formalities. This comprises a passport, valid for three months after the last day of stay; eight application forms per individual (two for a child); eight recent passport-size photos; proof of U.S. resident status; financial guarantees such as a letter

from your bank stating that you have sufficient means to live in France, or proof of a retirement pension; proof of medical insurance with coverage valid in France; a non–criminal record certificate to be obtained from the police in your current town or city.

Consulat Général de France, 4101 Reservoir Rd. NW, Washington, DC 20007-2185, 202/944-6195, fax 202/944-6148.

Embassy of France, 42 Sussex Dr., Ottawa, Ontario K1M 2C9, 613/789-1795.

The Language

Visiting France is always the cultural treat *par excellence* but how do many of us return the favor? We fly in like assassins and attempt to murder their language! Setting out on a French odyssey, many travelers may be concerned about encountering a language barrier the height of Mont Blanc. After all, the French have a worrying reputation for being snooty and offhand with linguistically challenged foreigners.

Well, even if your own French studies never went beyond your school days, (or even if you don't speak the language at all), you'll still find that many doors are open to you. Especially in Paris, Strasbourg, and along the

Riviera, most real estate agents and people in the professional and service industries speak English. If you're timid about speaking French, you can even rent vacation properties from English expatriates. However, do try to *parlez*, even if you have to painstakingly pick a path through a phrase book.

Numerous language schools are geared to teaching adults. For a 1–3 week intensive course, prices average around $200 weekly. If more leisurely progress appeals, (e.g., two-hour sessions totaling 32 hours per month), conversation classes cost approximately $300 monthly.

Alliance Francaise, 101 Boulevard Raspail, 75270 Paris, tel. 33/0-1-45-44-38-28, fax 33/0-1-45-44-89-42, email: info@alliancefr.org.

Cetradel Elysees, 120 Ave. des Champs Elysees, 75008 Paris, tel. 33/0-1-56-69-21-00, fax 33/0-1-56-69-21-01, email: cetradel@wanadoo.fr.

Elfca (Institut d'Enseignement de la Langue Francaise sur la Côte d'Azur), 66 Avenue de Toulon, 83400 Hyères, France, tel. 33/0-4-94-65-03-31, fax 33/0-4-94-65-81-22, email: elfca@elfca.com.

Information on accredited private language schools throughout France from Jean Petrissans, Souffle, Espace Charlotte, 83260, La Crau, France, tel. 33/0-4-94-00-94-65, fax 33/0-4-94-00-92-30, email: courrier@souffle.asso.fr.

Vacation Rentals

The French call a vacation rental property a *location saisonnaire*. The most inexpensive way to rent is directly from the owners. Paris rental apartments are discussed later, but the ideal way to experience rural France for a short period is by renting furnished holiday properties—*gîtes*. There is no

Colmar, in the Alsace region.

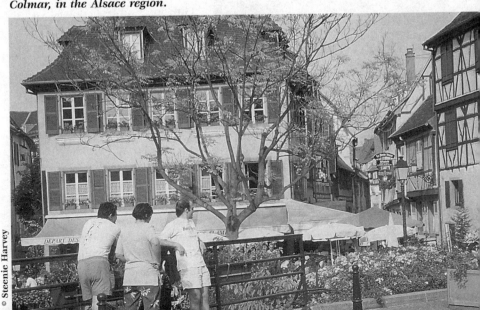

© Steenie Harvey

USEFUL HOUSING TERMS

arrondissements—districts
gîtes—furnished vacation properties
immobilier—a sales and rental agency
location saisonnaire—vacation rental property

meublé—furnished
non-meublé—unfurnished
vide—unfurnished
Visa de Séjour long—long-stay visa

typical *gîte* property—take your pick from simple cottages to converted watermills, seaside villas, and restored *bastide* (fortified) farmhouses complete with outdoor swimming pool.

Gîtes are found in every corner of France and rental rates depend upon property size and season. Off-peak weekly rents for modest properties can be as low as $190, and generally include allowances of electricity and bottled gas in the price. Needless to say, high summer is the most expensive period. Bookings usually run Saturday to Saturday and you may be asked for a security deposit (typically around $145 to $190), returnable on departure. Bed linens and towels aren't usually included, but most owners rent sets for around $15 per person weekly.

Fruit, vegetables, spices and all kinds of other goodies are sold at the open air market on Cours Saleya in Nice.

© Steenie Harvey

There are a number of umbrella organizations for *gîte* owners, both in France and overseas. With 55,000 holiday addresses on their books, the big player in the market is Gîtes de France. They sell a range of brochures including a countrywide guide to *gîte* properties and individual guides to France's 22 different administrative regions (further divided into *departements*).

Many holiday properties are owned by British expatriates. France is the most popular foreign country for U.K. second-home buyers—so if chattering away in the French language is a problem, you may feel happier dealing with English speakers. If so, get hold of a copy of Chez Nous, a brochure with descriptive property listings for hundreds of English-speaking *gîte* owners whom you then contact direct.

Maison des Gîtes de France et du Tourisme Vert, 59, rue St. Lazare, 75439 Paris CEDEX 09, tel. 33/0-1-49-70-75-75, fax 33/0-1-42-81-28-53, email: info@gites-de-france.fr. (CEDEX always indicates a box number.)

Chez Nous, Spring Mill, Earby, Lancashire, BB94 0AA Great Britain, tel. 44/0-8700-781-400.

Hideaways in the most desirable areas are quickly snapped up, especially in summer, so don't leave booking until the last minute. If you can access the Internet, some English-speaking owners also list their *gîtes* through online brochures. Two to try are www.francedirect.net and www.gite.com.

VACATION RENTAL AGREEMENTS

Whether it's a Paris flat or a rural cottage, and whether your stay is for a single week or a couple of months, you usually have to pay a deposit when booking in advance. Depending on the owner or agency, the balance may be due six to eight weeks beforehand, or when picking up the keys. Taxes are usually inclusive, but some establishments bill a local "tourist tax" separately. It's generally only a small payment, usually amounting to less than $1 per person daily.

Despite all the gingerbread cottages, this Alsace wine village is in France, not Germany.

© Steenie Harvey

Long-Term Rentals

Although it's a different story in Paris, large provincial towns, and along the Riviera, most properties for long-term rental in rural locations are unfurnished. Although it's possible to rent furnished homes in the countryside, the majority are rented by the week or month as vacation homes. However, you can sometimes rent these for longer periods at advantageous rates during winter.

For longer stays, the best thing to do is to get in touch with an *immobilier*—a sales and rental agency. Over 7,000 agents belong to FNAIM (Fédération Nationale de l'Immobilier) and they'll provide a list of member agents in your chosen area. The organization's website has a database detailing what kind of furnished and unfurnished properties are available in any given area—and at what price.

Each property description lists the relevant *immobilier* with office address and phone number. Once you've chosen a home, the agent arranges all the rental details with the owner, but note you'll be charged a "finder's fee." Generally amounting to one month's rent, it covers the drawing up of a written lease and inventory list. The advantage of dealing through licensed realtors rather than going it alone is that they can also provide various services such as arranging utilities and telephone installations, housing insurance (required to be paid by the tenant for unfurnished properties), and cleaning services.

FNAIM, 129 rue du Faubourg St. Honoré, 75008 Paris, tel. 33/01-53-76-03-52, fax 33/01-42-56-28-28, www.fnaim.fr, email: fnaim@fnaim.fr.

LONG-TERM RENTAL AGREEMENTS

The norm is to sign a one-year lease for furnished properties and a three-year lease for unfurnished properties. The law protects tenants and landlords cannot renege on an agreement without just cause. The scales are tilted in favor of the tenant as rental agreements for both furnished and unfurnished properties can be broken by the renter with three months' notice (one month's notice in the case of a job transfer). Rent is usually paid monthly in advance, but the owner cannot demand more than two months' rent as a deposit. Providing no damage is incurred, this deposit must be returned to the tenant within two months of the termination of the lease.

Although maintenance charges and habitation tax is usually included in short-term rental prices, this isn't generally the case for yearly or three-year leases. Habitation tax varies between areas, but is usually 2.5 percent of the basic monthly rent. It's charged to all tenants who are *in situ* on January 1st and is payable in a lump sum in November. Maintenance charges apply to apartment buildings and cover such things as staircase cleaning, concierge charges, elevator repair, etc. A typical charge for this is $35 to $75 monthly. Electricity and gas needs budgeting for too—average bills amount to $77 to $115 monthly. Tenants are also asked for financial proof of ability to pay the rent. To avoid the risk of debt, most *immobiliers* and agencies require your monthly income to be at least three times as high as the rent.

Short-term furnished contracts are renewable at the landlord's option, but tenants in unfurnished properties have a right to renew when the lease term expires. Those in unfurnished properties are responsible for insurance costs. A landlord is entitled to make you leave if you cannot produce proof of insurance.

Once You're There

Private medical insurance will cover hospital treatment, though for minor ailments the cost of visiting a doctor will probably have to come out of your own pocket. Expect to pay around $20 to visit a general practitioner and $32 to see a specialist in his or her office. If you need to call a doctor out, fees are higher for home visits and higher still for nighttime callouts, weekends, and public holidays. Within Paris, Neuilly suburb boasts the American Hospital, staffed by American and English-speaking personnel.

American Hospital of Paris, 63 Boulevard Victor Hugo, 92202 Neuilly, tel. 33/0-1-46-41-25-25.

Some Costs: baguette $0.85, 500 g (17.5 oz) coffee $4.50, 6 eggs $1.25, 1 kg (2.2 lb) rump steak $14.00, 1 kg (2.2 lb) chicken breasts $9.72, 1 liter (1.76 pt) milk $0.98, 1 kg (2.2 lb) sugar $1.49, 1 kg (2.2 lb) apples $2.22. Nothing beats buying a crusty baguette direct from the bakery, but food bills vary according to whether you shop at an out-of-town supermarket chain such as Carrefour or a more expensive local grocer. Movie tickets generally cost between $4 and $6.50, though you may pay around $9 in

Nice is a seaside city, wrapped around the Baie des Anges, the Bay of Angels.

© Steenie Harvey

Paris. English-language newspapers run $1.80 to $2.66. A week's car hire, economy model, from $175. Train ticket, Paris to Strasbourg, costs $35.15. Check out more train fares, routes and timings at www.sncf.fr.

Providing you have a residential address, you can hold a French bank account. It will be useful for setting up direct debits to pay utility bills and monthly rent. Banque Nationale de Paris (BNP), Credit Lyonnais, and Societe Generale are the main players in the banking world, all with nationwide branches. Opening hours vary but the norm is 9 A.M. to 4:30 P.M. weekdays. English-speaking expatriates can avail of full banking services through a number of well-known U.S. and British banks. They include:

Citibank, 125 Ave. des Champs Elysees, 75008 Paris, tel. 33/0-1-53-23-33-60.

Barclays SA International Branch, 6 Rond-Point des Champs-Elysées 75008, Paris, tel. 33/0-1-44-95-13-80.

At Home in Paris

Henry Miller got it right. This city of singing streets really does drip with history, glory, and romance. Yet you don't have to pay exorbitant amounts for a Parisian rental, not unless your heart is set upon an extremely fashionable residential neighborhood. Many expatriates are drawn to familiar place-names such as St. Germaine de Prés and the Latin Quarter, but the latest district to hit top desirability ratings in this ever-evolving city is the once staunchly proletarian Bastille Quarter. Here, amongst cobbled courtyards and narrow backways, many old *ateliers* (workshops) have been transformed into high-rent lofts, hip wine bars, and minimalist boutiques.

Although Paris isn't dauntingly huge, and the Métro tunnels its way into every neighborhood, it's still big enough to get lost in. If the capital is fairly unfamiliar to you, it helps to have some advance knowledge of the geographical layout. Getting your bearings is fairly straightforward—the River Seine divides the city into two main areas, the Left Bank (Rive Gauche) and Right Bank (Rive Droite). Look at a map and the Left Bank is south of the river, the Right Bank is north. The city is further divided into twenty separate *arrondissements*, or numbered districts, which spiral out in a clockwise direction—kind of like a snail shell—from the center. Low-numbered *arrondissements* (the 1st to the 7th) are central. The west of the city takes in the 8th, 16th, and 17th *arrondissements*; the 9th, 10th, 18th, and 19th are to the north; the 11th, 12th, and 20th are east; the 13th, 14th, and 15th south. The higher the number that each piece of the jigsaw puzzle carries, the further away you'll be from the city's heart.

Each neighborhood has its own distinct character—the sidebar in this chapter offers a taster of each *arrondissement*. For example, if you yearn to immerse yourself in the bewitching caldron of bohemian Paris, look for a home-away-from-home in the 5th *arrondissement*. Known to generations of foreign visitors as the Latin Quarter, the district lies east of Boulevard St-Michel. It supposedly got its name because Latin was the everyday language of resident students here up until the French Revolution.

Still the haunt of Sorbonne students, the 5th is the university district and part of the Left Bank. It's also a microcosm of provincial France and its former colonies—narrow streets are packed with Breton crêperies, Alsatian beer brasseries, and splendid family-run charcuterie shops where owners from the Auvergne make their own sausages and pâtés. The backstreets abound in tiny bistros charging ridiculously low prices—a simple lunch of salad, *moules* (mussels), and a slice of upside-down apple flan called *tarte tatin* costs less than $8.

And you don't have to traipse off to Istanbul, Algiers, or Tunis to take a *hamam* bath, hear the call of the muezzin, or to sip mint tea and feast on grilled *kefta* (a type of spicy meatball) and honeyed pastries—you can experience all those exotic delights in the oh-so-cosmopolitan Latin Quarter. A great way to get your first taste of its color and vitality is to stroll past the foodie shops and stalls of Rue Mouffetard, the district's street market. It's a fantastic area but there's one caveat—the ribbon-thin backstreets get horribly traffic-congested.

Like much of central Paris's housing stock, the majority of apartment buildings were built between 1850 and 1920. They're often known as Haussmann apartments as Baron Haussmann, Napoleon III's Interior Minister, initiated the housing program. Replacing the old Paris slums, these apartment houses were all built in similar style, elegantly simple, and usually six stories high. The ground floor was given over to shops and the 1st floor to shopkeepers, who often had to contend with mud-splattered windows from the carriage trade in the street below. With their high ceilings and the prerequisite balcony, the most sought-after apartments were on the 2nd and 3rd floors. The least preferable location was the 4th and 5th floors—not surprising when you realize that in pre-elevator days, tired tenants had to lug their heavy shopping bags up long flights of stairs.

Costs of renting a Parisian apartment depend on length of stay: you'll usually pay a premium to rent for a single week. Even so, it's still likely to be far less than hotel bills. If you're prepared to forgo a central location, small furnished studios and apartments with kitchen facilities rent for less than $342 weekly in the outer 9th and 18th *arrondissements*. Work it out for yourself how much the bill would be for a couple in a medium-class hotel! Even somewhere more central doesn't necessarily have to cost an arm and a leg. At the time of writing, a furnished studio apartment for two on the 5th *arrondissement*'s Rue de la Harpe rented for an equivalent $522 a week. Stay a month and the total cost is $1,231.

PARIS'S ARRONDISSEMENTS

The two numbers on the end of a Paris address are a code—they immediately explain in which *arrondissement* a place is located. Thus, Paris 75015 indicates an address in the 15th *arrondissement*; 75008 is in the 8th. Let's zip through them.

Romantic strolls in the Tuileries gardens, the Louvre museum on the doorstep. The central 1st *arrondissement* also takes in Châtelet, the Palais-Royal park and the old market of Les Halles, now a shopping mall. Very busy, it can be a pricey area for apartment-hunters.

The 2nd *arrondissement* is home to many lovely 19th-century shopping arcades and elegant department stores such as Printemps and Galleries Lafayette. Sentier, the traditional heart of Paris's garment trade, also falls into the boundaries. Very central, and though you can occasionally find reasonable-priced accommodations, apartment houses near the Opera and Madeleine command high rents.

Tiled passageways, cobbled courtyards, and thoroughly intriguing. The 3rd *arrondissement* bursts with character, though you may think that cafés that cater for philosophical debate take pretentiousness to new heights. Known as le Marais (the marshes), many gentrified houses here date from the 17th and 18th centuries. And though it might be a former swamp and birthplace of the Revolution, rents aren't at proletarian levels.

The chic Marais spills over into the 4th *arrondissement* and includes Rue des Rosiers, the hub of Paris's Jewish quarter. Alongside designer boutiques, kosher delis offer delicacies such as paprika cream cheese and stuffed vine leaves. The district's southside boasts the most famous Notre Dame church and the beautiful Place des Vosges, built in 1612, where Victor Hugo once lived.

The 5th *arrondissement* is the densely packed Latin Quarter, home to the Sorbonne University, and dozens of interesting streets. Bohemian booksellers along the River Seine's quays, wonderful foodie shops, and some reasonably priced accommodations for such a central location.

Stylish, bookish, and artistic, the 6th *arrondissement* is very upmarket and rents can be stratospheric. Perfect for gallery-browsing, the area takes in St. Germain des Prés and the Odéon. As most visitors with a guidebook soon discover, the St. Germain des Prés quarter was the birthplace of existentialism. It's almost obligatory to seek out cafés such as Deux Magots and Flore where luminaries such as J. P. Sartre and Simone de Beauvoir once held court.

The expensive residential streets of the 7th *arrondissement* include Avenue de Tourville, the highest value property in the French version of Monopoly. This area also takes in Les Invalides, a number of government ministerial buildings, and the unforgettable Eiffel Tower. A tourist cliché it may be, but come nightfall when it's lit up like a Christmas tree, the sight is heart-stopping.

The 8th *arrondissement* includes the Champs Elysées as well as many Parisian financial and corporate institutions. If you want to do lasting damage to your credit cards, the shops of rue St. Honoré will happily oblige.

Mainly a working-class district, the 9th *arrondissement* takes in the streets of Pigalle and Clichy, which can be rather sleazy at night.

As a quick rule of thumb, one-room furnished apartments average $1,120 to $1,580 per month, two rooms $1,230 to $2,410, and three rooms $1,630 to $2,750. Here are a few examples of what you can expect to pay. Sleeping two, a bijou apartment on Rue Pondicherry, close to the Champ de Mars and the Eiffel Tower, was recently available through Locaflat for an equivalent $1,653 per month. The same agency quoted $1,880 for another

Many Turkish and North African immigrants live in the 10th *arrondissement*—consequently apartment rents are fairly affordable. However, streets around the two stations (Gare du Nord and Gare de l'Est) aren't exactly inviting.

An up-and-coming neighborhood, the arty 11th *arrondissement* is the Bastille district, fast becoming a desirable residential location. Residents aren't too far out of the central Paris loop and the colorful Marché Richard Lenoir street market is the place to shop like a Parisian for your fruit and vegetables.

The 12th *arrondissement* is another evolving residential district and the once run-down streets around the Gare de Lyon are slowly being spruced up. Since the 15th century, this has been an artisan's quarter, particularly for furniture-making. If costs are a key factor, this is one of the best bets for finding an inexpensive location.

With more dim sum restaurants than you can shake a chopstick at, the 13th *arrondissement* includes Chinatown and the Bibliothèque de France complex. Can be a good value, but some charmless high-rises have been built here.

With no major tourist sites, the 14th *arrondissement* is a great bet for authentic Parisian living. Neighborhoods include Denfert, Porte d'Orléans, and Montparnasse, which it shares with the neighboring 15th.

The neighborhoods of the 15th *arrondissement* are now also extremely popular with middle-class Parisian families. Montparnasse was a magnet for foreigners before World War II, attracting giants of the artistic and literary world. The litany of famous names that found inspiration here includes Hemingway, Fitzgerald, Modigliani, and Picasso.

Quiet, staid, and proudly bourgeois, the 16th *arrondissement* has its share of prestigious addresses and can be very expensive. It's bordered to the west by the Bois du Boulogne.

If the 17th *arrondissement* were a psychiatric patient, the conclusion would be that it has a split personality. Locations are expensive for the moneyed residents who live around Parc Monceau, a pretty park brimming with follies and statuary. Things get more affordable around the working-class La Forche district.

Containing Paris's greatest concentration of immigrants, the 18th *arrondissement* wraps itself around the switchback streets of Montmartre. It's an inexpensive area with good Métro links to the center and some excellent markets. With more than 3,000 stalls, the Marché aux Puces Cligancourt is France's largest flea market, selling everything from household bric-a-brac to crystal chandeliers, carved African masks, and army surplus clothing on Saturdays, Sundays, and Mondays.

The 19th *arrondissement* is not a good choice for would-be residents with stars in their eyes. Too many parts are drab, depressing, and rife with drug addicts and dealers. It's definitely not for me, and it's probably not for you either.

The 20th arrondissement is just as affordable and much more pleasant—a blue-collar district with a vibrant mix of artists and ethnic restaurants. The major draw for visitors is a danse macabre through the Pere Lachaise cemetery, last resting place of Freddie Chopin, Oscar Wilde, Edith Piaf, and Jim Morrison of the Doors.

small apartment in the Latin Quarter, near Odeon Métro and Jardin de Luxembourg. Through MS Mesnil, a monthly rent of $2,028 secured a two-bedroom apartment in the 4th *arrondissement*.

Rents vary from one district to another and the swanky 16th *arrondissement* (on the Right Bank), and the Left Bank 6th and 7th *arrondissements* can be **formidable**. Depending on apartment size and address, monthly rents in these neighborhoods can reach $9,415 for something really special. If you're prepared to take out a six-month lease, MS Mesnil has two- to six-room duplex apartments in the 16th *arrondissement* between Avenue Foch and the Champs Elysées. This is the smartest residential quarter of central Paris, close to the business district known as *le triangle d'or*, the golden triangle. According to the bilingual agents, apartments have "luxuriously equipped" kitchens, videophones, and private parking. Furnished apartments (one bedroom) start at $2,318 per month.

Outside central Paris, the majority of flats and apartments are rented long-term on an unfurnished basis. The main market for them is the small ads pages of *Le Figaro* newspaper. There's also a free magazine called France-USA Contact (Fusac) which carries property listings in English. By renting from an individual, you can avoid commissions—most agencies charge fees of a month's rent on longer leases. However, do be wary of scams. Some foreigners have seen billboard advertisements and paid substantial sums in advance rent, only to find that the apartment's real owners were away on vacation and they've fallen victim to a con artist. For peace of mind, it may be worth paying an agency fee.

Furnished or non-furnished? While *non-meublé* or *vide* theoretically only means "unfurnished," in practice it also often means completely unequipped. When they move, former tenants are apt to take everything except the kitchen sink. Only around 15 percent of city rental properties come with basic furniture and essentials such as light fixtures, television antennae, carpets, and curtain rails. Unless you're planning to relocate to Paris for at least two years, it probably makes economic sense to rent furnished (*meublé*).

Paris has a host of rental agencies and most have at least one English-speaking staff member. For rentals of a month or longer, Apalachee Bay is worth noting, as they'll translate rental agreements into English. De Circourt has over 6,000 rental properties; Locaflat and Lodgis quote for both vacation and long-term rentals.

Multi Services Mesnil Immobilier, 10 rue Mesnil, 75116 Paris, tel. 33/0-1-56-26-57-56, fax 33/0-1-44-05-18-60, email: msmimmo@wfi.fr.

Locaflat, 63 Av. de la Motte Picquet, 75015 Paris, tel. 33/0-1-43-06-78-79, fax 33/0-1-40-56-99-69.

De Circourt Associates, 11 Rue Royale, 75008 Paris, tel. 33/0-1-43-12-98-00, fax 33/0-1-43-12-98-08.

Lodgis, 16 Rue de la Folie Mericourt, 75011 Paris, tel. 33/0-1-48-07-11-11, fax 33/0-1-48-07-11-15, www.lodgis.com.

Apalachee Bay, 21 Rue de Madrid, 75008 Paris, tel. 33/0-1-42-94-13-13, fax 33/0-1-42-94-83-01.

For information on the City of Light and a free monthly events guide, call the Paris Office du Tourisme, 127 Ave. des Champs Elysées, fax 33/0-1-49-52-53-00, email: info@paris-touristoffice.com.

The Luscious Languedoc

The Languedoc-Roussillon region is the hypnotically beautiful south of song and troubadours. The sightseeing is first rate, the golden landscape dotted with the imposing hilltop castles and fortified towns of the 13th-century Cathars who were slaughtered for their heretical beliefs by Crusaders' swords. The litany of must-see medieval gems is almost endless: For starters there's the walled and turreted town of Carcassonne—try to be here on Bastille Day when a fireworks extravaganza seems to turn the town ramparts into a sea of flames. Rose-pink Albi, the birthplace of Toulouse-Lautrec, is another beautiful town on the Tarn River, and the distinctly weird village of Rennes-le-Chateau comes complete with occult legends of buried Cathar treasure and rumors of the Holy Grail.

The countryside is a joy, a land of slumbering villages surrounded by vineyards and craggy mountains, often breached by rocky river gorges where eagles soar overhead and the warm air is heavy with the scents of lavender, wild mint, and thyme. The east of the region tumbles down over the Pyrennean foothills to the Mediterranean—don't miss the seaside town of Collioure, which has houses that resemble pastel-colored bon-bons, a cathedral that's really a lighthouse, and a castle that once belonged to the Spanish lords of Majorca. Artists are drawn by the luminosity of the light and the great Henri Matisse himself set up his easel on Collioure's wharf in 1905.

The coast and main towns like Carcassonne and Albi are well served by bus and train, but to make the most of the area, a car comes in handy. It's a region where you'll never run out of adventures, but if you fancy a change of scenery, all the glories of sun-drenched Spain lie waiting to the south.

Another great reason to come to Languedoc-Roussillon is for the food. Even far inland, seafood is always in plentiful supply, caught from the nearby Mediterranean and delivered to market the following morning. Try a dish of red mullet (*rouget*) baked in rosemary, sea bass (*loup*), or monkfish (*lot*). The cassoulets and spicy sausages are terrific, but unless you intend swallowing spit-roasted snails laced with garlic, don't go ordering *cargolade*. Local wines are addictive brews and include a headily potent red called Banyuls, the only wine that I know of that's paired with chocolate.

If you're seeking a vacation *gîte*, the region has some gems. On the river Orb, 45 minutes from the coast, village houses in medieval Roquebrun rent from $370 per week in the low season. In the heart of Cathar country, a luxury villa apartment sleeping eight at Lagrasse rents from $390 to $925 per week. If you're particularly interested in following the

Cathar Trail, a property near Carcassonne, Béziers, or Castelnaudary would be just the ticket. Many pretty village homes fall into the $290 to $610 per week bracket.

The local branch of Gîtes de France is at 78 rue Barbacane, 11000 Carcassonne, tel. 33/0-4-68-11-40-70, fax 33/0-4-68-11-40-72.

You can also find furnished vacation rentals through *immobiliers.* The regional tourist office produces a free booklet titled "locations de vacances" (holiday rentals), listing realtors who handle such properties. For this and general information about the region contact: Comite Régional du Tourisme, 20 Rue de la République, 34000 Montpellier, tel. 33/0-4-67-22-81-00, fax 33/0-4-67-58-06-10, email: contact.crtlr@sunfrance.com.

Furnished homes for long-term rent aren't exactly thick on the ground throughout rural Languedoc-Roussillon, but persevere and you should find something suitable. The following FNAIM realtors all had properties at the time of publication. They ranged from studio apartments in the Tarn town of Castres starting at $253 per month to four-bedroom village houses around Castelnaudary for $635 per month.

BSM Immobilier, 24 rue Alquier Bouffart, 81100 Castres, tel. 33/0-5-63-59-20-60, fax 33/0-5-63-59-06-12.

Celleneuve Immobilier, 29 route de Lodeve, 34080 Montpellier, tel. 33/0-4-67-75-20-26, fax 33/0-4-67-03-21-81.

Agence Lauragaise, 34-36 rue de Dunkerque, 11400 Castelnaudary, tel. 33/0-4-68-94-51-31, fax 33/0-4-68-94-51-30.

The Riviera and Provence

The Côte d'Azur has more than its share of foreign fans. This is the French Riviera of scantily clad starlets, golden beaches, and glittering casinos where you can lose all your holiday money on the whim of the roulette wheel. Strung out from Hyères to Menton, 26 resorts line this turquoise coast of rust-colored cliffs and sandy bays. The big Riviera magnets are St. Tropez, Cannes, and Nice, but also check out the coastal town of Antibes, a charming old port with an ancient core of tiny alleyways and medieval ramparts facing the sea. Flower, food, and flea markets can be found everywhere and Antibes's enticing covered market is the source of everything from briny black olives to lavender soap, and clay pots packed with the famously aromatic *Herbes de Provence.* Another lip-smacking regional specialty to look out for is jars of *tapenade*—a mousse of capers, garlic, olives, anchovies, and lemon which is delicious eaten with fresh, crusty bread.

However, some people may be disappointed that much of the Riviera isn't quite as glitzy as they imagined. Alas, the stardust is beginning to get a bit thin in places: Europe's budget-minded families come to pitch tents in downmarket camping and trailer sites, fast food joints abound, and St. Tropez is something of a biker's hangout. And despite the grand hotels that line the Promenade des Anglais and the delightful fish restaurants, much of Nice doesn't resemble a neat Riviera resort. You need some very dark shades to blot out the urban sprawl beyond the *vieille ville*, the medieval quarter.

That said, movie stars still flock to the Cannes film festival in May, and the so-called "beautiful people" continue flashing their platinum credit cards in the galleries and boutiques of the famous Croisette, the boulevard beyond Cannes marina. The villas are as palatial as ever, the sports cars will make you green with envy, and marinas remain packed with sleek, oceangoing yachts. Not your kind of hangout? Well, beyond the frenetic pace of the coast is an entirely different world. The hilly Provence hinterland is a picture book of sloping vineyards, olive groves, and pine forests. Wander through this paradise of poppy fields, lavender beds, and truffle oaks, and it really will make you want to grab a paintbrush and emulate Van Gogh and Cézanne. Provence's rustic villages seem straight from a bygone century, blessed with mossy fountains, ruined fortresses, and hilltop bell towers.

Go exploring. It's not necessary to rent a car as local buses serve many of the most interesting villages from resorts on the coast. The coastal towns are linked by the Paris-Marseille-Nice-Italy railway (day trips to the Italian Riviera are easy to do), and these fast trains can also connect you to more leisurely scenic splendors. One panoramic journey is the Chemin de Fer Provence, a narrow-gauge train line operating between Nice and Digne, a town buried in the mountainous back-of-beyond.

Above St. Tropez, on the slopes of the Maure Mountains, La Garde Freinet is a stunning old Saracen village; Lorgues and Cotignac are picture-perfect market towns of plane trees, sun-dappled squares, and pattering fountains. Frequent

Its harbor a forest of masts, Antibes is an attractive town on the Côte d'Azur.

© Steenie Harvey

buses ply from Cagnes-sur-Mer, Antibes, and Nice to the perfume town of Grasse, hemmed in by meadows of flowers—their aromatic scents are distilled and find their way into some of the best-known (and most expensive) perfumes in the world. Besieged by Saracens in the 9th century, Grasse is one of those places where time is imprisoned in the stones, a gorgeous old town of arcaded shops, intriguing arched alleyways, and medieval watchtowers.

Few of us can afford to splash out $10,000 to rent a top quality villa for a month, so don't get carried away by all the glamour—that's the kind of price you can expect to pay for the more palatial Riviera properties during July or August. Less-expensive options surface around the medieval stone villages of the Provençal hinterland, but we're still talking fairly steep prices—the average for a furnished holiday villa with garden, sea view, and private swimming pool is $1,180 per week or $3,800 monthly during high summer.

Happily you'll find cheaper vacation properties. An apartment or studio is the most affordable option and if you book early they are usually available in the Mandelieu/Cannes/Antibes/Juan-les-Pins areas. Outside the summer season, standard furnished studios and one-bedroom apartments rent for $290 to $360 per week, though prices can double and triple during July and August and you'll always pay twice as much for sea views. During spring or fall, modest village houses (without pool) start at $290 through most *gîte* agencies, so look there too if you fancy a sojourn in rustic Provence. The France Direct website has some gems, including an exceptionally pretty cottage in the lavender fields and olive groves of Cotignac for $375 to $525 weekly, www.francedirect.net.

Local tourist offices also keep lists of holiday rentals. If you long for familiar accents, quite a few American expatriates have settled around Aix-en-Provence. Fifteen miles from the flowery bastions of the Luberon hills, the town has an extensive range of vacation apartments and houses. The tourist office is used to non-French speakers and will locate accommodations for you.

Office Municipal du Tourisme, Place Générale de Gaulle, 13100 Aix-en-Provence, tel. 33/0-4-42-16-11-61.

Long-term rental prices in Provence depend on the type of property and lease length. Depending on whether they're furnished or unfurnished, studios in the backstreets of Nice itself (the cheapest Riviera location) average $360 to $615 monthly; one-bedroom flats start at $470. Small unfurnished villa properties (two bedrooms) begin at $845 monthly, but you'll probably have to pay at least $1,730 for an unfurnished property with swimming pool or sea view. Larger furnished homes cost a lot more. The built-in premium that operates between July and September means that you could easily multiply the above rates for villa properties by a factor of three.

Rental agencies are almost as numerous as in Paris. At the time of writing, properties available included two-room furnished apartments in Cannes and Cagnes-sur-Mer for between $525 and $615 monthly. For both holiday and long-term rentals try:

Cabinet Berge Michel, 91 bd Carnot, Residence Le Mallory, 06400 Cannes, tel. 33/0-4-93-68-30-25, fax 33/0-4-93-39-67-40.

Agence Ordimmo Orpi, 28 Bd Victor Hugo, 06000 Nice, tel. 33/0-4-93-88-08-53.

Declety Immobilier, 63 Blvd Marechal Juin, 06800 Cagnes-sur-Mer, tel. 33/0-4-93-73-24-24.

Agerim, 6 Ave de Suède, 06000 Nice, tel. 33/0-4-97-03-04-05.

Fried Immobilier, Palais Miramar, Suite 215, 65 La Croissette, 06400 Cannes, tel. 33/0-4-93-43-00-17, email: micheledelcroix@aol.com.

Strasbourg and Alsace

Germanic place-names, Riesling and Gewürztraminer wines, and half-timbered Renaissance houses straight from the pages of the Brothers Grimm—are you in France at all? The Alsace region lies between the Vosges Mountains and the Rhine, in eastern France. It's a place where eyes and tastebuds can get very confused indeed!

Hard against the German border, Alsace is an intriguing frontier region where Teutonic efficiency meets up with French *joie de vivre*. With excellent bus and rail links, the region's hub is Strasbourg, which (like Brussels) is one of the European Union's administrative centers. But don't let the thought of Eurocrats put you off—the European Council buildings don't detract from the beauty of Strasbourg, a provincial city whose intact medieval core is known as "Petite France." Slumbering beside riverbank walkways, this part of the city is a dreamy picturama of gothic spires and roofed bridges. Gabled houses have timbered fronts and windowsills bloom all summer long with bright yellow and red geraniums.

The perpetual turnover of European civil servants ensures Strasbourg has a glut of accommodations. Monthly rents for furnished studios and one-bedroom apartments start at less than $460 monthly. Four-bedroom houses (unfurnished) outside the city can be found for under $900 monthly, though furnished homes of similar size are likely to cost double that amount. There are numerous *immobiliers*—contact FNAIM for local members. They include:

Gestrim Alsace Nord, 11 place de Halle, 67000 Strasbourg, tel. 33/0-3-88-37-57-30, fax 33/0-3-88-37-57-37.

CT Bottier Immo du Rond Point, 1 Rond Point de l'Esplanade, 67000 Strasbourg, tel. 33/0-3-88-45-50-70, fax 33/0-3-88-45-50-79.

Agence Bintz, 21 rue des Francs Bourgeois, 67000 Strasbourg, tel. 33/0-3-88-15-20-50, fax 33/0-3-88-15-20-58.

Another type of city accommodation worth considering for both short- and long-term stays is an apartment hotel. You have all the comforts of a home, including a kitchen, but within a hotel setting. And if you feel too lazy to even brew coffee, you can order breakfast along with a wake-up call. Strasbourg has a number of apartment hotels—one is Victoria Garden. You can book in for a single night or for eternity, and prices reduce dramatically as a stay increases. Apartments are of various size: A studio apartment for two costs an equivalent $63 for an overnight stay; $56 per night for a five-night stay; $37 per night for a 14-night stay. If you stay for 60 nights, the rate falls to $26 per night. That's per apartment, not per person, and short stay prices (up to 14 nights) include all taxes, electric costs, TV, and linen rental. If you were staying as a long-term resident, taxes and maintenance charges are also included but you'll be billed for various things such as TV, linen rental, and electricity. All apartments come with a private number phone and calls carry a small tariff on top of normal charges.

Appart'hotel Victoria Garden, Strasbourg les Halles, 1 rue des Magasins, 67000 Strasbourg, tel. 33/0-3-90-22-43-43, fax 33/0-3-90-22-44-44, email: victoriagarden@strasbourg.com.

Alsace is predominantly rural, so you may want to rent a *gîte* as an alternative to Strasbourg. The local branch of Gîtes de France is Maison du Tourisme Vert, 7 Place des Meuniers, 67000 Strasbourg, tel. 33/0-3-88-75-56-50, fax 33/0-3-88-23-00-97. The best Internet site for finding Alsace *gîtes* is www.alsanet.com or for general information on the area contact Alsace Tourisme, 6 Avenue de la Marseillaise, 67005 Strasbourg, tel. 33/0-3-88-25-01-66, fax 33/0-3-88-52-17-06.

Above pine and beech forests, and vineyards down below, the high pasturelands of the Vosges Mountains are a magnet for summer ramblers and winter skiers. Look for storks on your travels—believed to bring good luck, these elegant long-legged white birds are regional mascots. Fifteen years ago, the storks had been hunted almost to extinction, but local people got a reintroduction project underway, setting up special bird rearing centers. Now safe from hunters, these summer migrants build their straggly nests atop houses and churchtowers along Alsace's Route du Vin. The road wends its way past vineyards and picture-book villages like Eguisheim, Obernai, and incomparable Riquewihr with its medieval streets and macabre carvings. This townlet really is magical and there's lots to see, including a castle, stork's nest houses, and the Thieves' Tower, where you can shiver at a torture chamber, rack, and dungeon. Buses to the wine villages run from Strasbourg and Colmar, another quirky medieval town groaning with colorful half-timbered houses, cloisters, and churches. Definitely worth sparing a day for, Colmar is on the railway between Strasbourg and Basel in Switzerland.

Although Strasbourg has countless gourmet restaurants, nothing beats a meal in a wooden-paneled rustic *winstub*, where patrons often sit at communal tables and plow their way through plates of *schiffala*, smoked pork with potato salad. Riquewihr has some excellent *winstubs* serving local specialty dishes such as a meat stew called *baeckoffa*, Munster cheese with caraway seeds, *tartes* made from golden mirabelle plums, and fruit brandies distilled from the produce of the Vosges orchards. (Expect to pay around $5 for starters, $11 to $15 for main courses). Another Alsatian staple for robust appetites is a mound of *choucroute*, topped with sausage or ham. Just in case you wondered, French pickled cabbage (*choucroute*) is indistinguishable from German pickled cabbage (*sauerkraut*). You can easily take trips from here into Germany's Black Forest region and try it for yourself.

Riquewihr's holiday homes include apartments in a 16th-century house belonging to the owner of Le Tire Bouchon *winstub*. Smaller apartments cost from $375 weekly. Contact Antoine Zimmer, 29 rue du Général de Gaulle, 68340 Riquewihr, tel. 33/0-3-89-47-91-61, fax 33/0-3-89-47-99-39.

Immobiliere Martin, 16 Rue Jacques Preiss, 6800 Colmar, tel. 33/0-3-89-24-13-01, fax 33/0-3-89-41-58-99. For long-term rentals within the town of Colmar, typical prices are $265 monthly for town center studios, $435/$660 for two- and three-bedroom apartments.

5 The Netherlands and Belgium

A lthough not obvious holiday destinations, the Low Countries have their high points. Both the Netherlands and Belgium have enough charm to warrant an in-depth look. It's not all beer, chocolate, tulips, and Old Masters. The capital cities, Amsterdam and Brussels, are likeable places with lots to offer. It's worth taking the opportunity to travel to less well known corners too.

THE NETHERLANDS

Often called Holland, the Netherlands lends itself to a multitude of visual clichés: everything from clogs and tulips to windmills and cyclists. And thousands of them. Europe's most bike-crazy country, The Netherlands's capital is Amsterdam; other major cities include Rotterdam, Maastricht, and The Hague (Den Haag). The Hague makes an interesting alternative base, especially if you're traveling with children. It's within easy reach of pretty towns like Delft and Gouda, the bulbfields, and the North Sea's silvery sands.

Netherlands Board of Tourism, 355 Lexington Ave. (19th Fl.), New York, NY 10017, 888/464-6552, fax 212/370-9507, www.visitholland.com.

Legalities

North Americans don't need visas for stays of under three months. However, unless you are being sent on a work assignment, or for study purposes, residency permits are difficult to obtain. Coupled with a chronic housing shortage, the Netherlands' generous social security benefits have led to an influx of refugees. Rigorous restrictions now apply to non-European Union nationals.

As everybody's circumstances differ, check with the Netherlands Embassy before making long-term plans. The first step is to apply for authorization for Provisional Sojourn. If you're given leave to stay, you'll still need a residency permit once you arrive. There are five different types of permits. To obtain one you'll have to register with both the local police and town hall within eight days of entering the country. Obtain more information from:

Netherlands Embassy, 4200 Linnean Ave. NW, Washington, DC 20008, 202/244-5300.

With boats and bikes for transport, Amsterdam doesn't suffer the same kind of traffic congestion as many other EU capitals.

© Steenie Harvey

Netherlands Embassy, 350 Albert St., Ottawa, Ontario K1R 1A4, 613/237-5030.

The Language

English is widely spoken but there are plenty of opportunities to learn Dutch, including courses offered by the *Instituut voor Nederlands als Tweede Taal* (Institute for Dutch as a Second Language.) Part of Amsterdam University, it offers programs for beginners as well as more advanced programs. Intensive summer courses (four weeks, 80 hours) cost approximately $770. Day or evening classes (48 hours) cost around $395.

Instituut voor Nederlands als Tweede Taal (Institute for Dutch as a Second Language), Spuistraat 134, 1012-VB Amsterdam, tel. 31/20-525-4642, fax 31/20-525-4429, email: isp@bdu.uva.nl.

Vacation Rentals

The tourist office boasts of having "the perfect holiday cottage for every holidaymaker." Some are close to beaches or deep in the woods; others are within a bike ride of villages and towns. However, a Dutch family's idea of a cottage may not be your idea of a cottage. When locals take home-based holidays, many prefer to stay in a *Recreatiepark* or *Vakantiecentrum.* These are orderly "parks" of vacation bungalows rather than the individual types of holiday cottages found elsewhere in Europe.

Although it sounds regimented, a *Vakantiecentrum* can be a good choice if you're traveling with kids. Many have excellent on-site facilities—outdoor swimming pools, "sub-tropical" indoor pools, miniature golf, go-karting, and lakes with pedal-boat and canoe rentals. During school holidays, larger parks organize recreation programs. Off-season prices can be as little as $159 per week, but in parks with extensive facilities, properties for six can top $600 weekly in summer.

Recreaticentra Nederland has 10 centers in various locations. Including

USEFUL HOUSING TERMS

In the Netherlands ...	in Belgium ...
huisart—general practitioner	*a louer*—to rent
Kamer te Huur—room for rent	*Gîte*—country cottage
Recreatiepark—vacation bungalow park	*te huur*—to rent
Vakantiecentrum—vacation bungalow park	*zu vermieten*—to rent
woonboot—houseboat	

linen package, final cleaning, tourist tax, and cancellation insurance, a one-week bungalow holiday for a family with two children in July/August costs approximately $551. For more ideas, get the tourist office's "Holiday Cottages" brochure. After choosing a *Vakantiecentrum*, you can either book direct or through the Netherlands Reservation Center. Or contact one of the 350-plus local tourist offices (VVV, also listed in the "Holiday Cottages" brochure). These have information on private holiday rentals in their own areas.

Recreatiecentra Nederland, Postbus 38, 3970 AA Driebergen. Telephone for brochures at Central Information, tel. 31/343-513547.

Netherlands Reservation Center, P.O. Box 404, 2260 AK Leidschendam, tel. 31/70-4195544, fax 31/70-4195519.

During spring and summer, reservations should be made as far in advance as possible. The bulb fields are a major springtime attraction with visitors from all over Europe, and Dutch families are keen on home-based holidays during July and August. Amsterdam can be surprisingly tricky on short notice. I visited in March, which is definitely an out-of-season month. I made my inquiries in February, but it was too late to book a houseboat—I had to be content with a canal-side apartment.

VACATION RENTAL AGREEMENTS

Holiday bungalows are generally rented by the week, but you can usually rent for long weekends or midweek breaks outside the summer season. City apartment stays are usually for three or four nights minimum. In most instances, heating and electricity is included. You may be requested to give

Many houses in Amsterdam's Jordaan district carry pictorial plaques.

© Steenie Harvey

credit card details as an assurance you'll turn up. If you don't, the cost of one night's stay is charged. In other instances you may be asked for an initial deposit or full payment before arrival.

Although city apartments include bed linens, holiday bungalows usually charge extra. (Dutch families load the car and bring their own with them.) Expect to pay approximately $8 per person for linens. Final cleaning isn't always included—$30 is average. In addition, some places charge a tourist tax, typically $7 weekly, per adult.

Long-Term Rentals

Finding reasonably priced accommodations within university cities such as Amsterdam, Utrecht, and Leiden can be difficult. The majority of families (57 percent) are tenants rather than homeowners, and current estimates put the housing stock shortfall at about 100,000 homes.

Within Amsterdam, prices range from $484 monthly for small studio efficiencies to around $4,850 for executive apartments. The average one-bedroom apartment fetches around $1,140 monthly. Most larger apartments go for between $1,444 and $2,375. Elsewhere in the country, rents are generally lower. For example, Bureau de Woonmarkt recently advertised a fully furnished apartment with central heating in west Rotterdam for $760 monthly. The rent included electricity and the property comprised two bedrooms, living/dining room, kitchen, shower, and toilet.

Along with local newspapers and the Wednesday edition of the national daily, *De Telegraaf*, private rentals can be found on noticeboards in shops and supermarkets. Many estate agencies also market rentals as well as home sales. For addresses of agents in a particular area, contact NVM, the official organization for realtors. Their members handle around 70 percent of all rentals. Although their website is in Dutch, and there are no links to actual rentals, it will point you toward member agents.

Although most of their properties are in The Hague (Den Haag) and Amsterdam, Bureau de Woonmarkt has a few rentals in other towns too. Have a look at the searchable database on their website, www.dewoonmarkt.nl. Most sections are in Dutch but click the *Woning* button for descriptions in English.

Furnished bungalows in holiday villages can often be rented at discount monthly rates. Open all year, Gran Dorado group has bungalow parks throughout the Netherlands—all with heated swimming pools on-site. Inclusive of utilities, cleaning, and weekly linen change, bungalows start at $1,254 monthly.

De Nederlandse Verenging van Makelaars (NVM), Fakkelstede 1, P.O. Box 2222, NL-3430 De Nieuwengein, tel. 31/0-30-608-5189, www.nvm.nl.

Bureau de Woonmarkt, Groot Heroginnelaan 13, 2517 Den Haag, tel. 31/0-70-3654447, fax 31/0-70-3655674, email: bdw@bureau-de-woonmarkt.nl.

Gran Dorado, Postbus 94510, 1090 Amsterdam, tel. 31/0-20-5606476, fax 31/0-20-5606151, email: info@grandorado.com.

LONG-TERM AGREEMENTS

Lease terms can be fairly flexible: Amsterdam's Briefcase Hometip agency reckons it can arrange rentals for periods between one week and several years. Agency fees vary. Some charge half a month's rent for rooms, and a full month's rent for studios, apartments, or villas. Others charge fees of half a month's rent for a six-month lease, and a month's rent for anything longer. The deposit almost always amounts to an additional one or two months' rent, paid when contracts are signed. Alternatively, you can sometimes pay the entire rent for the contractual period up front.

Once You're There

Health care is funded through a system of public and private insurance. However, low-cost public health-care insurance is only available to resi-

Clogs—rarely worn nowadays, but they make a colorful memento.

dents with modest incomes. Visitors seeking nonemergency treatment should consult a *huisart* (general practitioner) who will then refer you to a specialist if necessary. A visit to a general practitioner costs around $35 to $42.

Some Costs: bottle of white Bordeaux wine $3.41, 100 g (3.5 oz) coffee $2.05, 200 g (7 oz) liver sausage $1.50, bread $0.52–1.17, 1 liter (1.76 pt) of Coke $1.10, large chicken $4.09, 1 kg (2.2 lb) potatoes $0.53, six-pack of Amstel beer $3.05, 250 g (8.75 oz) butter $1.16, 200 g (7 oz) cheese $1.74, 0.5 l (0.88 pt) milk $0.82. A week's car rental, economy model, usually falls between $149 to $152.

Identification and an initial deposit are all you need to

open bank accounts. This is one of the few foreign countries where customers can obtain bank statements in English. Dutch banking's four major players are ABN-Amro, Rabobank, Postbank, and ING. Hours are usually weekdays from 9 A.M. to 4 or 5 P.M. with an extension to 7 P.M. on a town's "late shopping" day.

Amsterdam

Like most port cities, Amsterdam has a louche reputation. You could be forgiven for thinking that it's a place best avoided, a hotbed of vice whose citizens are an unsavory collection of spaced-out druggies, hard-bitten prostitutes, and predatory gays on the hunt for rough trade. Certainly the city has a sleazy side, so let's get that out of the way first. If you insist on taking a walk on the wild side, the Red Light district centers around the warren of alleyways between the Oude Kerk and Nieuwmarkt. A *Kamer te Huur* (Room for Rent) isn't hard to find, but they're not places where you'll be given the key to a pretty canalside apartment.

Not that you're likely to make the mistake—not when you see the window displays of semi-clad wenches. In this disreputable quarter, *Kamer te Huur* translates as Sex for Sale. The Red Light district is what many tourists come to gawk at, and although it may leave women visitors feeling uncomfortable, there's no need to be shy strolling through the district. However, don't take photos unless you want to cause a commotion.

Ordinary folk with families **do** live and work in Amsterdam. Sought-after residential districts include the area around the Vondelpark, Apollolaan, and Churchill-laan. My own favorite neighborhood is the Jordaan, hemmed in behind Prinsengracht canal, and only a 20-minute amble from Centraal Station. We stayed here in a studio flat on Lijnbaansgracht, the Tightrope-Walk Canal, a ribbon-thin waterway strung with houseboats.

A cat's cradle of alleyways, the Jordaan is Amsterdam's old proletarian quarter. Nowadays, though, it's an up-and-coming neighborhood. Moneyed professionals have recently been gentrifying its skinny canalhouses, many of which date from the 17th century. House facades often carry pictorial gable plaques—you see things like ships, livestock, and windmills, which are always an indication of the trades of former occupants. It's tremendous fun to play spot the miller, the brewer, and the clothing merchant, but watch your step! Jordaaners don't appreciate tourist obstacles, certainly not when they're pedaling to work. Heaven help the jaywalking visitor who steps into a cycle path in order to line up the perfect picture of bridges and canals.

Despite the new restaurants and designer galleries, the Jordaan oozes bohemian charm. It's still the kind of neighborhood where you'll find bicycle repair shops, hatmakers, seamstresses, and secondhand clothes outlets. And—needless to say—quite a few of those wacky "coffeeshops" where patrons can legally indulge in marijuana.

There are various notions as to how the Jordaan got its name. One school of thought reckons it originated from the Dutch word for Jews, *Joden*, when Sephardic Jews fled from 17th-century Spain and Portugal. Although most of Amsterdam's Jewish community had drifted east of the Amstel River prior to the Nazi occupation, some still had homes and businesses here. Listening to the Westerkerk's (West Church) carillon, I realized Anne Frank had heard these same bells when she spent two years hidden in the back rooms of her father's office premises on Prinsengracht.

The Jordaan's two square miles were made for wandering—and for seeking out some of the city's most convivial drinking dens. Known as "brown cafés" (*Bruin Koeg*), some of these tiled and timbered Dutch pubs date back centuries. Café Chris on Bloemstraat, for example, has been a taphouse since 1624. Cornering Prinsengracht and Brouwersgracht, Café Papeneiland (Pope's Island) is another 17th-century oldie with a handsome facade of stepped gables. Its first owner reputedly made coffins as a sideline.

Trash-and-treasure stores abound. On Wolvenstraat, *Knopenwinkel* sells nothing other than buttons. Runstraat's White Teeth Shop (*Witte Tanden Winkel*) is a kind of toothbrush emporium. Leliegracht's *Gone With the Wind* is a source of painted wooden tulips and a menagerie of mobile hangings: parrots, tropical fish, and butterflies. Top score in the browsability contest goes to *De Looier* on Elandsgracht, a covered antiques market of around 100 stalls.

Lindengracht hosts a Saturday general market. Locals come out in force, filling bags with everything from sausages and golden cannonballs of cheese to flowers and cut-price socks. The market stretches the length of Lindengracht, something of a misnomer as the canal itself has been filled in. Beside the Noorderkerk church, another Saturday farmers' market sells provisions as well as second-hand bikes, books, and budgerigars.

If you do wash up on the Jordaan's shores, trams 3 and 17 rattle along Marnixstraat, the neighborhood's western edge, but the most useful is No. 20, the Circle Line. As well as Marnixstraat, there are additional Jordaan stops at Elandsgracht and Westermarkt. Tram 20 serves Centraal Station, Dam Square, and the museum quarter where Rembrandt's *Night Watch* takes pride of place in the Rijksmuseum, and sunflowers are always blooming in the Van Gogh Museum. Tram 20 also stops at Leidseplein, focal point of Amsterdam's nightlife.

Our studio-for-two cost $100 nightly, all-inclusive. Landlords Hans and Marlene van Vliet also own the nearby Acacia Hotel and rent houseboats. These start at $91 nightly if you fancy trying the lifestyle of Amsterdam's

2,000 canal dwellers. Book early. Even at two months' notice, we were too late for a *woonboot*. Acacia Hotel & Studios, Lindengracht 251, 1015 Amsterdam, tel. 31/0-20-622-14-60, fax 31/0-20-638-07-48, email: acacia@hotelnet.nl or acacia.nl@wxs.nl.

More apartments and houseboats are available through Amsterdam House. Prices range from $109–142 nightly for one-bedroom apartments and houseboats to $280 for three-bedroom houseboats. Amsterdam House, Amstel 176, 1017 Amsterdam, tel. 31/0-20-626-2577, fax 31/0-20-626-2987, email: info@amsterdamhouse.com.

In the museum and theater district, Canal Apartments charge weekly rates of $432, or per night at $67. Canal Apartments, Niewe Achtergracht 67-3A, 1018 Amsterdam, tel. 31/0-20-625-7238, email: canalapp@hotelnet.nl.

Holiday apartments can also be booked through Amsterdam Tourist Service, Damrak 7, 1012 Amsterdam, tel. 31/0-20-520-7000, fax 31/0-20-624-5999, www.amsterdam-ts.nl, email: sales@amsterdam-ts.nl.

Regarding long-term stays, Briefcase Hometip carries around 600 furnished rentals on its database. Rental periods can range from one week to several years, with prices varying from $484 to upwards of $3,230 per month. Sample properties include a three-bedroom apartment on one of central Amsterdam's main canals, the Keizersgracht, for $1,508 monthly. A five-room townhouse near Amsterdam's zoo/planetarium, rents for $2,371 monthly.

Churning a passage down Amsterdam's Prinsengracht

© Steenie Harvey

Run by English-speaking expatriates, Homeseekers agency caters to both individuals and the corporate market. Another agency, Have Vastgoed, is across the road from Centraal Station. Check out Bureau de Woonmarkt too. (address above in Long-Term Rentals). Their properties recently included a two-room furnished apartment in Amsterdam's Jordaan neighborhood for $1,235 per month, and a fully furnished four-room house off one of the city's prettiest canals, Prinsengracht, for $2,370.

THE GREATEST FLOWER SHOW ON EARTH

For your Amsterdam home-away-from-home to be authentically *gezellig* (cozy), you'll need some blossoms. Every street market sells flowers, but the Singel Canal market is a special treat. During March, it's thronged with locals buying *tulpen*: tiny parrot tulips striped yellow and zingy orange, showy scarlet tulips the size of teacups, velvety Queen of the Night tulips that look black from a distance, but are actually deep purple.

If you're visiting in springtime, don't miss Lisse's Keukenhof Gardens. Midway between Amsterdam and the Hague, this 60-acre flower garden is one of the world's largest. Between late March and May, it lays on a six-million-bulb spectacle—rainbow palettes of crocuses, daffodils, narcissi, and hyacinths, followed by dazzling arrays of tulips.

Around 10 miles of footpaths meander past lakes, fountains, and through woodlands. Bring a picnic if you want, but there are several restaurants here where you can lunch or snack on *poffertjes*—Dutch pancakes. You can reach Keukenhof by public transport: take the train to Leiden and then one of the frequent buses to Lisse from outside the station.

The Netherlands grows around 8.5 **billion** bulbs annually. Not far from Lisse, the seaside resort of Noordwijk is at the heart of the bulb-growing area, which comprises a massive 42,000 acres. The beach here stretches for miles and you'll see many Dutch families out walking or bicycling through the bulbfields. Noordwijk's tourist office (VVV) can make reservations for cottages or seaside chalet apartments. For example, Bad Noordwijk's 25 apartments are open all year and rent from $115 to $365 weekly.

VVV Noordwijk, Postbus 1508, 2200 BE Noordwijk, tel. 31/71-3619321, fax 31/71-3616945.

Bad Noordwijk, De Ruyterstraat 49, 2202 KH Noordwijk Zee, tel. 31/71-3611196, fax 31/71-3620208.

Briefcase Hometip, Sarphatistraat 484, 1018 Amsterdam, tel. 31/0-20-6254443, fax 31/0-20-6257098. You can also make contact through their website which carries sample rentals, www.hometip.com.

Homeseekers, Sarphatistraat 77, 1018 Amsterdam, tel. 31/0-20-4286973, fax 31/0-20-4286983, email: info@homeseekers.nl.

Have Vastgoed, Prince Hendrikkade 24, 1012-TM Amsterdam, tel. 31/0-20-4288876, fax 31/0-20-6249408, www.havevastgoed.nl.

The Hague (Den Haag)

Although the seat of government is usually in a country's capital, the Dutch parliament meets in den Haag, not Amsterdam. The city is also home to the royal family, the International Court of Justice, most foreign embassies, and a clutch of museums and art galleries. The Mauritshaus, a 17th-century palace, houses a collection of Dutch Masters as well as Andy Warhol's peculiar portrait of Queen Beatrix.

Den Haag can seem rather genteel and staid compared to Amsterdam. However, it does host free summer pop concerts, the North Sea Jazz Festival, and trams rattle along the short five-mile stretch to the country's top seaside resort, Scheveningen. There are more sandy beaches at nearby Noordwijk and Katwijk, but don't be surprised to see topless sunbathing and even complete nudity amongst the sheltered dunes. Like Germans and Scandinavians, most Dutch people aren't prudish.

If you have toddlers in tow, take them to Madurodam, den Haag's most popular family attraction. Midway between the city and Scheveningen, Madurodam is the Netherlands in miniature, a toy-town version of the country's showpiece sights. In the space of an afternoon you can stroll the canals and bridges of Old Amsterdam and visit the cheese market at Alkmar, the port of Rotterdam, and Schiphol airport.

As most places within the Netherlands lie within a day trip of den Haag, it makes a good base for forays to smaller towns. If you've a yen for cheese visit Gouda; if your tastes are more ornamental, putter around Delft. Only a half-hour journey on the train, this tranquil town is synonymous with porcelain. Mementos range from windmills and miniature clogs to high-priced antique Delftware.

Den Haag's nearest *Vakantiecentrum* is at Kijkduinpark, a country estate just 500 meters from Kijkduin Beach. The estate boasts 230 villas and 100 chalets available for rental and you can also rent bikes. Within the estate are traces of an old Roman settlement and a "Coliseum" has been built where kids can take part in real musicals as well as organized games. Low-season weekly prices range from $286 to $320; high-season from $751 to $818.

Vakantiecentrum Kijkduinpark, Machiel Vrijenhoeklaan 450, 2555 NW Den Haag, tel. 31/70-4482100, fax 31/70-3232457, email: info@kijkduinpark.nl.

Sample long-term furnished rentals include one- and two-bedroom apartments in seaside Scheveningen for $594 and $1,078 monthly. Near den Haag's Belgische Park, within biking distance of beach and dunes, a two-bedroom furnished

Tourist cruisers are a popular way to explore Holland's canals.

© Steenie Harvey

EFTELING—THE FAIRYTALE FOREST

Since it opened its gates in 1952, Efteling has had over 70 million visitors. Seven miles from the southern Dutch town of Tilburg, this is one of Europe's oldest theme parks. For older children there are white-knuckle roller-coaster rides, for little ones a Fairytale Forest whose life-size characters are based on legends from all over the world. Strolling along the woodland paths, you'll meet Sleeping Beauty, Rumpelstilt-skin, Little Red Riding Hood, and other fairy-tale folk. There's even a gingerbread cottage where poor Gretel is working in the kitchen and Hansel is being fattened up in readiness for the witch's dinner.

The park's attractions include a dragon that roars if you finger his treasure, a for-tune-telling troll king, and Bird Rok—a hair-raising indoor coaster ride inspired by Sinbad the Sailor's voyages. Other rides include the Pirana white-water boats, the "Forbidden City" of Fata Morgana and a Dreamflight which ascends through misty mountains to floating castles and back down to a netherworld of trolls and dwarfs. Haunt of a brigand, Villa Volta is a mansion whose walls and floor move. Then there's Laaf Land with its giggling stairs, slides, and wobbly bridges. Complete with school, brewery, and bake-house, this is the village of local elvish creatures, the Laafs.

Open between late April and late October, admission costs approximately $22 for both adults and children (under age four free). Efteling, Europalaan 1, 5171 Kaatsheuvel, tel. 31/0-416-288111, www .efteling.com.

Railway stations sell discounted tickets that include rail fare to Tilburg, bus trans-fer to Efteling, and park entry. (With an early start, it's feasible to visit Efteling on a day trip from Amsterdam, 60 miles away.) The nearest self-catering accommo-dation is at De Rosep, a small bungalow park east of Tilburg, set in a nature reserve. Depending on the season, bunga-lows (sleeping up to six people) rent for $263 to $496 weekly.

Gran Dorado runs a larger *Vakantiecen-trum* at Weerterbergen, close to the Belgian border, but still within easy reach of Eftel-ing. Facilities include miniature golf, *boules* (a game similar to bowls), tennis, squash, water bikes, canoeing, clay pigeon shoot-ing, and wagon excursions into the woods. Like all Gran Dorado villages, Weerterber-gen has a "subtropical water paradise" with an indoor pool heated to 32°C. Although centers are self-sufficient with supermar-kets and restaurants on-site, you're encour-aged to venture into the wider world. In Weerterbergen's case, it's to the nearby Groote Peel nature reserve and the town of Thorn with its whitewashed houses and streets paved with glittering *Maaskeitje* cob-blestones. Depending on the season, a four-night midweek break in a cottage sleeping four costs from $253 to $610. For more ideas check out the website: www.grandorado.com.

De Rosep, Oirschotsebaan 13, 5062 TE Oisterwijk, tel. 31/0-13-5232100.

Gran Dorado Weerterbergen, Tra-cheeweg 7, 6002ST Weert, tel. 31/0-495-530055.

apartment rents for $1,520 monthly. For the budget-conscious and students hunting for efficiencies, this can be a very affordable area. Partially fur-nished rooms (shared kitchen and bathroom) start at $175, fully furnished rooms from $276 monthly. Bureau de Woonmarkt (address above in Long-Term Rentals) has a wide choice of properties.

BELGIUM

Poor, forgotten Belgium. It is not Europe's number one choice for vacationers, and you shouldn't encounter problems with finding accommodations at short notice at any time of year. Business, rather than pleasure, brings many foreigners to Belgium. They're usually bound for Brussels, the capital, which also serves as the European Union's political hub. Often dubbed Euroland, it's where politicians and civil servants rub shoulders with the international business world. More than 2,000 foreign corporations have headquarters here.

Although an obvious base for travelers, Brussels isn't the only option. Much lies within a 70-mile radius of the capital. In the densely populated north, Flanders, there are the great medieval art cities of Antwerp, Ghent, and sleeping beauty Bruges with its looking-glass canals and the steeply gabled houses of 16th-century wool merchants.

South of Brussels lies Wallonia and the hummocky hills of the Ardennes—a wooded region whose oak forests are still home to deer and wild boar. Crisscrossed with country roads and sparkling trout streams, the Ardennes are thickly dusted with castles, monasteries, and only a short hop from cities such as Liège, Namur, and Tournai.

Belgian Tourist Office (Headquarters for U.S. and Canada), 780 3rd Ave., Ste. 1501, New York, NY 10017, 212/758-8130, www.visitbelgium.com.

Legalities

Stays of less than three months only require a passport. However, foreigners staying in Belgium for longer than three months are classed as residents and must conform with formalities regarding residential and any necessary work permits. Temporary residence permits are obtained from Belgian diplomatic or consular offices. On arriving in Belgium, and within three working days, future residents must register with the Population or Aliens department of their *commune* of residence and obtain a Certificate of Registration for Foreigners. Initially valid for one year, this is your proper residence permit. Depending on personal circumstances, it can be renewed annually.

Freelancers must also apply to the *commune* (equivalent to a town hall) for a *carte professionnelle*. Issued for a five-year period, it includes a description of the authorized activity. For non-EU students, a residence permit is limited to the period of study at a recognized college or university. You'll be issued a residence permit, initially valid for three months. Depending on the studies you're undertaking,

after you've submitted all relevant documents, you'll get a one-year residence permit, which can be extended.

Persons of "private means" who don't need to work for a living must apply for residence permits through the Belgian Embassy or Consulate. You need to show that you have sufficient means at your disposal and that income can be transferred to Belgium. You must also prove you have ties with Belgium. For more information contact:

Embassy of Belgium, 3330 Garfield St. NW, Washington, DC 20008, 202/333-6900, email: Rudi.Veestraeten@diplobel.org.

Embassy of Belgium, 80 Elgin St., Ottawa, Ontario K1P 1B7, 613/236-7267.

The Language

"To rent" translates as *a louer*. Or *te huur.* Or *zu vermieten*. Belgium has three official languages: French, Dutch (also called Flemish), and German. Mercifully you probably won't have to worry about the latter as it's only spoken by a few Belgians near the German border to the east. The good news is that English is widely understood, especially in Brussels.

Flanders, the northern part of Belgium, is Dutch-speaking. The southern half of the country, Wallonia, speaks French. However, just to confuse matters, Brussels is more of a French-speaking city, even though it's in the northern half of the country. Here street signs operate a bilingual system of French and Dutch. As relationships between north and south can sometimes be prickly, a Flanders shopkeeper will be more appreciative of your attempts to speak Dutch rather than French. And vice versa. Don't use Dutch to seek directions in Wallonia—you'll likely be sent in the wrong direction.

Private lessons from individuals cost around $40 per hour and numerous language schools offer intensive courses in French and Dutch—Berlitz has seven Belgian centers. Fondation 9 is a nonprofit organization created by the Free University of Brussels. A one-week intensive course costs $247.

Fondation 9, 485 Avenue Louise, 1050 Brussels, tel. 32/0-2-627-52-52, fax 32/0-2-627-51-00, email: fondation9@ulb.ac.be.

Berlitz School of Languages, 306-310 Avenue Louise, 1050 Brussels, tel. 32/0-2-649-61-75, fax 32/0-2-640-11-37, www.berlitz.com.

Vacation Rentals

Where else besides Brussels? Dutch-speaking Flanders is the most industrialized part of Belgium and it's not overly blessed with rural options. Holiday accommodations tend to be in historic art cities or in North Sea resort villages. Although northern Belgium isn't my idea of seaside heaven, the contrary-minded can get information on coastal holiday homes from Toerisme Vlaanderen (Flanders). They're based at the main Belgian tourist office, which also provides listings of Brussels vacation apartments:

Toerisme Vlaanderen, Grasmarkt 63, B-1000 Brussels. tel. 32/0-2-504-03-90, fax 32/0-2-504-02-70, email: info@toerismevlaanderen.be.

The Ardennes hills of French-speaking Wallonia abound in country cottages and rural *gîte*-type properties. For instance, you could stay beneath the turreted walls of a 17th-century "farm castle." Modern lodges in the castle grounds sleep 4–6, and rent for $252 weekly low season, $304 high season. Details from: Mme. Masschelein, Ferme Chateau de Laneffe, Grand Route 47, B5651 Laneffe, tel. 32/0-71-65-58-32, fax 32/0-71-65-16-85.

For more ideas contact Gîtes de Wallonie or the tourist office for their "Holiday Accommodation Belsud" brochure. Prices are given by the week, but discounts apply for longer stays: 5 percent reduction for two weeks to 15 percent for four weeks.

One little house in Bruges that had a **Te Huur** *(to let) sign in its window.*

© Steenie Harvey

Office de Promotion du Tourisme Wallonie-Bruxelles, Rue Marché-aux-Herbes 61, 1000 Brussels, tel. 32/0-2-504-03-90, www.opt.be.

Gîtes de Wallonie, Avenue Prince de Liège 1B, B-5100 Namur, Belgium, tel. 32/81-31-18-00, fax 32/81-31-02-00.

VACATION RENTAL AGREEMENTS

Gîte (country cottage) properties can be booked through the tourist office's central reservations. The charge, including cancellation insurance, is $7. They'll forward the official contract, which you'll also get if booking with the landlord. Owners generally supply sheets and towels, but often charge extra for utilities. Many properties require a security deposit. The typical amount is $110 to be paid in cash or covered by a Eurocheque. This will be returned to you, either on departure or within a week. Tenants are expected to clean the property—otherwise you'll be charged for this too. Any tourist tax is mentioned under the lodging description in accommodation brochures.

Long-Term Rentals

Accommodation ranges from studio flats to apartments in modern buildings or converted town houses. Expatriate families often opt for villas—large detached houses set in leafy suburban gardens. Both furnished and unfurnished rental accommodations aren't too difficult to find. The main English language paper for expatriates is *The Bulletin,* and you'll also find

The Vismarkt, or Fish Market, in Bruges gets underway very early in the morning.

© Steenie Harvey

details of rentals in French-language publications such as Friday's *Le Soir*, or Thursday's *La Libre Belgique* and *La Lanterne*. If Dutch is more your strong point, check out Friday's *Het Laatste Nieuws* and Saturday's *De Standaard* or *Het Nieuwsblad*.

Many landlords find tenants by hanging out an orange *te huur/a louer* sign. Websites for hunting down rentals include www.expataccess.com and www.expatriate-online.com. There's a fair choice of studio flats and one-bedroom apartments priced between $355 and $560 monthly, particularly in Brussels. Most have separate shower rooms and what's often described as "an American luxury kitchen." Some ads say "no charges"; others might be worded "x monthly + x charges." These charges relate to entranceway cleaning fees, communal lighting, garden maintenance, etc.

With links to dozens of agents all over the country, probably the best website for tracking down long-term rental listings is www.immoweb.be. You can also find rentals through real estate agents. To obtain a list of agents in your chosen area, contact:

Institut Professionnel des Agents Immobiliers, Luxemburgstraat 16B, 1000 Brussels, tel. 32/02-505-38-50, fax 32/02-503-42-23.

One large agency is ERA, with 50 offices throughout Belgium. Although it's currently only partly in English, check out their website at www.era.be or contact their head office: **Era Belgium,** Antwerpsesteenweg 68-2, 2630 Aartselaar, Belgium, tel. 32/323-227-41-85, fax 32/323-227-41-82.

LONG-TERM AGREEMENTS

Although it's possible to find hassle-free rentals for a one-month to one-year stay, most leases run for either one, three, six, or nine years. Be careful what kind of lease you're putting your name to as signing the contract means you accept all clauses. Landlords usually favor a long lease, but nine years? Sounds scary, almost like penal servitude, but it certainly doesn't mean staying in Belgium for a lifetime. However, breaking the lease attracts financial penalties and you can effectively bid farewell to your deposit.

Any lease can be broken at any time during the first three years, subject to three months' notice and payment of a fixed sum. In the first year, that fixed sum "fine" amounts to three months' rent. In the second year, it reduces to two months' rent, and in the third year to one month's rent. If you're into your fourth year or more of rental, three months' notice is required but you won't have to pay a financial penalty.

A deposit of three months' rent is usually sought. By law, this amount has to be transferred to a blocked bank account that carries both your signature and that of the landlord. The deposit, plus any interest, is repaid when vacating the property. That's assuming no damage has been incurred and you haven't broken your lease agreement.

Before moving in, it's usual to get a survey—a detailed description of the premises and their fixtures and fittings. Costs of obtaining a survey are usually split 50-50 between landlord and tenant. This survey is attached to your lease and registered with it. When vacating the property, an exit survey is carried out and compared with the original entry survey.

Unless you stay in an apartment-hotel, you'll have to budget for insurance as well as such things as minor maintenance repairs and even chimney cleaning. Under Belgian law, tenants are responsible for insuring their landlords' property.

Once You're There

Belgium's health care service has over 30,000 doctors and 80,000 hospital beds for a population of around 10 million. There are both private and state-run hospitals, which are usually affiliated with universities. Travelers should obviously arrange health insurance; if you need to visit a doctor the embassy can provide names of English-speaking physicians. Consulting hours are usually Monday to Friday but weekend emergency services are available at hospitals, clinics, or for home visits.

Health insurance is mandatory. Expatriates can choose whatever doctor or specialist they want, but a visit to the doctor's office is another excuse for Belgian red tape. You pay up front, the doctor issues a receipt of different numerical codes for services rendered, which you then remit to the insurance company or *mutuelle*, a mutual health insurance fund. Those working in Belgium will find more information on the country's healthcare system through their company, but people in Belgium for a shorter stay should make sure they are covered by travel insurance.

Some Costs: fresh-baked croissants $0.47, bottle of Alsace sylvaner wine $4.45, Bordeaux white $2.80, *punnet* (small basket) of cherry tomatoes $1.75, six brioches $1.23, 1 kg (2.2 lb) steak $9.94, 250 g (8.75 oz) coffee $2.17, 3 kg (6.6 lb) potatoes $1.59, 250 g (8.75 oz) butter $1.52, 1 liter (1.76 pt) milk $0.61, 750 g (26 oz) Kellogg's cornflakes $2.41, 20 Stuyvesant cigarettes $3.46. A week's car rental, economy model, averages between $122 and $200. Train ticket, Brussels to Bruges, $9.78.

Those in Belgium for a lengthy period may want to use a bank accustomed to dealing with expatriates. Global giant Citibank has 260 branches throughout Belgium and offers a full range of services. Another large bank offering an expat service is BBL. In Belgium, contact their information service at 02-481-33-38.

Citibank, Expatriates Marketing, 263G Blvd Général Jacques, 1050-Brussels, tel. 32/0-2-626-50-50, fax 32/0-2-626-55-98, www.citibank.be.

Brussels

Most people associate Brussels with bureaucrats and the European Parliament buildings. And bureaucrats means boring, right? Wrong—this unsung city of stroll-around streets and boulevards has a surprising core of medieval alleyways chock-full of atmospheric shops and dimly lit taverns. It's just like finding an unexpectedly delicious filling in one of those famous Belgian chocolates.

Start your explorations on the ancient cobblestones of the market square, the Grand Place, where bright tapestry flags flutter from Flemish guild houses. Dominated by a Gothic town hall, lined with pavement cafés and flower sellers, Grand Place is a real showstopper. Through an archway beside the town hall is a bronze figure called t'Serclaes. His right hand gleams like polished gold—there's a legend that any unmarried wench who clasps it will be wed within the year.

Time for a beer? Brussels caters to serious thirst-quenching with over 350 varieties of ale available: fruit-flavored beers, Trappist beers brewed by monks, beers with weird names like Lucifer, Judas, and the irresistible-sounding Forbidden Fruit. Roy d'Espagne is a huge pub on Grand Place and, no, you're not seeing things. For some odd reason, there's a stuffed horse in the room.

The city's unofficial symbol is the Mannekin Pis who does his stuff at the corner of Rue du Chene, a short stroll from Grand Place. In case you didn't know, the Mannekin is a fountained statue of a little boy. The reason he's a major tourist attraction is—how can I put this?—well, let's just say

In the cosmopolitan city of Brussels, you can eat your way around the world's cuisines.

© Steenie Harvey

he's taking a leak. One story goes that a bold youngster decided to relieve himself against a house door where the fountain now stands. Trouble was, the house belonged to a witch—she was so furious that she cast a spell and turned the culprit into a statue.

Grand Sablon is the area for antique lace and beer tankards, 1930s comic books, Meerschaum pipes, and other offbeat mementos. Surrounding streets are crammed with antique shops and there's an outdoor market on Saturdays and Sundays. Even if you're not interested in shopping opportunities, there's a park next door called Le Petit Sablon, which is worth a visit. A nice spot for a stroll, the park is surrounded by 48 little statues representing the city's medieval guilds.

When it comes to food, there's more to tempt the palate than *moules* (mussels) and mayonnaise-smothered *frites*. You may not want to eat in every night and for Belgian specialties, Aux Armes de Bruxelles is a good bet. You'll find it on Rue des Bouchers, a street completely lined with restaurants. I was too timid to try a dish translated as "eels in green sauce," but the *Carbonnade de Boeuf a la Gueuze* was delicious. Flemish beefsteak, and guess what it's cooked in? Yes, beer. Most main courses are around $17 but you can also choose from the fixed-price menu—just under $34 for a three-course spread.

Tarte tatin, charlotte russe, and wickedly sticky *rum babas*—can't you feel your cholesterol levels skyrocketing already? Along with pastry shops galore, Brussels is also home to countless *praliniers* and *chocolatiers* with their sumptuous assortments of handmade chocolates. Some are filled with

Brussels has a large expatriate population, and it's easy to catch up on all the latest news from home.

© Steenie Harvey

crème fraiche, others with caramel, orange fondant, and—if my eyes weren't deceiving me—beer. The Neuhaus and Corne de la Toison d'Or stores are two best bets if you want to experience Death by Chocolate. Both are in a long glass-covered gallery called Galerie de la Reine, between Grand Place and the Mort Subite tavern. (The name Mort Subite means Sudden Death. It sounds alarming, but is actually derived from an old dice game.)

Along with legions of career-minded bureaucrats, Brussels has a long-established expatriate community, many working for multinational giants. Singles tend to live in the city; families gravitate towards the wooded suburbs of Uccle, Woluwe-Saint-Lambert, and Woluwe-Saint-Pierre. Long-term monthly rents for furnished studio flats and city-center apartments start at around $589 and $712, respectively, though top-quality homes can fetch as much as $2,280. A town house/duplex with one bedroom, bathroom, and fully furnished kitchen costs $706 monthly. A two-bedroom apartment in Uccle rents for $942. Three-bedroom villas in Woluwe-Saint/Lambert start at around $1,045.

Eurorent, 24 Rue Buchholz, 1050 Brussels, Belgium, tel. 32/2-646-26-86, fax 32/0-2-646-74-44.

Victoire Properties, Avenue de Tervueren 418, B-1150 Woluwe-Saint-Pierre, Brussels, tel. 32/0-2-771-12-40, fax 32/0-2-772-31-06, email: rent@victoire.

Office des Proprietaires, Avenue Emile de Mot 19-21, B-1050 Ixelles, Brussels, tel. 32/0-2-626-08-26, fax 32/0-2-626-08-38, email: info@op.be.

If you're going to be in Brussels for at least a month (the minimum rental period), consider Rue Souveraine, in the central Avenue Louise area. A street of adjoining town houses has been renovated into more than 100 fully furnished luxury apartments, many with private gardens and terraces. Lease terms are flexible and the owners promise "red tape eliminated." With discounts for longer stays, prices start at $1,330 monthly for one-bedroom apartments, $1,672 for two-bedroom apartments, and $2,042 for three-bedroom apartments and houses. Residents can avail of a fully equipped fitness center and all apartments include cable TV and private telephones with calls charged at standard rate. Charges for utilities are extra. Depending on usage and the size of the property, they should be somewhere between $71 to $166 monthly.

Ixelinvest, Souveraine House, 40 Rue Souveraine, 1050 Brussels, tel. 32/0-2-512-34-00, fax 32/0-2-511-20-29, www.ruesouveraine.com, email: rue.souveraine@btinternet.com.

For shorter stays, plenty of apartment-hotels offer various sized apartments. Contact the Belgian Tourist Office for details. One option is the New Continental. For studio apartments sleeping two, they charge $86 daily for stays up to seven days; $62 for stays up to two weeks. Prices are inclusive of utilities, taxes, bed linens and weekly cleaning.

New Continental, Rue Defacqz 33, B-1050 Brussels, tel. 32/0-2-536-10-00, fax 32/0-2-536-10-15, email: info@ncf.be.

The Walloon-Brabant countryside is only 20 minutes away from Brussels. With good public transport links into the city, the area around Braine-L'Alleud was the site of the Battle of Waterloo. Depending on the season, you could rent a village cottage here for $195 to $256 weekly. Leaf through the Belsud accommodations brochure for more ideas, or go to www.opt.be.

Bruges

Romance turned to stone. The Four Horsemen of the Apocalypse, Michelangelo's marble Madonna, a belfry whose 47-bell carillon has been ringing out the quarter-hours for the past seven centuries....Sixty miles from Brussels, and only five miles from the North Sea coastline, Bruges is a Dutch-speaking city and the favorite Flanders cultural heavyweight for visitors doing the "Museums and Old Masters" circuit. Known to its Flemish inhabitants as Brugge, it's a delightfully Gothic city of cobbled squares and innumerable canals spanned by stone bridges. In the coldest winters, the canals freeze and locals skate over these icy white ribbons like characters from a turn-of-the-century Christmas card.

Despite first impressions that Bruges is a kind of open-air museum that somehow got trapped in aspic, it's not. There's a thriving café society, honky-tonk piano bars, and in summertime a student jazz band floating along the waterways may even serenade you. In addition to art treasures and lace shops,

The Beguinage, still home to nuns, in Bruges.

© Steenie Harvey

there's much to enjoy if you simply amble down laneways, or drift down canals and soak up the musty atmosphere of the High Middle Ages. Here a little row of almshouses, there the cloistered enclosure of a *beguinage*—not quite a convent, but a house of seclusion where genteel laywomen once lived, going out to tend to the poor and sick, or spinning bobbins of lace.

Herrings for breakfast? Early risers and insomniacs can follow their noses to the Vismarkt, Bruges' fish market which gets underway at the unearthly hour of 6 A.M. We stayed nearby, on Hallestraat, a traffic-free shopping street only a step away from the main Marketplace. With excellent kitchen facilities, the cozy (but unpronounceable) Koffieboontje flats and studios adjoin a small hotel of the same name. Various-sized apartments sleep up to six people. In the low season, a three-night weekend stay in a studio for two costs a total of $142, with each extra night charged at $32.

Lokkedizze's self-catering apartments are above a jazz and blues bar. Daily rates equate to $58 for two people, $83 for three people and $94 for four-person apartments. Get a list of other self-catering options from the Bruges tourist office.

Flats Koffieboontje, Hallestraat 4, B-8000 Brugge, tel. 32/0-50-33-80-27, fax 32/0-50-34-39-04.

Lokkedizze, Korte Vulderstraat 33, 8000 Brugge, tel. 32/0-50-33-44-50, fax 32/0-50-34-76-50.

Bruges/Brugge Tourist Office, Burg 11, B-8000 Brugge, tel. 32/0-50-448686, fax 32/0-50-448600, email: toerisme@brugge.be.

For long-term rentals, Bruges would certainly be worth considering for anybody who might be relocating to Brussels for work purposes. Only an hour from the capital by train, it feels more intimate. The dimly lit streets are safe to walk about at night, and although a provincial town, it's no cultural backwater. We attended a performance of the *Barber of Seville* at Bruges' magnificent Baroque theater, the Stadsschouwburg. Tickets were a steal—$20 for the best seats in the house.

Along with some excellent *charcuteries* (delicatessens), a couple of good supermarkets are within a five-minute walk of the Grote Markt, Bruges' central square, where Wednesday morning markets are held. If you want to eat out, there's an incredible choice of restaurants and bistros. Order mussels in cream and what appears to be half the mussel stocks of the North Sea arrives at your table in a bubbling cauldron. The beers are good too— try one of the local brews like Straffe Hendrik (Strong Henry) or shock the tastebuds with a cherry-flavored Kriek beer.

Most Bruges leases run for a year, with the majority of properties rented on an unfurnished basis. Studios start at around $225 monthly, two-bedroom apartments from $370 monthly and bungalows/villas from $855 monthly. However, furnished apartments and houses in nearby seaside villages can be rented for a two- or three-month period. It's not impossible to

find furnished properties in Bruges itself, either. The ERA office had furnished studios from $370; Dewaele had one-bedroom apartments from $310
and a three-bedroom villa at $736 monthly. De Smet & Poupeye's furnished
rentals included studios from $251 to $370 and two- or three-bedroom apartments from $380 to $710. Many Bruges agents advertise in a weekly paper
called *Vlan*, which is also online at www.vlan.be. You'll also find local
agents on the www.immoweb.be website.

De Neve & Partners, Katelijnestraat 150, 8000 Bruges, tel. 32/0-50-34-
38-48, fax 32/0-50-34-25-20.

Adviesburo Dewaele, Vlamingstraat 32, 8000 Bruges, tel. 32/0-50-44-
49-99, fax 32/0-50-44-49-90, email: adviesbureau@dewaele.com.

ERA Belgium, Hoogstraat 30, 8000 Bruges, tel. 32/0-50-33-19-32.

De Smet & Poupeye, Hoefijzerlaan 1, 8000 Bruges, tel. 32/0-50-47-00-00.

PART IV

Germany, Austria, and Switzerland

6 Germany

Germany, Europe's industrial and economic powerhouse. That's how most people see it. But there's far more to this country than BMW, Mercedes Benz, and the Ruhr Valley steelworks. Ever since I came here on a school exchange as a 13-year-old, I've always enjoyed coming back and discovering new places. Foreign vacationers are relatively few—you never get the feeling that you're just one of the crowd.

For me, much of Germany's charm lies in the regional character of its towns and cities. All are very different, from high-tech Frankfurt to booming Berlin to the picture book towns of Bavaria. My last trip was to Saxony and the Harz Mountains, two regions of the old East Germany. Despite the former Communist regime, this part of the country brims with romantic imagery—steam trains chugging through gratifyingly gloomy forests, towns and villages of crooked streets and half-timbered houses, and mountains wreathed in mist and legends.

German Tourist Office, 122 E. 42nd St., Chanin Building, 52nd Fl., New York, NY 10168-0072, 800/637-1171, www.visits-to-germany.com.

German Tourist Office, Toronto, Ontario M4K 3Z2, 877/315-6237.

Legalities

For stays of 90 days or less, North American citizens don't need visas. If you intend on staying longer, you'll need a residence permit from the German embassy or consulate. This can take up to three months. Documentation to be submitted is a valid passport, two application forms, photographs, and proof that you can support yourself. Students need to provide an admissions certificate from a German university.

German Embassy, 4645 Reservoir Rd., Washington, DC 20007-1998, 202/298-4000.

German Embassy, 1 Waverley St., Ottawa, Ontario K2P 0T8, 613/232-1101.

The Language

During my Saxony trip, I only met a handful of English speakers. The older generation expects you to speak their language. Things are easier in cities accustomed to tourists and international business travelers: places like Berlin, Munich, and Frankfurt. Even so, don't be surprised if you're dreaming in German by the end of your trip.

Offering various language courses, the Goethe Institute has both U.S. and German branches. A twice-weekly, five-week program costs around $460; customized intensive courses start at $1,420. Within Germany, the Humboldt Institute has 15 centers. An intensive 30-lesson, week-long group course costs around $540; 40 one-on-one lessons, $1,650.

Goethe House, 1014 5th Ave., New York, NY 10028, 212/439-8700, www.goethe.de.

Humboldt Institute, Schloss Ratzenried, D-88260 Argenbuehl, Germany, tel. 49/0-7522-9880, www.humboldt-institut.org.

Vacation Rentals

Without Internet access, obtaining names and addresses can be lengthy. Once you've contacted the German tourist office, the next step is to decide which *Land* (region) most appeals. Write to the regional office and they'll then send you tons of information on their area. Watch for the poor post-man crumpling at the knees and you'll know your package is about to thunder into the mailbox!

Now wade through this lot to get the name of the actual tourist office (*Fremdenverkehrsbüro*) in whichever place you want to stay. It's no exagger-ation to state there are hundreds—even the smallest village seems to have one—and it's these places that send out accommodation booklets. And, even though you never requested it, you'll get information about cycling routes, steam railways, and every single monument, restaurant, and *wan-derweg* (walking trail) within a 10-mile radius.

Information isn't always in English but figuring out what's what isn't impossible. Rummage through your garage or wherever you've decided to locate your German information center: Dig out the *Gastgeberverzeichnis* booklets—by now you'll have dozens of them. Relevant pages are at the back of the booklet and headed *Ferienwohnungen* (vacation flats and apart-ments); and *Ferienhäuser* (vacation houses). Cheapest of all are *Privatzim-mer* (private rooms); if there's a bullet in the column headed *Kochgelegen-heit*, they have cooking facilities.

Unless it's the height of the tourist season and somewhere popular like the Black Forest, it's usually possible to stay in rental accommodations for a couple of days rather than a whole week. Prices are generally given by the day, with reductions for stays over three days. Although prices are a good indication of standards, you can sometimes be caught by surprise. We got a swanky apart-ment with state-of-the-art kitchen near the *Marktplatz* in Goslar, a medieval sil-ver mining town on the edge of the Harz Mountains, for $30 a night. Traveling into the old DDR, to Quedlinburg, we paid the same for camp beds, a grimy stove, and the shabbiest armchairs I've ever seen. At the bottom of the owner's garden, our *Ferienhaüs* was sturdy enough, but it resembled a converted shed.

Business travelers may want to consider a serviced apartment. The Appartementhaus company has properties in Munich, Frankfurt, Dussel-dorf, and Hamburg. Daily rates start at around $88 for studios.

USEFUL HOUSING TERMS

Devisen-Ausland—nonresident bank account
Devisen-Inland—resident bank account
Ferienhäuser—vacation houses
Ferienwohnungen—vacation flats and apartments
Fremdenverkehrsbüro—tourist office
Haftpflichtversicherung—personal liability insurance
Hausratversicherung—household insurance
Kaution—deposit
Kochgelegenheit—cooking facilities
Möbliert—furnished
Privatärzte—private doctors
Privatzimmer—private rooms
unmöbliert—unfurnished
Vertragsärzte—social security system doctors
wanderweg—walking trail

Schaper Apartment, Rothenbaumchausse 112, D-20149 Hamburg, tel. 49/0-40-41333957, fax 49/0-40-4101958, email: marketing.sales@ schaper-apartment.com.

VACATION RENTAL AGREEMENTS

In all our trips through Germany, we've never once been asked for a damage deposit. Nor have we had to sign any agreement. Utilities and bed linens are normally included in the price; the only extra is likely to be a small tourist tax, which is charged in some villages. It rarely amounts to more than $3 a day.

Long-Term Rentals

If you're planning to use newspaper advertisements or the Web to find accommodations, plenty of private landlords and agencies are out there but information is almost always in German. If you have a smattering of the language and Internet access, one useful site is www.immowelt.de. The recent property count topped 13,500 and there were good links to realtors with rentals in cities such as Berlin, Munich, Frankfurt, and Dresden. Re/Max has moved into Germany, but at present most of their rentals are in Berlin (www.remax.de).

Although prices are self-explanatory, it's worth learning some key words. Negotiating German sites is fairly easy once you've cracked the code. *Möbliert* means furnished; *unmöbliert* means unfurnished. Anyone considering renting an unfurnished property should bear in mind that it could be quite costly. Germany's rental market is unusual in that you often have to provide your own kitchen. The realization that former tenants have taken away everything right down to

Shoppers in the old market square.

© Steenie Harvey

the kitchen sink can come as a big shock. Unless you're going to be in one place for a lengthy duration, furnished rentals are probably the way to go.

Tenants normally pay agency commission fees. For residential rentals, this is limited by law to the amount of two months' rent.

LONG-TERM AGREEMENTS

Most landlords prefer tenants who are willing to rent for lengthy periods, and leases are often fixed for between three and five years. The typical rental contract cannot be cancelled by giving three months' notice, so ensure you know what you're putting your name to. What if your firm sends you home on short notice? The thing to do is to negotiate for what's called a "diplomatic clause" to be included which allows you to give a two- or three-month notice period.

Rental payments are due in advance, according to the lease terms. The deposit (*Kaution*), normally three months' rent, is held for the duration of the tenancy. It goes into a blocked bank account and the interest belongs to the tenant. However, you may not get it all back. Left a cigarette burn on the coffee table? Landlords can deduct amounts to offset costs incurred for cleaning, repairs, or replacement items. Most leases require tenants to accept responsibility for gas, electricity, telephone, and water bills, but utilities are occasionally included.

Before taking on a tenancy, comprehensive details of the condition of the premises and its contents will have been prepared by the landlord. This inventory includes the state of the decor, as well as listing every item of furniture down to the last cushion. On moving-in day, you'll be met by an inventory clerk who carries out an inventory check-in. You're asked to sign a declaration confirming that all items listed have been seen.

It's advisable to arrange personal liability insurance (*Haftpflichtversicherung*) and household insurance (*Hausratversicherung*). In the case of a burglary, the tenant is liable to pay for any replacement items or damage. Personal liability insurance covers any damage you may cause accidentally to others. Household insurance protects your belongings against theft and burglary, and also covers fire, water, and storm damage. Although landlords are liable for major interior and exterior repairs, tenants are responsible for decorating and minor repairs. Tenants are also usually required to keep the sidewalk outside their apartment building free of snow and ice.

Once You're There

If you need medical attention, you can choose any doctor: whom you go to isn't dependent upon your address. Some doctors charge their patients according to the Social Security system's fee schedule—these are known as *Vertragsärzte*. Private doctors, *Privatärzte*, charge higher rates.

Some Costs: 1 kg (2.2 lb) chicken breasts $9.66, 10 kg (22 lb) potatoes $3.42, 100 g (3.5 oz) coffee $5.31, six large eggs $1.09, 1 l (1.76 pt) milk $0.94, 500 g (17.5 oz) cornflakes $3.38, 200 g (3.5 oz) cheese $1.64. A household's average yearly costs for heating and electricity amounts to $1,761; water $618. If you drive, filling your tank with gas will set you back around $53. A week's car rental (economy model) starts at around $179.

Banking hours are Monday to Friday, usually 8:30 A.M. to 12:30 P.M. and 1:30 to 3:30 P.M., though many city banks stay open at lunchtime. Citibank has numerous branches; other principal banks are Commerzbank, Deutsche Bank, Dresdner Bank, Postbank, and Sparkasse. Provided you have a residential address, you can set up banking facilities. Depending on length of stay, and your own tax situation, you may want to hold a nonresident (*Devisen-Ausland*) account rather than a resident account (*Devisen-Inland*).

Berlin

With a population of around 3.5 million, Berlin is Germany's largest city. Until the fall of the Wall, this historically weighty metropolis had the distinction of being the easternmost city in Western Europe, and the westernmost outpost of the Eastern Bloc. Having replaced Bonn as the capital, Berlin is still a kind of crucible where the diverse political, cultural, and historical experiences of east and west have finally come together.

It has two separate centers. The heart of old West Berlin still beats around Kurfürstendamm; the East around Alexanderplatz and Friedrichstrasse. The subway, above-ground commuter trains, and an extensive bus network make getting around fairly painless. Passing through the symbolic Brandenburg Gate and strolling down Unter den Linden was a memorable experience, but I must admit that Berlin doesn't engage my affections. Too big, too noisy.

Surveying the skyline of cranes and brand-new apartment blocks, listening to the constant thrum of pneumatic drills, diggers, and earth-moving machines, you could say that Berlin is still a work in progress. Yet despite the noise and dust, it won't resemble a gigantic construction site forever. Entire new neighborhoods are being created, and the blizzard of building work in the last few years has increased the supply of affordably priced housing stock.

With little space for single family homes in the inner city, it has long been customary for Berliners to rent their homes. Only when suburbs and garden cities such as Frohnau or Zehlendorf were developed did owning one's home become a realizable option for some. Old ways die hard and for many locals, the idea of living in the *Kiez*, or local community, is far more enthralling than home ownership. People still like to meet in the corner pub or at the market, local theater, or swimming pool. The local community can be an important part of life and Berlin *Kiez* culture still flourishes. For example, there's the jazz festival in the Bergmannstrasse in Kreuzberg, the Turmstrasse street party in Moabit, and the annual Reich-strasse Day in Charlottenburg.

Many apartment buildings date back to the mid-19th century and an earlier building flurry when Berlin was bulging at the seams. Still considered desirable today, many of these renovated apartment buildings were built around a series of courtyards. Often decorated with gothic motifs, some have elegant reception rooms facing the street, while other rooms look out into the inner courtyard.

The Charlottenburg neighborhood has always been chic, and here apartments can vary from cramped student digs (41 sq m/443 sq ft) for $210 monthly to a more spacious 132 sq m (1,425 sq ft) for $1,280 monthly. Many sought-after neighborhoods are now in East Berlin. Newly fashionable districts include Prenzlauer Berg and Kreuzberg, whose 19th-century *Altbau* apartment blocks are enjoying a renaissance. There's no typical long-term rental price; much depends upon the specific area. Three-room flats around the Tiergarten go for $735 monthly, while similar-sized apartments near Friedrichstrasse or in Prenzlauer Berg can cost upwards of $1,025 per month.

Berlin is likely to remain Europe's biggest construction site for many years to come.

© Steenie Harvey

Housing advertisements appear in newspapers such as the *Berlinermor-genpost* and *Tagespiegel* and on websites like www.berlinonline.de and www.zweitehand.de. Rental agencies include Re/Max, which has a number of city offices. Berlin is surrounded by a countryside of lakes and forests and the Rudow office was offering rentals in the Golfplatz apartments, set in a country park with excellent recreational facilities. Thirty minutes by public transport to Ku'damm and the Reichstag building, three-bedroom apartments (88 sq m/950 sq ft) rent for $432 monthly. For $1,496 monthly, the Friedrichstrasse office has a two-bedroom family house at Karlshorst, 15 minutes from central Berlin on the S-Bahn.

Wohn-Agentur Freiraum has apartments around Kreuzberg district from $190 per month, and rooms from $166. Commission fees depend upon length of contract: 28 percent of the monthly rental for stays up to a month, 100 percent for six months, and 175 percent of the monthly rent for terms of over a year. This agency can also arrange short-term apartment stays if you're only in Berlin for a short while, or want to spend time checking out various long-term options. Price per couple is $45 nightly.

Leonhard Willems Gmbh, Erich Weinert Strasse 11, 10439 Berlin-Prenzlauer Berg, tel. 49/0-30-446904-0, fax 49/0-30-446904-5, email: info@leonhard-willems.de.

Re/Max Immobilienring, Schönefelder Strasse 11B, 12355 Berlin, tel. 49/0-30-66-52-75-00, fax 49/0-30-66-52-75-01, email: mail@remax-immobilienring.de.

Walk through Berlin's Brandenburg gate and you enter what used to be Communist East Germany.

© Steenie Harvey

Ruth Schaloske Immobilien, Friedrichstrasse 95, 10117 Berlin, tel. 49/0-30-50-89-81-60, fax 49/0-30-50-89-81-62, email: info@schaloske.de.

TIB Immobilien, Kurfürstendamm 69, 10707 Berlin, tel. 49/0-30-3244678, fax 49/0-30-3233639, email: info@tib.de.

Wohn-Agentur Freiraum, Wiener Strasse 11, 10999 Berlin, tel. 49/0-30-6182008, fax 49/0-30-6182006, email: info@freiraum-berlin.com.

Munich and the Bavarian Alps

Munich, or *München* to give it its German title, is the perfect city for a longer-term stay. Most people associate it with the Oktoberfest and beer gardens, but it's also a wonderful base for discovering the castles of Mad King Ludwig, numerous fairy-tale towns, and the Bavarian Alps. The public transport system is excellent and the Austrian city of Salzburg is only 90 minutes away by train.

A university city, the heart of Munich beats around Marienplatz and its pedestrian-only shopping area. Bordered on one side by the Englischer Garten, stylish districts include Schwabing, now more of a center for nightlife rather than the traditional "artists and students quarter." (Although Schwabing still has a *Studentenstadt*, the bohemians have drifted south into the Haidhausen neighborhood, a former proletarian stronghold.) Trim residential districts march north from Swabing towards Olympiapark, venue for the 1972 Olympics, and west towards Nymphenburg where summer operas and concerts are held in the grounds of the local castle.

Ever had one of those recurring nightmares where you're stark naked in the middle of a city? Well, Munich is likely to prove an eye-opener in more ways than one. If you're shocked by nudity, steer clear of the Englischer Garten. When the sun comes out, Germans are fanatical about getting their kit off and in summer this public park becomes a center for mass exhibitionism. If you want to bare all, you won't be alone—the old, the young, and the distinctly unbeautiful don't show a whit of shyness about putting themselves on public display. Lunchtimes are particularly hectic with office workers and businessmen grabbing the chance of some all-over sun therapy.

Long-term rental accommodations are fairly easy to come by. Monthly rents average $390–565 for one-bedroom flats, $785–1,130 for two-bedroom apartments, $960–1,530 for a three-bedroom place, and $1,980–2,455 for houses. It's also possible to rent short-term accommodations—ask Munich's tourist board for their leaflet on private accommodations and apartment sharing. The list includes a number of privately operated business agencies which can coordinate apartment sharing as well as arranging stays in nonshared furnished apartments and houses. A *Mitwohnzentrale* charges commission based on rent and length of stay—usually around 20 percent for short stays.

MAD KING LUDWIG'S CASTLES

Covering 120 km (74 miles) and marked with signs showing a blue K and crown, Germany's most trodden footpath is Bavaria's *König-Ludwig-Weg*. The starting point of King Ludwig's Way is also the country's biggest tourist attraction—Schloss Neuschwanstein. Everybody's image of a storybook castle, it inspired the Fantasyland castles of Disney's theme parks.

Near the town of Füssen, Neuschwanstein is a kind of *memento mori* to the crazy excesses of King Ludwig II of Bavaria, who lived from 1846 to 1886. Ludwig craved castles like vampires crave blood and his passion for building romantic follies threatened to bankrupt Bavaria. By all accounts the king wasn't merely eccentric, he really was as mad as a hatter.

Although a recluse, Ludwig liked to dress for dinner—sometimes as a carbon copy of Louis XIV, the Sun King of France, sometimes as the swan-prince Lohengrin. Sleeping all day in a boat-shaped bed that took two years to carve, he would often demand to be taken on nighttime sleigh rides through the mountains.

It's not surprising that Ludwig became a fanatical admirer of Richard Wagner. Both were obsessed with Germany's mythical past. Many of Neuschwanstein's rooms are decorated with huge murals depicting Lohengrin, Siegfried, and Parsifal, all major figures in Wagner's operas. Neuschwanstein's top floor was designed as a concert hall where these marathon operas could be performed...usually to an audience of one.

Ludwig spent his teenage years at Hohenschwangau Castle, a medieval fortress down the mountain from Neuschwanstein. The signs of instability were already in evidence. Here Ludwig's black-ceilinged bedroom is drilled with holes. He demanded that his servants shine spotlights through it from above, so he could lie back and imagine he was watching stars wheeling across the night sky.

A few miles east of Hohenschwangau and Neuschwanstein, Schloss Linderhof is more modest. Even so, the castle grounds are dotted with more romantic follies and pavilions including a Venus Grotto. It was based on the stage set of the Wagnerian opera *Tannhäuser*. It must have been a sight to behold when the king emerged from the grotto to ride across the lake in a gigantic golden conch shell. Ludwig's grandiose schemes were so much of a financial drain that his subjects eventually had him certified as insane. Schloss Herrenchiemsee, an island castle on the Bavaria's largest lake, the Chiemsee, seems to have been the last straw. Ludwig planned to build a replica of Louis XIV's palace of Versailles, but the money ran out before it could be completed to his satisfaction.

The Ludwig Trail ends at Starnberg and Schloss Berg, a few miles southwest of Munich. After being declared insane, the king was placed under house arrest here. Under mysterious circumstances, both Ludwig and his psychiatrist met their ends in the cold waters of Lake Forggen. A theater seating 1,400 has recently been built on the lakeshore. Costing around $50 million, it's a fitting tribute to the Mad King, and was built to stage the world's most expensive musical: *Ludwig II—Longing For Paradise*. How long the show will run is hard to guess; much depends on whether tour groups will go for what's billed as "sex and crime in the royal palace." One thing's certain—King Ludwig himself would have thought it money well spent.

As in most large cities, you can also find plush serviced apartments. Within walking distance of the town hall, the Opera, and a huge open-air fruit and vegetable market called the *Viktualienmarkt*, Appartementhaus Maximilian is situated in a quiet residential area of Munich. Daily rates for studios start at $77 and go up to $270 daily for a three-bedroom apartment.

City of Munich Tourist Office, Sendlinger Strasse 1, D-80331, München, tel. 49/0-89-2-33-03-00, fax 49/0-89-23-33-02-33, email: tourismus@ems.muenchen.de.

Appartementhaus Maximilian, Hochbrückenstrasse 16, 80331 München, tel. 49/0-89-24258-0, fax 49/0-89-24258-199, email: maximilian@schaper-apartment.com.

Mr Lodge Agentur, Barer Strasse 32, 80333 München, tel. 49/0-89-340-8230, fax 49/0-89-340-82323 (apartments and flats; one month and longer).

City Mitwohnzentrale, Adaldbertstrasse 6, D 80799 München, tel. 49/0-89-28-66-060, fax 49/0-89-28-66-06-24 (rooms, apartments, flats, houses; four nights and longer).

If you want to avoid agency fees, private landlords advertise for tenants in newspapers such as the *Süddeutsche Zeitung* (Wednesday and Saturday), the *Abendzeitung* (Saturday), the *Münchner Merkur* and *TZ* (Thursdays and Saturdays). If you're traveling in summer, another possibility is to look at the bulletin board at Munich's University on Leopoldstrasse. Students often sublet apartments during the summer break.

One hundred km (62 mi) south of Munich, the frescoed villages of the Bavarian Alps make a gorgeous holiday destination both in winter and summertime. Garmisch-Partenkirchen and the Passion Play village of Ober-ammergau are on the tourist map, but I would recommend a stay in the "village of a thousand violins"—Mittenwald. It's just as pretty as any of the really well known alpine villages of Switzerland and Austria. As Mittenwald has its own railway station, it's easy to reach from Munich. You can also get direct trains from Innsbruck, over the Austrian border.

Mittenwald's most famous son was Mathias Klotz. The son of a tailor, he trained in the Italian city of Padova in the 17th century, eventually returning home as a master violin-maker. His grandson made Mozart's concert violin and the tradition of the Mittenwald fiddle-makers has survived ever since. The School for Violin-Makers has being going for around 140 years and whereas some villagers hang out laundry in the garden, in others newly varnished violins are hung out to dry!

When Goethe came here in 1786, he described the village as *ein lebendiges Bildenbuch*: a living picture book. Most village houses are of the traditional alpine chalet variety, overhung by decorative gables and with flowers spilling from the balconies in summertime. Like the baroque tower of the parish church, Mittenwald's older houses are decorated with frescoes and wall paintings with a religious theme—a local art form known as *Lüftlmalerei*. Served by a cable car, the mighty Karwendl massif (2,244 m/7,360 ft) and the Wetterstein Mountains are Mittenwald's backdrop, but there are also gentle walks through the Isar Valley, or to small lakes, waterfalls, and the Leutaschklamm gorge.

Around 25 of Mittenwald's chalets have been converted into *Ferienwohnungen*, or holiday apartments. Depending on the time of year, prices range from $29 nightly for one-person studios to $78 for flats sleeping six.

Haus Försterchristl, Familie Tolle, Rehbergstrasse 2a, D-82481 Mittenwald, tel. 49/0-8823-5918, fax 49/0-8823-5831. Studios and apartments for 1–6 persons from $31-80 nightly.

Haus Rustikana, Familie Merk, Goethestrasse 21, D-82481 Mittenwald, tel. 49/0-8823-8633, fax 49/0-8823-932390. Apartments sleeping 2–4 persons from $36-75 nightly.

For more apartments, contact Mittenwald Tourismus, Dammkarstrasse 3, D-82481 Mittenwald, tel. 49/0-8823-33981, fax 49/8823-2701. If your German is up to scratch, you can request information by filling in a form on the www.mittenwald.de website.

Frankfurt am Main

Martin Luther described Frankfurt as "a pot of gold and silver." The imagery still applies to this wealthy metropolis on the River Main, home to countless multinationals as well as the European Central Bank. Nicknamed "Mainhattan," this is the country's commercial and financial hub, a modern international city of skyscrapers, banks, and trade fairs. If you're being sent to Germany on a company assignment, there's a good chance that your temporary home will be in Frankfurt. And even if you're not, its geographical position makes it an excellent base for discovering more of central Germany.

Frankfurt's city center was blitzed by allied bombers during World War II. Although the medieval *Altstadt* has been partly restored, (before 1944 it was the largest in Germany), the city planners were more interested in embarking on a program of modernization. The outcome was mainland Europe's largest airport, its busiest railway station, and a skyline that seems to rightly belong in New York. Yet despite the fact that the wheels of commerce oil this dynamic city, its residents aren't constantly engaged in moneymaking. You'll find markets, museums, leafy parks, and a thriving art scene.

For a taste of traditional Germany, head for Sachsenhausen, one of Frankfurt's southern suburbs. The cobbled-street neighborhood is famed for *Ebbelwei* (apple wine) and taverns where aficionados sit at long tables, sampling wine from jugs. Some apple-wine houses are in the open-air, others are in cellars, and just about all serve food. The staple accompaniment is either a plate of cheese and raw onions or pork chops with sauerkraut.

Those who want to be on top of their work may want to live in the Westend, Frankfurt's financial district. It's one of Frankfurt's most expensive residential neighborhoods with luxury condos renting out at between $2,435 and $3,825 per month. However, the public transport system of

buses and U-Bahn (underground trains) runs like clockwork and the suburbs are only minutes away. Along with Sachsenhausen, other desirable
neighborhoods include Bockenheim, the university district. Adjoining Westend and the *Palmengarten* (Botanical Gardens), this district also takes in the
diplomatic quarter, the *Diplomatenviertel*. Bockenheim's most exclusive
addresses are Zeppelinallee and Lilienthalallee, where condos rent for
between $2,010 and $2,920 monthly.

Ballwanz and Noor agencies both have furnished and unfurnished long-
term rentals in various Frankfurt neighborhoods. Priced by the month,
unfurnished rentals start at $1,015 for a two-room apartment in the West-
end and $1,150 for a studio in Sachsenhausen. Sample furnished rentals
include a two-room apartment in Bockenheim for $1,216, a three-room
apartment in the Westend for $1,650 and a "luxury" three-room apartment
in the diplomatic quarter for $1,900 monthly. In less swish districts,
monthly rentals start at around $590 monthly for unfurnished studios, $640
for two-room apartments, and $715 for three-room apartments.

If you're only here for a short business trip, Appartementhaus Westend
has serviced apartments in Frankfurt's financial district. Daily rates start at
$88 for studios and go up to $460 daily for luxury suites.

Ballwanz Immobilien GmbH, Corneliusstrasse 7, 60325 Frankfurt am
Main, tel. 49/0-69-787030, fax 49/0-69-78703285, email: mail@ballwanz.de.

Noor Immobilien, Meisengasse 11, 60313 Frankfurt am Main, tel.
49/0-69-20401, fax 49/0-69-20404, email: service@noor.de.

Schaper-Apartment Westend, Feuerbachstrasse 14, 60325 Frankfurt
am Main, tel. 49/0-69-970907-0, fax 49/0-69-970907-199, email: westend
@schaper-apartment.com.

Saxony

Most people have heard of Dresden and its neighboring porcelain town,
Meissen. Yet the rest of Saxony, the largest *Land* (province) in former East
Germany, is practically uncharted territory. Bordering both Poland and the
Czech Republic, this is the farthest east you can travel and still remain on
German soil. As yet, few foreign travelers have rummaged through Com-
munism's rubble and discovered *Sachsen*'s secret places.

You'd be wrong to think that eastern Germany offers nothing other
than an endless vista of decaying housing blocks complete with tattooed
Neanderthals scowling from the balconies. Our visit took us to tower-ringed
towns whose belfries and pattering fountains rightfully belong in the Middle Ages. An industrial wasteland? Here were mountains, forests, and pastoral villages of timber-framed farmsteads where chickens roam about
cobble-paved roads.

Public transportation is excellent. All sizeable towns are on the rail network, and buses serve even the smallest village. During our three-week trip, we stayed in flats and private households that had their own cooking facilities. The norm was $38–47 per couple, per night. As prices may have increased a little, contact local tourist offices (address at the end of this section) for up-to-date listings.

Some of Saxony's easternmost towns are real showstoppers. One place you shouldn't miss is Görlitz. Linked by a bridge to Zgorzelec in Poland, it rises above the banks of the river Neisse, on what was once an important trading route for medieval cloth merchants. It belonged to Bohemia for much of its 1,000-year-old history and managed to survive World War II virtually intact.

Thankfully the former Communist authorities didn't tamper with Görlitz's old town, or *Altstadt*, whose twisting alleyways remain full of character. Here an elaborate sundial, there the Rathaus clock—decorated with a man's face whose chin drops with each passing minute. Look out too for the *Flüsterbogen*, a whispering arch that carries secrets to listeners on the far side of its portals. For me, the town's most unexpected sight was the *Heilige Grab*, or Holy Grave. A replica of the Garden of Gethsemane, its chapels and crypt were built in 1504 by a wealthy citizen who had made a pilgrimage to the Holy Land.

An hour away on the train is Bautzen, its skyline bristling with defensive towers of all shapes and sizes. Here it's not only statues to long-forgotten Bohemian kings that disorient you—street signs are exotically bilingual. Bautzen's alternative name is Budysin and it's the cultural capital of Germany's ethnic minority, the Sorbs. The Sorbisches Museum at Castle Ortenburg explains their folklore and history: One colorful tradition is that of decorating eggs with intricate patterns at Easter. The town's many peculiar buildings include the *Hexenhauschen,* the "Witch's House." Beside the fledgling river Spree, this ancient fisherman's cottage earned its nickname through miraculously surviving a number of fires. Somewhat mysteriously, all the neighboring cottages burnt to the ground.

Another appealing time warp town is Zittau, in Saxony's southeast corner. Founded by a King Ottokar in the 13th century, its medieval core is another Bohemian Rhapsody of baroque guild halls and sun-dappled squares, each showcasing an ornate fountain. You can plot a course from the Mars fountain to fountains dedicated to Hercules, the Good Samaritan, a Green Child, and a group of swans.

For a taste of the authentic Saxon countryside, you couldn't do better than stay in Waltersdorf. On a bus route from Zittau, right on the border with the Czech Republic, this semi-alpine village has 230 houses dating from the 16th and 17th centuries. Known as *Umgebindehäuser*, these vernacular Saxon dwellings combine half-timbering with thick black jackets of

▼ If you're feeling energetic, St. Anton-am-Arlberg, in Austria, is an excellent area for hiking.

© Steenie Harvey

▲ The Tyrol's main town, Innsbruck, is surrounded by mountains.

▼ In the Alstadt, the medieval part of Switzerland's Lucerne, many buildings are decorated with colorful frescoes.

© Steenie Harvey

▲ The exterior of Denmark's Rosenborg Castle has not changed since it was built in 1633 by King Christian IV. The castle and its adjoining gardens are especially beautiful in springtime when the crocuses bloom.

▼ The picturesque ship-lined dock of Denmark's Nyhavn formed the heart of the old sailor quarter of Copenhagen. It was also the home of Hans Christian Andersen for three periods of his life.

▲ In Colmar, many houses have timber trimmings, an architectural style that the French call *colombage*.

▼ The modern and the medieval in Colmar, France.

© Steenie Harvey

▲ Bautzen's towers and turrets make it one of the most picturesque towns in the former East Germany.

▼ Görlitz, on Germany's eastern border, is an attractive old town linked by a bridge to Zgorgelec in Poland.

▲ Spooky Glamis Castle is reputedly the most haunted castle in the Scottish Highlands.

▼ Derbyshire's hills and dales are wonderful for a hiking holiday in England.

© Steenie Harvey

▲ Azure blue and dazzling white are the colors of the Greek flag,
and of most houses on the Cyclades islands.

▼ Clonakilty is one of county Cork's attractive coastal towns.

© Steenie Harvey

▲ Ireland's Kylemore Abbey

▼ Siena, for many visitors, is the prettiest Italian town in the province of Tuscany.

▲ Amsterdam's Jordaan neighborhood is full of boats, canals, and tall, skinny houses.

▲ Medieval magic—the tranquil Rosenhoedkai in Bruges, Belgium.

© Steenie Harvey

▼ The Mateus Palace, nestled in the heart of northern Portugal's vineyards, may look familiar. Its picture appears on the label of bottles of Mateus Rosé wine.

© Steenie Harvey

▲ The spires of Santiago di Compostela in Spain.

wood paneling. We stayed in a holiday apartment in the village's former customs house. Peter and Gaby Landrock, a watchmaker and his school-teacher wife, now own it. Contact them at 166 Hauptstrasse, 02799 Walters-dorf, Sachsen. Peter speaks a little English and can be contacted at his workshop (tel. 49/0-35841-35068).

Waltersdorf was our base for hiking the hilly countryside and exploring neighboring villages. The village is a way station on the Oberlausitzer Berg-weg, a 115-km (71-mi) walkers' path switchbacking through the meadows and forests of Saxony's southern frontier. Sculpted into bizarre shapes by time and weather, the path is marked with curiously named rock forma-tions such as the Blacksmith's Forge, the Devil's Mill, and the Organ Pipes.

One of the prettiest stops on the trail is Oybin, a spa town that was off-limits to Westerners during the Communist era. Overlooked by a spooky castle and monastic cloisters, the village also has a *Märchenspiele* (an illu-minated fairy wonderland), and a steam railway that chugs up narrow gauge tracks back to Zittau.

Another walkers' path from Waltersdorf meanders its way into the Czech Republic. One Sunday afternoon we tramped to the nearest Czech village, Dolni Svetla, with its beat-up *Skodas* (popular car in the Czech Republic) and *Umge-bindehäuser* in various states of dilapidation. Housewives doing their spring cleaning had the entire contents of their farm-steads spread out in the gar-dens; chickens were clucking underfoot everywhere. It all seemed strangely old-fashioned, almost like slipping through a crack in time, and from one house we heard the distinctive tinny sounds of a wind-up gramophone. And while the women worked, guess where the men were? Yes, having their own kind of Bohemian Rhap-sody in the village inn.

Contact local tourist offices for private accommodation lists. We didn't make any weeks-in-advance bookings—I simply phoned around the night before

The Meissen porcelain factory in Saxony is open to visitors.

© Steenie Harvey

we moved on to our next stopover. In Görlitz, we stayed in a 19th-century apartment house, though be warned that landlord Herr Appelt doesn't speak English (Peter Appelt, 1 Wielandstrasse, 02826 Görlitz, Sachsen, tel. 49/0-3581-404148).

Eurotourismus Zentrum, Obermarkt 29, 02826 Görlitz, Sachsen, tel. 49/0-3581-47570.

Bautzen-Information, Hauptmarkt 1, 02625 Bautzen, Sachsen, tel. 49/0-3591-42016.

Tourist-Information, Rathaus, Markt 1, 02763 Zittau, Sachsen, tel. 49/0-3583-752137.

Fremdenverkehrsbüro, Dorfstrasse 93, 02799 Waltersdorf, Sachsen, tel. 49/0-35841-60980.

The Harz Mountains

Straddling the border of what was once East and West Germany, the Harz Mountains have a reputation for mythic weirdness. A bewitching region of medieval mining towns and shadowland forests, the mountains belong to the province of Sachsen-Anhalt—confusingly, an entirely different province from Saxony. The towns of Goslar, Wernigerode, and Quedlinburg are all picturesque bases for exploring this region but if you're here on April 30th, make your way to Schierke village. Off-limits to western travelers for decades, its *Walpurgisnacht* celebrations attract around 6,000 visitors. *Walpurgisnacht* is the spookiest date in the Teutonic calendar, a trysting-time for ghouls, ghosts, and witches. Folklore deems this to be the night when the northern winter makes a final stand, when Dame Holda's witches gather in lonely places to dance away the snow. Their diabolical shenanigans reputedly take place on Harz peaks such as the Bockberg and Brockenberg. According to Jacob Grimm, both were once sites of sacrifice to pagan gods.

Buried deep in enchanted forests, Schierke village huddles below the sinister-looking Brockenberg, at 3,747 feet the Harz's highest "mountain." Grim legends swirl around the Brockenberg—legends that were heard by Johann Wolfgang von Goethe who paid a visit in 1777. The Brocken was where he set the witches' sabbat in *Faust*, the story of a man who sells his soul to the devil.

May Eve begins with puppet shows, folk choirs, and Schierke's schoolkids parading in witch and devil costumes. Faces painted with freaky makeup, the littlest ones from the Kindergarten are wheeled in strollers to see the arrival of a miniature train, a "Hexenexpress" festooned with witch puppets. By nightfall, though, all baby witches are tucked up in bed. Now it's time for more dubious-looking souls to go on the prowl: kobolds, werewolves,

vampires, and phantoms of the opera; crones with floppy hats and broom-
sticks; gangs of horrible hunchbacks whose devilish horns glow in the dark.

The local Kurpark gets crowded with beer tents, food stalls, and fortune-
tellers. Evoking all the fun of a medieval fair, here you'll find fire-eaters,
sword-swallowers, and booths where you can stock up on three-cornered
mirrors, crystals, amulets, hunting horns, witches' hats, and other *Walpurgis*
mementos. Before the witching-hour fireworks, a play of Wagnerian length
is performed on an open-air woodland stage. My non-German-speaking husband wasn't relishing the prospect of three hours of "devilish dances and
bucolic music" but the entertainment was an easy-to-follow pantomime
about Holda the Hexe (witch) and her cronies.

The spirit of choice for serious tipplers is *Schierke Feuerstein*, made from
herbs and bitters and a knock-your-socks-off 35-proof. A local apothecary,
Willi Druber, concocted this throat-searing brew in 1908. Bottles are still sold
in the old apothecary shop, *Zum Roten Fingerhut*, the Red Thimble. If you
want to pay your respects to Willi, he lies in the village cemetery. His tomb-
stone carries a deliciously chilling inscription, warning you to hurry away
before he rises from his grave and joins you for a drink.

To purge any *Walpurgisnacht* excesses, pull on your hiking boots and
head into the Brocken National Park. The forest is spellbindingly eerie, latticed with paths that double as cross-country winter ski trails. These are
trails to fire the imagination, marked with bizarre rock formations like the
Witch's Altar (*Hexenalter*) and Devil's Pulpit (*Teufelskanzel*). Was that an

*Village children enjoying Walpurgisnacht, or May Eve, the spookiest date in
the German calendar. Folklore deems it to be a trysting time for witches,
ghosts, and demons.*

© Steenie Harvey

ordinary rock outcrop or something more sinister squatting in the spruce thickets? To my bleary eyes it resembled a malevolent dwarf.

Handily linked to Schierke by steam train, Wernigerode is a beautiful little town and a good base for further explorations into the Harz Mountains. Its *Altstadt* is straight from the Middle Ages, a place of labyrinthine lanes and half-timbered houses overlooked by a 19th-century Romantic castle. The highlight is undoubtedly its *Rathaus*, a town hall that's three parts Disney, one part nightmare. With its vivid orange roof and spiky lead steeples, the only possible architectural description is Gothic-gone-mad.

Quedlinburg is another Harz town that time and everyone else forgot. Over 1,600 half-timbered houses crowd its laneways and on the *Marktplatz* one stallholder was doing a roaring trade in pots of liquid cheese. The variety remains a mystery. All I could glean from the man's unfathomable dialect was "typical." Yes, but typical of what? Its chokingly ripe aroma lingered in my backpack for weeks.

With its 1200 Fachwerk (half-timbered) houses dating back six centuries, Quedlinburg seems to have slipped through a crack in time, destined to forever remain in the Middle Ages.

© Steenie Harvey

Trains run between Quedlinburg and Thale, Schierke's main Harz rival for *Walpurgisnacht* revelries. The town lays on theatrics at the irresistibly named *Hexentanz-platz*, the witches' dancing place. Cable cars are the easy route to this pagan disco above the Bodetal Valley, a densely forested river chasm banked by towering rock walls. It's a lovely place for walks with clearly marked trails and information boards detailing the local animals, birds, and plantlife.

If this area intrigues you, contact Harz Tourism's Goslar office or check their website at www.harzinfo.de. The site is in German with villages listed under *Ort* and holiday accommodations under *Art*. Depending on property size and season, most self-catered accommodations rent for between $32 and $65 per day. Options range from mountain villages to medieval towns. However, book well in advance to rent a property in Schierke for *Walpurgisnacht*. Its central street is Brockenstrasse. Here Ferienhaus Amkurpark sleeps four and rents for $30–48 per day; Ferienhaus Hesse sleeps three and rents for $33–52 daily. The village only has 15 holiday homes and if they're full, try Wernigerode. Trains and buses run between the two places and Wernigerode has over 150 holiday apartments and houses. For example, Haus Lerchenfeld sleeps four and rents for $47 per day. Regarding long-term rentals, Oppermann and Pfützner are realtors with properties in Wernigerode and surrounding Harz villages.

General Harz information and holiday homes brochure: **Harzer Verkehrsverband,** Marktstrasse 45, 38640 Goslar, tel. 49/0-5321-34040, fax 49/0-5321-340466.

Schierke accommodation lists: **Verkehrsamt,** Brockenstrasse 10, D38879 Schierke, tel. 49/0-39455-310, fax 49/0-39455-403 (Ferienhaus Amkurpark 8, Brockenstrasse 8, D38879 Schierke; **Ferienhaus Hesse,** Brockenstrasse 38e, D38879 Schierke).

Haus Lerchenfeld, Im Lerchenfelde 31, 38855 Wernigerode, tel. 49/0-2052-5538.

Oppermann Immobilienvermittlung, Burgstrasse 15, D-38855 Wernigerode, tel. 49/03943-5496-0, fax 49/03943-5496-66.

Pfützner Immobilienmakler, Sandbrink 21, D-38855 Wernigerode, tel./fax 49/03934-602856.

7 Austria and Switzerland

Europe's most magnificent scenery is to be found in the lakes and mountains of Austria and Switzerland. Picture either of these alpine neighbors and it's probably a wintertime scene: icy peaks thrusting into jewel-blue skies, skiers plowing through fresh snow, and sun-spangled icicles hanging from the eaves of frescoed Hansel and Gretel chalets. But the mountains are just as magical in summer. Cowbells clunk in meadows, chalet-owners display their window-boxes of geraniums, and steamers churn a passage between lakeside towns.

You don't have to be forbiddingly fit to enjoy holidays here. Pulling on moleskin breeches, wearing clumping hiking boots, and then scaling your way up 12,000 feet of mountain isn't compulsory! Exploring the foothills, riding to flower-studded plateaus in cable cars, and rambling along lakeshore paths is the order of the day for most visitors. The north face of the Eiger? No, thanks. Having a view of the Alps is satisfaction enough.

AUSTRIA

Austria is made up of nine provinces, or *Bundesländer*. Vienna, the capital, has its own province as does Salzburg; the others are Upper Austria, Lower Austria, Burgenland, Carinthia, Steiermark, Vorarlberg, and Tyrol. Vienna is one of the great European cities—a tangible reminder of the wealth and influence of the Hapsburg dynasty who ruled the mighty Austro-Hungarian empire. Cradled by mountains and built on a smaller scale, Salzburg is a Renaissance stage-set that exudes an almost Italianate elegance. And Innsbruck is the gateway to numerous alpine villages.

Austrian National Tourist Office, P.O. Box 1142, New York, NY 10108-1142, 212/944-6880, www.austria-tourism.at/us.

Austrian National Tourist Office, 2 Bloor St. E #3330, Toronto, Ontario, 416/967-4101.

Legalities

North American tourists don't need visas to visit Austria for periods of up to three months. If your stay is going to be more than three, but less than

six months, a visa is needed. To obtain one, forward your passport, a recent photograph, a copy of your round-trip ticket, and proof of sufficient funds and health insurance to the Austrian Consulate General. Students need a letter from the relevant Austrian school or university. A visa with a six-month maximum validity will be issued free of charge.

Residency permits are required for stays of more than six months. You have to report to local authorities within three days by means of a special form called a *Meldezettel*.

Embassy of Austria Consular Section, 3524 International Ct. NW, Washington, DC 20008-3035, 202/895-6767, fax 202/895-6773, email: obwascon@sysnet.net.

Embassy of Austria, 445 Wilbrod St., Ottawa, Ontario K1N 6M7, 613/789-1444, fax 613/789-3431.

The Language

Although dialect survives in remote areas, standard German is Austria's official language. Many Austrians do speak English, but it's polite to make the effort to speak German. Easy words to sprinkle around include *Bitte* (please), *Danke* (thank you), and *Grüss Gott*—the standard Austrian greeting which translates as "may God greet you."

There are numerous language schools, with Vienna having the most options. Vacationers could take one of Actilingua's two-week courses, which include cultural activities too—learn to waltz, discover hidden Vienna, and explore the villages of the Vienna Woods. The city's green lungs, this wine-growing region is famous for its Heuriger taverns where connoisseurs come to sample the young wine of last year's grape harvest. Actilingua can also arrange apartment stays. Including accommodations, standard two-week courses start at around $548.

Actilingua Academy, Gloriettestrasse 8, A-1130 Wien, tel. 43/0-1-877-6701, fax 43/0-1-877-6703, email: german@actilingua.com.

Österreichische-Amerikanerische Gesellschaft, Stallburggasse 2, A-1010 Wien, tel. 43/0-1-512-3982, fax +43/0-1-513-9123.

International Language Center, Moosstrasse 1060, A-5020 Salzburg, tel. 43/0-662-824617, fax 43/0-662-824555.

Vacation Rentals

Short-term accommodations can be reserved through local tourist offices or by contacting the owners directly. If you're online, going to a search engine and typing in the name of a village and "tourism" yields good results. If you're unsure where to go, there's a comprehensive overview of Austria's holiday areas at www.tiscover.com. Most summer and winter resorts have websites which include accommodation sections. For example, www.mayrhofen.com leads into the Zillertal valley and the Tyrolean village of Mayrhofen, a summer resort popular with families. Plenty of gentle pursuits are available as well as more adventurous activities such as caving, kayaking, and summer skiing on the Hintertux glacier. Daredevils can even jump off a mountain and go paragliding.

Throughout much of the Tyrol, many families still derive their income from farming.

© Steenie Harvey

Regarding planning and cost questions, it all comes down to when you aim to go to Austria. In the mountains, there are two main seasons. The Christmas/New Year's period is when skiers from all over Europe want to head for the snowy peaks. Prices are at their steepest, and accommodations are thin on the ground. If you plan to visit at this time, book as far in advance as possible—in really popular resorts such as Kitzbühel and St. Anton, accommodations fill up incredibly fast. The period from mid-July to the end of August is also peak season for the peaks. Many European families with children have to take their main vacation during the summer school break. Again, start making plans as far in advance as possible.

For a city stay, say in Vienna or Salzburg, it can often be tricky to find accommodations at short notice during major cultural events. The Vienna Festival is in May/June and the Salzburg Festival usually takes place sometime between the end of June and the beginning of September. Check with the tourist office to see if a big musical festival coincides with your planned dates—if it does, start taking some action on the accommodation front.

Village churches often have unusual, onion-shaped domes, such as this one in St. Anton-am-Arlberg.

© Steenie Harvey

Depending on season and location, 2–4 person apartments usually run between $46 and $68 daily. Prices generally include electricity and heating, though sometimes you pay extra for bed linens, towels, and final cleaning. Although you'll almost certainly be asked to pay an advance deposit for a booking during the peak season, at other times it's quite possible that you won't. It all depends on the individual owner. As to the minimum time period for renting a property, most owners will be looking for weekly bookings over Christmas/New Year's and in high summer. Outside of those dates, you shouldn't have any difficulty in finding accommodation for a three-night stay. One umbrella group for holiday rentals has a website at www.privatzimmer.at. Or write to:

Anton Schachinger, Dach-verband der Österreichischen

Privatvermieter, 5322 Hof bei, Salzburg NR 104, tel. 43/0-6229-2361, email: office@privatermieter.at.

Long-Term Rentals

In Vienna and other major towns, most people live in apartment houses. Monthly rents for two-bedroom apartments with bathroom and kitchen vary from $880 for something basic to $3,700 for something really special. That's not to say you can't find less expensive properties. Student bedsits—often a room in a house, where you share kitchen and bathroom facilities—are available in Vienna for $390 or so, though don't expect to find one in a baroque palace for that price. Detached family homes (two bedroom) in rural areas average $1,350 per month. Most properties are rented on an unfurnished basis (*unmöbliert*), as when Austrians move home they take everything with them. However, tenants are sometimes offered the opportunity to buy essentials such as refrigerators, washing machines, and stoves.

More landlords are finding tenants through the Internet, but practically all advertisements and websites are in German. When conducting a search, vital keywords are *vermieten* (to rent) and *Wohnungen* (apartments). One useful site (374 available flats for Vienna alone) is www.immobazar.at. Other ways to find long-term rentals is by scouring the *Wohnungsmarkt* section of local newspapers or contacting rental agents. Obtain lists of agents (*Immobilien*) in your chosen area from:

Österreicher Verband Der Immobilien, Favoritenstrasse 24/11, A-1040, Wien, tel. 43/1-505-48-75, email: office@ovi.at.

Rental Agreements

The Austrian Information Service warns that rent laws are complex and advises seeking legal advice before signing a lease or rental agreement. Including security deposit, expect to pay a total of three or four months' rent in advance. If using an agent, you'll have to pay a commission fee too, usually one month's rent. Leases can be lengthy: it's not uncommon to see five- and 10-year terms quoted. If you break the lease, the amount you paid up front is effectively gone for good.

Once You're There

Health insurance is a prerequisite for living in Austria. Foreigners can pay premiums (around $270 monthly) to an Austrian provider, but you'll need to be living in the country for at least six months. When visiting a doctor, it's customary to pay in cash and then obtain refunds from your insurance company. Typical charges are $57 for an examination by a general practitioner and $71 to visit a specialist's clinic. For minor ailments, most people take whatever remedy the local pharmacist recommends.

Some Costs: bread $1–1.90, 10 eggs $1.30, 500 g (17.5 oz) Gouda cheese $3.75, 250 g (8.75 oz) butter $1.30, 500 g (17.5 oz) sausage $3.75, 10 kg (22 lb) potatoes $6.50, 1 kg (2.2 lb) rice $2.36, 1 kg (2.2 lb) tomatoes $1.62, 1 kg (2.2 lb) apples/bananas $1.30, 500 g (17.5 oz) coffee $4.13, 1 liter (1.76 pt) milk $0.82; 1 liter (1.76 pt) orange juice $1.21. A week's car rental, economy model, starts at $220.

Main banks include Bank Austria, Creditanstalt, and Österreichishe Postsparkasse. Weekday hours are generally 8 A.M.–12:30 P.M. and 1:30 P.M.–3 P.M., with an extension to 5:30 P.M. on Thursdays.

Vienna

Austrians call their capital Wien. Synonymous with Strauss waltzes and the (usually gray) Blue Danube, this city of parks and palaces was at the center of one of Europe's longest surviving empires. The Hapsburg dynasty took control of Austria in the 13th century, ruling their mighty Austro-Hungarian empire from Vienna for almost 700 years. The Viennese calling card is as long as your arm, scripted with a myriad cultural experiences: glittering opera balls, angelic-voiced boy choristers, and the high-stepping white horses of the Spanish Riding School. Oh, and with *Sachertorte*, *Apfelstrudel*, and countless other calorifically rich pastries.

Above the Volksprater pleasure grounds, the red gondola cars of the *Riesenrad* make their umpteenth revolvement. Since 1898, this giant Ferris wheel has been giving fairgoers a bird's-eye view of their grandiose city. It evokes images of that classic movie of postwar occupation, *The Third Man*, and Harry Lime plunging into the underworld of the Viennese sewers. Thankfully there are better ways of having a change of scenery. Crisscrossed with hiking trails, the *Wiener Wald* (the Vienna Woods) are only a few kilometers away.

Although Vienna is now one of central Europe's most modern capitals, it has something of a decorous and starchy reputation. Perhaps that's because it has so many glittering memories on which to draw. Illustrious former residents include Mozart, Schubert, Freud, and Leon Trotsky, who argued and played chess with his revolutionary colleagues in the coffeehouses of the old part of the city, the *Innere Stadt*.

Since the late 17th century, the *Kaffeehaus* has been a Viennese institution. These dark and cozy wood-paneled cafés serve an array of pastries and coffees, some of which are a real adventure for the tastebuds. Does

Starbucks have anything to rival the *Kaisermelange*? Served with egg yolk and a shot of brandy, this is coffee fit for an archduke or one of those Hapsburg princes. Or how about a *Fiaker*? Named after Vienna's horse-drawn carriages, this strong black brew is laced with *kirsch* (cherry) liqueur and topped with cream and a maraschino cherry.

Ordering coffee isn't simple. You'll probably be glad that the waitresses move at a snail's pace. Deciding whether you want it with cream (*schlag*) or without is only the beginning. Depending on which of the 300 or so coffeehouses you visit, as many as 40 different coffee types may be available. Variations generally include *Melange* (black coffee with milk **and** whipped cream), *Mokka Gespritzt* (black coffee with cognac), *kleiner or grosser Mokka* (small or large black coffee), *Einspänner* (served in a tall glass, a large Mokka with cream and a sprinkling of cocoa), *kleiner or grosser Brauner* (small or large black coffee with a little milk), *Kapuziner* (small black coffee with one drop of cream, named for the color of a Capuchin monk's habit), *Franziskaner* (slightly more cream and the color of a Franciscan habit), *Piccolo* (black coffee in a miniature cup served with or without whipped cream), *Milchkaffee* (half coffee and half hot milk), espresso (thick, highly concentrated coffee in a small cup), and cappuccino (coffee with milk, whipped cream, and sprinkled cinnamon).

Students pore over essays, pensioners read free newspapers, businesspeople conclude deals, matronly shoppers rest their feet and indulge in gossip. In the days before World War I, the coffeehouses operated as both offices and a forum for debate. Mail was held for regular patrons, and headwaiters would usher politically minded coffee drinkers to tables where they could join soul mates engaged in radical or conservative discussions. Café Central on Herrengasse was Trotsky's favorite *Kaffeehaus* and Lenin also came here during his exile. Café Museum on Freidrichstrasse appeared in *The Third Man* and it's the place to go for a game of chess.

Linked by subway and an old-fashioned tram system, the city is divided into 23 districts called *Bezirke*. It's fairly easy to get your bearings and most locals either walk or use the public transportation system. Vienna's heart is the first *Bezirk*, the atmospheric old city known as the *Innere Stadt*. Surrounding this quarter is Ringstrasse, a circular road lined with palaces, monuments, and parks. Beyond the Ring, the inner suburbs of the second to ninth *Bezirke* have a city feel, while the outer suburbs are mostly residential.

If you're seeking an apartment in a baroque palace, most are located in the inner city. Depending on apartment size, most monthly rents range between $911 and $2,630. A bedsit (room with shared kitchen and bathroom facilities) or studio apartment goes by the name of a *garconniere*— expect to pay around $415 for one of these in a less swanky district. Furnished two-room apartments (*komplett möbliert*), start at around $565. Long-term rental agents include:

Barcelo Immobilien, Lambrechstrasse 16, A-1040 Wien, tel. 43/0-1-585-5151, fax 43/0-1-585-5150, email: office@barcelo.at.

Mobilreal, Mariahilfer Strasse 103, A-1060 Wien, tel./fax 43/0-1-595-2525, email: office@mobilreal.com.

Westpoint Immobilien, Floriangasse 41, A-1080 Wien, tel. 43/0-1-408-8604, fax 43/0-1-408-2915, email: immobilien@westpoint-immobilien.com.

Vienna's tourist office keeps lists of *Ferienwohnung*, holiday apartments. Some landlords also advertise in online brochures such as Apartment Service Vienna at www.apartment.at. Familie Rohacek have three apartments on this website. Sleeping two, the properties rent for between $49 and $76 per day. Vienna Apartments has a wide range of holiday apartments; the Dr Riess agency can arrange both short- and long-term rentals. Another option is Mitwohnzentrale, a private agency that arranges accommodations in rooms or apartments for minimum stays of at least three days.

Vienna Tourist Information, Kärntner Strasse 38, A-1010 Wien.

Vienna Apartments, Lorenz Mandlgasse 62/12, A-1160 Wien, tel. 43/0-1-49-33-257, fax 43/0-1-49-33-257-22, email: office@apartments.at.

Dr Riess Apartments, Zeltgasse 3/13, A-1080 Wien, tel. 43/0-1-402-5701, fax 43/0-1-402-5701-21, email: apartment@riess.co.at.

Mitwohnzentrale, Laudongasse 7, A-1080 Wien, tel. 43/0-1-402-6061.

Familie Rohacek, Apartments Ferchergasse, Ferchergasse 19, A-1170 Wien, tel. 43/0-1-484-4522, email: office@rohacek.at.

Salzburg and the Lakes

The hills are alive with the sound of music ... the famous Julie Andrews film about Maria, the singing nun, put Salzburg on the moviegoers' world map. Every summer, coachloads of fans come to pay homage, but don't let that put you off. This is a marvelous place for a lake and mountain holiday—and enjoying classical concertos. The surrounding hills echoed to the sound of music long before that sickly sweet ditty about raindrops on roses was ever written.

On Austria's border with Germany, Salzburg is a lovely riverbank town of red-roofed houses, cobbled streets, and baroque churches. Home to around 180,000 citizens, its crowning glory is the Hohensalzburg, a medieval fortress perched on a miniature mountain called the Mönchsberg. The city center is under a preservation order designed to prevent any unsightly new building. The quaintest part is on the left bank of the meandering Salzach River.

Salzburg's *Altstadt* is a wonderful jumble of alleyways, arcaded courtyards, and elegant houses. The people who live here are proud as punch
of their most famous son—Mozart. He was born on Getreidegasse, a
pretty street where houses are festooned with wrought-iron balconies and
gilded shop signs, and his house probably looks much the same as it did
in his lifetime. Mozart concerts are ten a pfennig, but Salzburg does allow
other composers an airing during its July-September Music Festival, one
of the most prestigious in Europe. And don't miss the palaces of Schloss
Mirabell and Schloss Hellbrunn with their ornate gardens and tricksy
water fountains.

Salzburg Tourist Office has a list of holiday apartments owned by private individuals. For example, Dr. Minnich has a fully equipped apartment
within walking distance of the *Altstadt*. Sleeping four, it rents for $69 daily.
For long-term rentals, Immobilien-Kanzlei had two-room apartments from
$503 monthly and four-room apartments from $780 monthly.

East of Salzburg beckons the spectacular Salzkammergut lake district.
Check its website at www.salzkammergut.at. Some gorgeous lakeside villages are linked to Salzburg by bus. Fuschl, for example, is only 12 miles
away. With over 60 miles of marked paths leading around tranquil lake
Fuschlsee and up into the mountains, the village is an excellent center for
walking. From St. Gilgen village, four miles away, you can take a steamer
down Lake Wolfgangsee to St. Wolfgang, once an important pilgrimage site.
St. Wolfgang apparently chucked an axe into a thicket and decided to build
a hermit's cell on the spot where it landed.

St. Wolfgang's 15th-century Pilgrims' Church has an incredibly ornate
altar, but nowadays the village is better known as a summer resort. There's
a wide choice of holiday apartments here—67 at the last count—and daily
rates mostly fall into the $38–62 range. Obtain a list from the tourist office.
Frescoed shops and houses line the cobbled village streets and there are
many hiking paths to local beauty spots. In the evenings you can listen to
operettas in the White Horse Inn, string quartets on the lakeshore, or brass
band concerts in the village square.

Salzburg Information, Auerspergstrasse 7, A-5020 Salzburg, tel. 43/0-
662-889870, fax 43/0-662-88987-32, www.salzburg.info.or.at.

Dr. Minnich, Vogelweiderstrasse 38B, A-5020 Salzburg, tel. 43/0/699-
11-55-78-06.

Immobilien-Kanzlei (Arthur Segur Cabanac), Aspergasse 11, A-
5020 Salzburg, tel. 43/0-662-624770, fax 43/0-662-624770-4, email:
segur@immobilien-salzburg.at.

Lake Wolfgang Tourist Office, Mozartplatz 1, 5340 St. Gilgen, tel.
43/6138-2239, fax 43/6138-2239-81, email: info@wolfgangsee.at.

Mountain Magic

Few villages in Austria's mountainous western provinces, Tyrol and Vorarlberg, are likely to disappoint vacationers. Just stick a pin in the map and off you go. One of my favorite places is St. Anton-am-Arlberg, on the railway from Innsbruck. Although best-known as a winter ski resort, summertime here is glorious—and accommodation costs fall substantially.

The ideal time to come is July: mountains are clothed in greenery and meadows are in full bloom. Late May and June can actually be a rather difficult time to find accommodations. Once the skiing season ends, many resorts go into slumber mode for a few weeks. Everything gets repainted in readiness for the walkers and amateur botanists.

Hiking paths are lined with wild strawberries and blueberries; the alms and meadows a constantly changing flower show with vivid blue gentians giving way to a profusion of wild orchids, lupines, and alpine roses. Although there are laws in place to prevent meadows being stripped of blooms, it's not totally *verboten* to pick a bunch of wildflowers to decorate your dining table. Just look for the signs which indicate "picking forbidden," "five flowers per person," or the invitation to put together a bouquet. If signs are missing, it's usually okay to gather blossoms where a whole meadow is in bloom, but leave single flowers alone.

You can wear your hiking boots out in St. Anton. There are lots of short walks, but to work up an appetite take the four- to five-hour-long trail to neighboring St. Christoph. Christened the St. Anton Historical Path, the trail leads past forests, mountain streams, and a small chapel. And you

In summer, this kindergarten in Innsbruck is held in the open air.

© Steenie Harvey

don't have to retrace your steps homeward—simply catch the bus back from St. Christoph.

During winter, the village attracts skiers from all over the world. The Arlberg "ski circus" covers over 260 km (161 mi) of piste, linking St. Anton with Lech, St. Christoph, Stuben, and Zurs. For advanced skiers, there are 30 challenging black runs, but intermediates and beginners are also catered to. Off the slopes there's curling, bowling, tobogganing, and sleigh rides. There are literally dozens of holiday apartments to rent here in chalet-style houses. For a full list, contact St. Anton's tourist office. (Addresses seem peculiar here because there are no village street names, only house numbers.)

The Tyrol's main town is Innsbruck, famous for its *Goldenes Dachl*, or Golden Roof, which dates from 1496. Great shops and an intriguing old quarter, but it isn't that strong on holiday apartments. However, there are lots available in surrounding villages, many of which are reachable by bus. Contact the Innsbruck tourist office for a brochure. Two nearby villages are Igls and Patsch, the latter six miles from Innsbruck on an old Roman road to the Brenner Pass. A feature of the region is the painted farmhouse murals, many from the 16th century and depicting scenes from peasant life. Patsch offers its visitors two outdoor pools, tennis courts, and weekly guided walking tours in summer. And, of course, winter skiing. One good place to stay is Tiroler Alpenhof—apartments sleeping between two and seven rent for $29–85 daily, depending on the season.

Alber Edmund, A 6580 St. Anton-am-Arlberg, St. Jakob 81, tel. 43/0-5446-2061. Apartments sleeping 2–6, $56–102 summer, $111–152 winter.

Arlberg Apotheke, St. Anton am Arlberg 485, Tyrol A-6580, tel.

The village's main street in St. Anton-am-Arlberg.

© Steenie Harvey

43/5446-2061, fax 43/5446-206185. Apartments sleeping 2–6. $35–48 summer; $69–207 winter.

St. Anton Tourismus, Arlberghaus, St. Anton am Arlberg, Tyrol A-6580, tel. 43/0-5446-22690, fax 43/0-5446-2532, email: st.anton@netway.at.

A WINTRY ALPINE WONDERLAND

Austria and Switzerland offer some of Europe's most enjoyable skiing. Tucked away in snaking valleys are numerous towns and villages where youngsters hit the nursery slopes as soon as they can walk. Unlike France's resorts, which were built specifically for vacation purposes, these are real communities. Their year-round population mostly live in Heidi-like chalets which have wooden balconies and walls decorated with hand-painted murals. And you don't have to ski to appreciate the winter wonderland scenery—walking along a cleared path around a frozen lake on a crisp, sunny day, admiring the glittering mountain backdrop, is a joyous experience. Lunchtime gondolas are often packed with ladies in fur coats rather than ski jackets, on their way to meet friends in a mountain restaurant. The following places have plenty of alternative daytime activities as well as jolly nightlife.

Kitzbühel (Austria). Guarded by the *Wilder Kaiser*, or Wild Emperor mountains, Kitzbühel is a "villagey" town. Main streets are pedestrian-friendly and some of its painted medieval houses and concealed passageways date back to the 14th century. Midway between Salzburg and Innsbruck, the town holds annual World Cup races, and advanced skiers can tackle the moguls of the famous Hahnenkahm downhill course. With 158 km (98 mi) of piste, 60 lifts, and 45 km (28 mi) of cross-country trails, the resort caters to skiers of all levels. It's also a good choice for nonskiers, as there are plenty of other activities: an aqua center with mud baths and saunas, skating, curling, sleigh rides, and afternoon tea dances. It has its own railway station if you fancy a sightsee-

ing trip across the German border to Munich. There were 157 holiday apartments here at the last count—contact the tourist office for details. Daily prices for studios start from $38 in summer and $62 in winter. Modest four-person apartments average $69 daily.

TourismusVerband Kitzbühel, Hinterstadt 18, A-6370 Kitzbühel, tel. 43/0-5356-621550, fax 43/0-5356-62307, email: info@ kitzbuehel.com.

Seefeld (Austria). Cross-country rather than downhill? With 250 km (155 mi) of groomed trails, Seefeld is Austria's *langlauf* capital. If you've never tried cross-country skiing before, you can hire equipment for around $10–13 per day. Be warned, though—it's tougher than it looks and plays merry hell on the leg muscles. Along with 80 km (50 mi) of cleared paths, the village also offers gentle alpine skiing—perfect for beginners who don't know a snowplow turn from a schuss. Or why not rent a toboggan or snowboarding equipment? Other facilities include curling alleys, indoor swimming pools, and romantic rides through the glittering Tyrolean landscape in horse-drawn sleighs. Trains run to Innsbruck and the tourist office can book apartments. Prices average $42–66 daily for accommodations sleeping two or three; $57–106 daily for four.

Tourismus-Verband Seefeld, Klosterstrasse 43, A-6100 Seefeld, tel 43/0-5212-2313, fax 43/0-5212-3355, www.seefeld-tirol.com, email: info@seefeld.tirol.at.

Wengen (Switzerland). Unless you're prepared to descend the north face of the Eiger, mountain railway is the only way to reach Wengen. Surrounded by the sparkling panorama of the Jungfrau range, Wengen's

Innsbruck Tourismus, Burggraben 3, A-6020 Innsbruck, tel. 43/0-512-59850, fax 43/0-512-59850-7, email: info@innsbruck.tvb.co.at.

Tiroler Alpenhof Ferienwohnungen, Familie Klocker, Serlesweg 5, A-6082 Patsch, tel./fax 43/0-512-377635.

picture-perfect ambience is preserved by a ban on cars. Perched on a sunny balcony above the Lauterbrunnen valley, it's an excellent choice for young families as it has some of the Alps best beginners' slopes and an English-speaking kindergarten. Taking in neighboring Grindelwald, the skiing area has over 185 km (115 mi) of well-marked piste and 48 lifts. All the usual winter sports are on offer, but don't miss taking the train to the summit of the famous Jungfraujoch with its glittering ice caves. Apartments can be booked through the tourist office. Most properties are rented on a weekly basis with studios starting at $171 during the off-peak winter season. In skiing resorts this would be mid-October through Christmas. However, you could pay $995 for a four-person apartment at the height of the season.

Tourist Office, CH-3823 Wengen, tel. 41/0-33-855-14-14, fax 41/0-33-855-30-60, email: information@wengen.com.

Engelberg (Switzerland). An hour's train journey from Lucerne, Engelberg is central Switzerland's largest holiday resort. Surrounded by three mountain ranges, the settlement dates from the 12th century when the Benedictus monastery was founded. High above Christmas card scenes of frozen waterfalls, cable cars journey across the gaping crevasses of the Titlis glacier and on to the mountaintops. From the sun terraces, views stretch from the Valais and the Bernese Oberland all the way around to the Jura and Germany's Black Forest. The skiing is superb and within the village is a huge complex, Sporting Park Engelberg, with a climbing wall, fitness center, skating rink, tennis, badminton courts, etc. Apart-

ments for two start at around $51 daily, with most four-person apartments renting for $74–106 daily.

Engelberg Tourism, 6390-Engelberg, tel. 41/0-41-639-7777, fax 41/0-41-639-7766, www.engelberg.ch, email: tourist.center @engelberg.ch.

St. Moritz (Switzerland). Sophisticated St. Moritz has lots to do if you don't want to stomp around in skiing boots or tackle the Cresta ice chute and Bobsleigh runs. Split into two areas—fashionable St. Moritz Dorf and quieter St. Moritz Bad—its alternative pursuits include curling, skating, tennis, squash, horse-drawn sleigh rides, and squandering Swiss Francs in the casino. During January and February, the frozen lake also hosts the unlikely activities of cricket and polo. You could say that St. Moritz is the birthplace of alpine winter tourism. In the summer of 1864, the Kulm Hotel's owner invited some British visitors to return in January for a free stay. Herr Badrutt was so confident that they would be smitten by the beauty of the Engadine Mountains that he offered to refund their travel costs if skies were gloomy. The visitors returned, the sun shone down, and St. Moritz found itself at the forefront of the classic winter holiday. Along with 350 km (217 mi) of piste, there are 150 km (93 mi) of cross-country trails. Again, you can book holiday accommodations through the tourist office. Daily rates for two-person studios start at $56, six-person apartments from $119.

Tourist Office, Via Maistra 12, CH-7500 St. Moritz, tel. 41/0-81-837-33-33, fax 41/0-81-837-33-77, www.stmoritz.ch.

SWITZERLAND

Pine-scented mountain forests, ice-blue glaciers, deep alpine lakes...the landscapes are fabulous and the streets are spotless, but Switzerland can do horrendous damage to your bank account. Those nightmare stories about the cost of living are—unfortunately—fairly accurate.

That said, it would be a shame to write off Switzerland completely. Indeed, you may not have an option if work purposes are bringing you to a financial center such as Zürich, or Geneva, where many international organizations are based. Because the country is so small, and transport systems are so well integrated, many residents live in one city and commute to another. For example they might work in Zürich, but live in Lucerne. Although long-term stays aren't an option for most visitors, certainly try and budget for a few days' vacation here.

Swiss Tourist Office, 608 5th Ave., New York, NY 10020, 877/794-8037, fax 212/262-6116, www.myswitzerland.com.

Switzerland Tourism, 926 East Mall, Toronto, Ontario M9B 6K1, 416/695-2090.

Legalities

North American citizens don't need visas for stays up to 90 days. The basic rule is "three months and you're out," though impoverished backpackers may find it's financially prudent to move on after three days. Of course, costs prob-ably won't worry anybody in the happy position of having net wealth exceeding two million Swiss francs (US$1,140,000). If that describes you, the authorities may decide you can  afford the lifestyle of a Swiss resident and grant what's called a "B permit." However, you would be expected to make your home in Switzerland on a more or less permanent basis.

Another way to gain long-term residency is by working for a multinational or international organization based in Switzerland. On the open job market, you'd need to be a highly skilled professional such as an engineer or university professor. Swiss jobs tend to go to Swiss people and many trades are protected by guilds, which put a block on employing foreigners. For more information, contact:

Embassy of Switzerland, 2900 Cathedral Ave. NW, Washington, DC 20008, 202/745-7900, www.eda.admin.ch.

Embassy of Switzerland, 5 Marlborough Ave., Ottawa, Ontario K1N 8E6, 613/235-1837.

The Language

Switzerland is multilingual with the majority of the population speaking *Schwyzerdeutsch*, the Swiss-German dialect. Although it's incomprehensible to pure German speakers, just about everyone also speaks standard German. In western Switzerland, around Geneva, French is the language of choice. As you near the Italian border, the language changes to Italian, spoken by the 10 percent of the population who live in Ticino canton. The fourth official language is Romansch, a hybrid of Latin and Etruscan, which is spoken by around 1 percent of the population. As almost all professional people speak English, it's easy to get by with just a smattering of French and German.

Vacation Rentals

Local tourist offices can arrange stays in holiday apartments. The minimum stay is usually three or four nights, but during the main winter and summer seasons some property owners will only rent out accommodations

Distinctive blue and white trams rattle around the city of Zurich.

© Steenie Harvey

by the week. As in Austria, Christmas/New Year's and July/August are both high-season periods in Switzerland, so if you're looking to go during this time, you should book as far in advance as possible. Extras include bed linens and towels—usually charged at around $12 per set. Most properties also charge for final cleaning—approximately $42 for studios and $55–60 for larger apartments.

Long-Term Rentals

Swiss immigration laws make long-term rental prospects an almost impossible dream. However, a job contract may lead to a residency permit. If you understand German, one useful website for finding private rentals is www.immob.ch.

Most people live in apartment houses. Sample monthly prices in various Swiss cities are $455 for a Lucerne studio, $845 for a two-room apartment in Zurich, and $1,030 for a three-room apartment in Berne. Most listings are for unfurnished properties, and you may have to resort to agencies to find a ready-to-move-into apartment. In German-speaking Switzerland look for an *immobilien*; in French-speaking areas a *régie*.

A "human statue" makes an appearance beside the Chapel Bridge in Lucerne.

© Steenie Harvey

While furnished rentals are fairly hard to come by, there are possibilities, especially in western Switzerland. Thanks to its international profile, Geneva is the easiest place to find a furnished apartment (*location meublée*), particularly if you're only planning to stay for a few months. Much depends on the area, but monthly rents for one-bedroom apartments average $955 to $1,360. You may also find someone willing to rent for the short term, though this will generally be for a minimum three-month period.

Apartments are usually described by the number of

rooms (*Zimmern* in German, *pièces* in French). Fairly self-explanatory, you may think. Yes, but in Geneva canton, kitchens are counted as rooms, whereas in Vaud they are not. In some other cantons, a "three-room apartment" nets two bedrooms plus kitchen and bathroom, so make sure you know exactly how many rooms you're getting for your money! "Charges" are normally listed separately from the rent, and cover heating, hot water, and the services of the building's caretaker.

Rental Agreements

Standard lease durations are normally one year with a three-month notice period. However, shorter periods, notably in summer, can sometimes be negotiated for furnished accommodations. Although leases cannot be broken, they can be transferred to someone else with the landlord's written permission.

The agent makes a detailed inventory on the day you move in. A damage deposit (*Kaution* in German, *garantie loyer* in French) amounting to three months' rent is required, normally paid when signing the lease. Your bank holds this money and, providing no damage has been caused, it's refunded when the lease is terminated and the inventory re-checked.

Once You're There

Ensure you're covered by health insurance. Tumbling down one of those mountains could be very expensive and even the most accomplished skiers have accidents. If you need to visit a doctor, you normally have to pay the first $30 to $50 of any costs up front. Even though Swiss hospitals are reputed to be among the world's best, they are not places for uninsured travelers. Depending on the necessary treatment, those without insurance have to pay deposits of between $1,320 to $6,600. Health insurance is mandatory for all Swiss residents—standard premiums covering 90 percent of health care costs start at around $143 per month.

Some Costs: 500 g (17.5 oz) bread $0.85, 1 liter (1.76 pt) milk $1.02, 200 g (7 oz) butter $1.98, 1 kg (2.2 lb) Berner cheese $11.50, 10 eggs $3.16, 1 kg (2.2 lb) pork cutlets $12.60, 1 kg (2.2 lb) steak $28.50. The prices were gleaned from Migros, a large supermarket chain.

Swiss residents can avail of both checking and savings accounts as well as foreign currency accounts. The two major retail banking groups are Credit Suisse and UBS (United Bank of Switzerland), though there are many smaller cantonal banks too. City banking hours are generally 8:30 A.M. to 4:30 P.M. weekdays, and Saturdays from 9 A.M. to 4 P.M.

Geneva

A snowball's throw from the French border, chic Geneva is Switzerland at its most cosmopolitan. A French-speaking city, it provides a temporary home-away-from-home for a large foreign population. The United Nations, the Red Cross, the World Health Organization, and over a hundred other major international organizations maintain European headquarters here. Anchored to the western end of Lac Léman (Lake Geneva), the city has an immensely charming *vieille ville,* or old quarter, full of art and antique galleries, jewelry and watchmakers' stores, and plenty of stylish boutiques.

If you want to emulate the fur-coated residents and take your perfectly groomed poodle for a walk, head for the lakeside promenade, where yachts share the mirror-clear water with swans. The city has numerous landscaped parks, a lot easier to negotiate than the cobblestones of the old quarter—especially if you're a "woman of substance," wearing the obligatory high heels.

Strolling down Rue du Rhône, past the luxurious stores, you can almost smell the money that Geneva generates. Only the window-shopping tourists look poor! And although the city's banks and businesses have adopted the Protestant work ethic, there's certainly not much evidence of Protestant austerity. Odd to think that Geneva was once under the control of John Calvin, one of the founding fathers of the Reformation.

Unfurnished studios start at around $462 monthly, two-room apartments from $515, and three-room apartments $790. A small five-room garden villa rents for $3,630 monthly. Agents such as Rosset and Grange, Corthay, Volpé have a wide selection of unfurnished rentals. However, supply and demand ensures that there's no such thing as a cheap furnished rental in Geneva. Nor in its equally expensive lakeside neighbors, Lausanne and Montreux.

With minimum rentals of three months, one agency specializing in furnished rentals is Home Sweet Home. Within walking distance of Lake Geneva and the business district, $1,455 monthly rents a one-bedroom flat in a turn-of-the-19th-century apartment building. The flat also comprises a living room, bathroom, and fully equipped kitchen.

Gerald Rosset, 28 Rue des Charmilles, 1203 Geneva, tel. 41/22-339-39-39, fax 41/22-339-39-00, email: info@rosset.ch. (Also has offices in Lausanne and Fribourg)

Grange, Corthay, Volpé, 21 Chemin de Grange-Canal, 1211 Geneva, tel. 41/22-707-10-10, fax 41/22-707-10-00, email: contact@grange.ch.

Home Sweet Home, Rue de Pré-Naville 6, 1207 Geneva, tel. 41/22-736-93-56, fax 41/22-736-93-55.

Zürich

"The Gnomes of Zürich"... the phrase sounds almost as enticing as "An important center of international finance." Until I went there, I must admit that the prospect of spending time in a city full of dull gray men in drab gray suits seemed more of a penance than a pleasure. However, just because Zürich is Switzerland's main business and insurance hub doesn't mean that it's a disagreeable place to live. Or to spend a few days on vacation. If you can afford it, the shopping on Bahnhofstrasse is world-class and the Alps are only a short train ride away.

Unless you're coming here for work purposes, you probably won't even be aware of the city's commercial activities. A German-speaking city, Zürich is chained fast to two rivers, at the western end of a placid lake called the Zürichsee. On the east bank of the Limmat River, the old center is very lively at night, with bars staying open on weekends until four o'clock in the morning.

If you plan on being in Zürich for at least a two-month minimum period, one option for a furnished rental is Haus zum Schwertgut, in Höngg, a leafy residential suburb beside the Limmat River. Originally surrounded by vineyards, this apartment house was built in 1640 for a city official. Only a few streetcar stops from the city center (you can be there in 15 minutes), it contains seven apartments of various sizes. Prices range from $2,400–3,900 monthly.

If you're looking to rent by the week rather than the month, an American company, Villas International, has furnished apartment houses in

Admiring the view over Lake Zurich.

© Steenie Harvey

Zürich's residential districts. Studios (for 1–2) from $875 weekly, one-bedroom apartments (for 2–4) from $1,490, and two-bedroom apartments (for 4–6) from $2,050.

Zürich's tourist office provides details on holiday apartments. In some cases discounts apply if your stay extends to a month. Most vacation rentals are priced nightly, but there's usually a minimum rental period of at least three nights and sometimes a week. Pension St-Josef has furnished studios and apartments with kitchen facilities. Nightly rates are $93 for a single-person studio, $119 for two people, $132 for three, and $142 for four.

Haus zum Schwertgut, Limmatalstrasse 111, CH-8049 Zürich. If you're telephoning, the apartment manager, Jürg Fischer, can be reached at Stockerstrasse 60, CH-8002 Zürich, tel. 41/1-201-5055, fax 41/1-210-5045, email: manager@schwertgut.ch.

Villas International, 4340 Redwood Highway, Suite D309, San Rafael, CA 94903, 415/499-9490, email: villas@villasintl.com.

Frau K. Schmitt, Pension St-Josef, Hirschengraben 64, Zürich, tel. 41/1-250-5757, fax 41/1 251-2808, email: st.josef@bluewin.ch.

Lucerne

A swan-clustered lake backdropped by the snow-capped peaks of Mount Rigi and Mount Pilatus—romantic or what? Called *Luzern* by its German-speaking inhabitants, Lucerne is the quintessential storybook town, a place of "Once Upon A Time" fantasies. Seeing its spires and Rapunzel-style turrets, you can almost imagine that you've fallen through a crack in time and landed in the High Middle Ages.

The town makes an excellent base for day trips. Cable cars and funiculars scale the surrounding mountainsides; paddle steamers churn their passage across Lake Lucerne, journeying to smaller lakeside towns and villages such as Hergiswil, Flüelen, and Rütli. One popular excursion is to the summit of Mount Pilatus, traveling by paddle steamer, cable car, and mountain railway.

Lucerne's *Kapellbrücke*, or Chapel Bridge, carries a pictorial record of the town's past. Although the pictures weren't added until the 1600s, the bridge itself was built in the 14th century, shortly after the octagonal *Wasserturm* (water tower). Gaze up to the gable rafters and you're delving into Lucerne's annals. Here are medieval battles and oath-taking ceremonies; the lives of Leodegar and Mauritius, the local patron saints; the hungry flames of the great fire of 1400. (History almost repeated itself in 1993 when the·*Kapellbrücke* was damaged by fire, but restorers have done an incredible job of bringing it back to its former glory.)

Another covered bridge crosses from Old Lucerne to the newer town across the Reuss River. Further downstream, the *Spreuerbrücke*, or Mill Bridge, bears some soul-chilling messages and a grim nickname. I soon realized why it's also called the *Totentanzbrücke*, the "Dance of Death Bridge." Above my head, some ghastly looking skeletons were prancing merrily in a ring.

Built in 1408 as part of Lucerne's fortifications, the *Spreuerbrücke*'s pictorial decorations date from the 1620s. Over a nine-year period, an artist called Kasper Meglinger painted 67 triangular panels in which the specter of death takes center stage. Armed with a sickle, wearing a crown, shaking his bones, the Grim Reaper appears in various guises. In some paintings he carries an hourglass, in others a spade or a scythe. In one disturbing image, a skeletal figure reaches out toward a rosy-cheeked baby gurgling in a cradle. These paintings were designed to tell the townsfolk that rich and poor alike should prepare for mortality.

The *Altstadt,* or Old Town, has plenty of curiosities among its ribbon-thin alleyways. A number of its squares have tales to tell. They include Hirschenplatz, named after a medieval inn, and Kornmarkt, where the town hall and Pfistern guildhall are festooned with gorgeous frescoes. Another must-see is Lucerne's Lion, the *Löwendenkmal*. Carved out of the natural rock in 1820, the dying lion commemorates the Swiss mercenary soldiers who lost their lives in 1792 at Paris's Tuileries during the French Revolution. The American writer Mark Twain described it as "the most mournful piece of stone in the world," and you'll probably agree.

The Chapel Bridge is Lucerne's best known landmark.

The best way to find holiday homes is to contact the tourist office for a list of *Ferienwohnungen* in both Lucerne and nearby lakeside villages.

Residence an der Reuss, Gütschstrasse 2, 6003 Luzern, tel. 41/0-41-240-01-23, fax 41/0-41-240-01-27. Lucerne studios for $330–610 weekly, one-bedroom apartments for $376–726, and two-bedroom apartments for $521–1,070, depending on season.

Residence Zum Löwen, Friedenstrasse 2A, 6004 Luzern, tel. 41/0-41-418-47-47, fax 41/0-41-418-47-49, email: LuzernHof@swissonline.ch. Apartments sleeping one or two people. $93–132 nightly.

Lucerne Tourist Office, Bahnhofstrasse 3, CH-6002 Luzern, tel. 41/0-41-227-17-17, fax 41/0-41-227-17-18, email: luzern@luzern.org.

PART V

Italy, Greece, Cyprus, and Malta

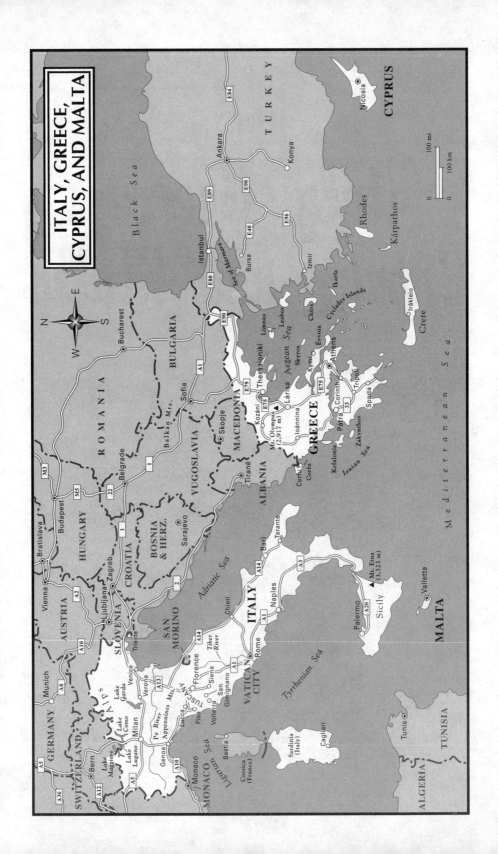

ITALY, GREECE, CYPRUS, AND MALTA

8   *Italy*

Sending out its siren song to the senses, Italy is a great place to find an extra-special home-away-from-home. Visiting Italy is not the same as living in Italy, and I can imagine nothing more beguiling than wending your watery way home on a *vaporetto*, knowing you have your own key to an apartment in a timeworn Venetian palace. Unaffordable? Not at all. Despite Venice's expensive reputation, palatial vacation properties with the very same views that entranced Canaletto rent for prices that are probably way less than you imagine. A long-stay home in Florence or Rome? Yours for as little as $730 a month.

The jewels in the Italian crown are its cities, and it's an impossible task to decide whether Florence, Venice, or Rome comes out tops. Back in the 18th and 19th centuries, it was almost obligatory for wealthy Europeans from other countries to take what was known as the Grand Tour. On their Italian leg, they spent months, not weeks, in each of the above cities. You may want to do the same, but thankfully you won't have to contend with horrors that plagued earlier travelers. The chief complaints seem to have been about bone-rattling carriages, tiresome servants, and voracious bedbugs!

But don't confine yourself to city life. The Tuscan countryside is a delectable feast; so too is neighboring Umbria, the gentle green province of St. Francis of Assisi. Then there's the Italian Lake district—Lake Garda is only a short hop from the pretty town of Verona, where you can thrill to opera under the summertime stars. If you want to be within sight of the sea, consider the offbeat Aeolian Islands, much more authentically traditional than Sorrento or Capri, which are always flooded with foreign tourists. For more ideas look at the www.enit.it website or contact:

Italian Government Travel Office, 630 5th Ave., Ste. 1565, New York, NY 10111, 212/245-5618 or 212/245-4822, fax 212/586-9249.

Italian Government Travel Office, 175 Bloor St. E, Ste. 907, South Tower, Toronto, Ontario M4W 3R8, 416/925-4882, fax 416/925-4799.

Legalities

North American citizens, traveling as tourists, don't need visas to stay in

Italy for up to 90 days. Remaining for a longer period requires you to obtain a long-stay visa from an Italian consulate. Within eight days of arrival in Italy, you then have to register with the local police authority (*Questura*) in order to obtain a Residence Permit (*Permesso di Soggiorno*), which is the only document that legitimizes the stay of a foreign citizen in Italy. Without this permit, you won't be able to rent a long-term apartment, sign contracts with utility and telephone companies, open a bank account, or even borrow books from a local library.

Embassy of Italy, 3000 Whitehaven St. NW, Washington, DC 20008, 202/612-4400, fax 202/518-2154.

The Language

Non parlo Italiano. Although it's feasible to arrange accommodations in Italy's more well trodden parts without speaking a word of the language, it would be silly to travel further afield without a phrase book. The further you venture from the tourist trail, and particularly in the deep south, the less likely you are to find English speakers.

If you're planning on staying for a lengthy period, why not enroll for some lessons at a local language school? You'll find them in all the major cities—the Italian tourist office has details or check www.it-schools.com.

Through Scuola Leonardo da Vinci, which has centers in Florence, Rome, and Siena, two-week general courses start at around $250.

Scuola Leonardo da Vinci, via Bufalina 3, 50122 Firenze, tel. 39/055-294420, fax 39/055-294820, email:florence@scuolaleonardo.com.

Italiaidea, Piazza della Cancelleria 85, 00186 Roma, tel. 39/06-68307620, fax 39/06-6892997, email: info@italiaidea.com.

Although you may be tempted to buy a "Teach Yourself Italian" tape, don't place too much reliance on it. After six months of dogged home study, I felt fairly confident with my new-found linguistic skills. Stepping off the plane in Rome, I was flabbergasted to find everybody jabbered away at least four times faster than they did on the cassettes—I could only understand the odd words here and there. The good news is that the more you hear and attempt to speak the language, the more you'll understand.

Vacation Rentals

Tourist organizations are an excellent starting point for finding vacation properties. Italian territory covers 21 regions, each further divided into several provinces. Listings of vacation homes to rent can be had through local tourism offices, known as *Ente Provinciale Turismo, Azienda Autonoma di Soggiorno e Turismo,* or *Azienda Promozione Turistica.* Every provincial town has a branch so initially contact the Italian tourist office for listings of local agencies and addresses. There are more than 100 of them, all producing accommodation brochures with rooms and apartments listed under *affittacamere* (rooms to rent) or *esercizi ricettivi extralberghieri* (other accommodation facilities). Choose an off-the-beaten-track location and prices for a couple can be as low as $160 weekly.

This is the method I used to find a seaside vacation flat on Lipari, one of the seven volcanic Aeolian Islands that lie between Sicily and Italy's southernmost region, Calabria. Perhaps because of their black sand and pebble beaches, the pervasive smell of sulfur, and a rather alarmingly

USEFUL HOUSING TERMS

affittacamere—rooms to rent
alimentari—grocery stores
Ente Provinciale Turismo,
Azienda Autonoma di Soggiorno e Turismo,
Azienda Promozione Turistica—local tourism offices
esercizi ricettivi extralberghieri—other accommodation facilities

immobiliari—sales and rental agents
Permesso di Soggiorno—residence permit
Proposta di Locazione—rental offer
Questura—local police authority
spese condominiali—common charges
vaporetto—public boat transport

active volcano, the islands see relatively few foreigners. But what's wrong with not being part of the crowd? The ambiance on Lipari is wonderfully Italian and it's easy to take boat trips to neighboring islands: Vulcano with its bubbling hot springs and alfresco mud baths; Stromboli, where you can see slow-moving lava flows and nature's fireworks shooting from the volcano; and Salina, which produces an unusual sweet wine called Malvasia. Get up-to-date accommodation lists, ferry schedules, and tons of information about these geologically peculiar islands from:

Azienda Autonoma di Soggiorno e Turismo delle Isole Eolie, Corso Vittorio Emanuele 202-98055 Lipari, tel. 39/090-9880095, fax 39/090-9811190.

To rent accommodations in advance, you may have to write an inquiry letter in Italian to the apartment owner. Help is at hand through the main Italian tourist office—ask for their Travelers' Handbook, which contains an example letter for booking accommodations. Of course, you'll need a phrase book to unscramble the reply. And once you get to Italy, an example letter isn't much use when figuring out how to buy a train ticket or shop for food in local *alimentari* (grocery stores), so be sure to pack that phrase book!

Sketch artist outside the Uffizi Gallery in Florence

© Steenie Harvey

Within the cities, there's a proliferation of accommodation agencies, many geared toward dealing with foreigners. The price of water, electricity, and any agency fee is normally included in prices for vacation rentals, but you're often asked to provide a security deposit against causing any damage to the property. You'll also be able to rent town and countryside vacation properties from companies in the United States, and there's an excellent U.K. agency that can arrange a stay in a Venetian palazzetto. You can also find holiday rental accommodations through numerous websites: www.emmeti.it is one of the best, particularly if you're seeking villas in the Tuscan countryside.

What's the minimum period you have to rent a property for, and how far in advance should you book? To answer the first part of the question, the minimum period is usually a week if it's in July or August and you're looking for a place in rural Tuscany, the Italian Lakes, or near the ocean. And, for these months, book as far ahead as possible. That said, I found our *agriturismo* cottage near San Gimignano, in Tuscany, with six weeks' notice—and the owner was happy to take a three-night booking.

Italy is such a big country it's hard to provide specifics, but as a rule, if you're planning to book a vacation apartment in Rome, Easter is always a busy time. So, of course, is Carnival in Venice. It usually takes place in February, but dates depend on when Easter falls, so always check with the tourist office. I think July and August are the very worst times to visit Italy's major cities—Florence, Rome, and Venice—for despite the sweltering heat, this is when all the foreign visitors swarm in. Don't leave bookings for these places until the last minute. In most cases, you should be able to rent a city apartment for three days rather than a week.

Long-Term Rentals

Furnished properties are probably the way to go as unfurnished rentals are even more bereft of fixtures and fittings than in France: Italians will even take the toilet seat when they move home! Plus there's a chronic shortage of accommodations within some major cities—Rome especially. Unless you're quick off the mark (and have an excellent command of the language), scouring local newspapers for accommodation is likely to prove very frustrating. Although it sometimes costs the equivalent of a month's rent, the hassle-free way of finding homes is through agencies.

Italian sales and rental agents are called *immobiliari* and almost 6,500 of them belong to FIAIP (Federazione Italiana Agenti Immobiliari Professionali). Contact them for names and addresses of agents in your chosen area or check out their website at www.fiaip.net. All member agents are listed, though few individual agencies are on the Web.

FIAIP, Piazzale Flaminio 9, Rome 00196, tel. 39/06-3219798, fax 39/06-3223618, email: info@fiaip.it.

When it comes to long-term rentals, most *immobiliari* and rental agencies ask you to pay the first three months of rental up front, and you may also have to provide the equivalent of another two or three months' rent as a security deposit. Providing the property is in the same condition as when you moved in, this deposit is returned at the end of the lease period. The agency's finder's fee is paid by the tenant and generally amounts to around 10–15 percent of the first year's rent.

Additional costs depend on where you choose to live—and also what kind of luxury level you require. Most urban folk live in apartment buildings and some of these edifices often look as if they were built at around the same time Rome was founded. Fine if you like the distressed look, and although kitchens are generally huge, unmodernized buildings don't usually have elevators or central heating. In provincial towns, the rental price of a basically furnished one-bedroom apartment in a crumbling old property can be as little as $460 monthly, slightly more in major cities. A back-to-medieval-basics two-bedroom apartment averages around $565 monthly.

A higher standard two-bedroom apartment is likely to cost somewhere between $650 and $710 monthly. However, comfort comes at a cost and you will have to budget for what's called the *spese condominiali,* or common charges, for an apartment building. Depending on what services are offered, central heating, hot water, elevator maintenance, external lighting, and the man who comes to clean the foyer could add an additional $88 to $178 to your monthly bill. And, of course, you'll have to pay electricity and telephone bills.

Rental Agreements

Under Italian law, all rental contracts must be registered. Registration fees, normally divided equally between landlord and tenant, are 2 percent of the annual rent for unfurnished properties, 3 percent for furnished. Once you've found a property to suit, you'll initially be asked to sign a *Proposta di Locazione,* or rental offer, which is legally regarded as a pre-contract. Make sure that it really is the property you want, since you will have to provide the deposit at this time. Change your mind and you are unlikely to get your money back.

If you're looking for a six-month or year lease, university towns and cities that are accustomed to overseas visitors are probably your best bet. Otherwise, the normal lease in most provincial towns is for three or four years. However, the tenant can break the lease,

Summer in Tuscany: the rural hideaway we rented at Casnova di Pescille, near San Gimignano.

© Steenie Harvey

subject to giving six months' notice. Rent is normally paid in advance every three months.

Once You're There

Under Italian law, all non-EU citizens must be covered by private health insurance during their stay. The embassy can supply a list of English-speaking health professionals in the larger cities. Unless you require emergency hospitalization, you will undoubtedly have to pay as you go, then reclaim from your insurance provider. A visit to most doctors costs between $65 and $85; a visit to a hospital emergency room for patching up cuts and bruises around $23; blood and urine tests $64.

Some Costs: 1 kg (2.2 lb) chicken breasts $9.10, 200 g (7 oz) cheese $2.68, 1 kg (2.2 lb) potatoes $0.74, 100 g (3.5 oz) coffee $3.40, six eggs $1.07, 1 liter (1.76 pt) milk $1.05, 500 g (17.5 oz) cornflakes $2.80. A week's car rental, economy model, from $200. Train fare, second-class single, Verona to Florence $22, Verona to Venice $9. Italian rail fares are state subsidized and astoundingly cheap. Check out schedules at www .fs-on-line.com.

Banking hours are 8:30 A.M.–1:30 P.M. and 3–4 P.M. Monday to Friday. To open a bank account you'll need to have your *Permesso di Soggiorno*. Once you have a current account, it may be worthwhile to have a Bancomat card to go with it. This can be used to withdraw cash from ATMs all over the country—they work like a debit card. Most supermarkets, gas stations, and restaurants take them too.

Florence and Tuscany

Arriving in Tuscany really is like being transported into the canvas of a Renaissance masterpiece. Washed in mellow, golden light, the reach-for-a-paintbrush landscapes are just as you imagined: dreamy hilltop villages, seas of vibrant yellow sunflowers, column after column of cypress trees standing guard like sentinels. The tranquil countryside is sublime, a celestial patchwork that begs you to pull on your hiking boots and wander the ancient hills like a footloose gypsy or a medieval pilgrim.

The only word to describe Tuscany's towns and cities is unforgettable. Lots of places are close to Florence, so go exploring—there are good public transport links to towns like Siena, Volterra, Pisa, Lucca, and San Gimignano, each with their own cache of wonderful medieval treasures. Steeped in centuries of history, they greet you like images from a faded Book of Hours, their bell towers, churches, mansions, and palaces glowing in warm, antique colors. San Gimignano is particularly beguiling—with its 14 towers that stab the skyline it has been likened to a medieval Manhattan. You can only imagine what the town must have been like in the Middle Ages when 76 towers reached heavenwards. But wherever you base yourself, it's impossible to absorb all of Tuscany's glories in a few days. You could spend a lifetime immersing yourself in the study of paintings and frescoes alone.

The food is something else to savor—there's lots more on the menu than just the famous *bistecca* (steak) *alla Fiorentina*. Regional specialties include a salami flavored with fennel seeds (*finocchione*), a soup made from beans and black cabbage (*ribollita)*, and a pasta dish made from wide ribbon noodles, topped with a rich sauce of fried bacon, tomatoes, and rabbit simmered in wine (*pappardelle con la lepre*). Favorite puddings include chestnut cake (*castagnaccio*) and pastries stuffed with spices, nuts, and candied fruits (*panforte di Siena*). Chianti is the best-known red wine of the region, or ring the changes with a bottle of Brunello di Montalcini. Tuscan white wines aren't considered as prestigious as the reds, but most people will find that they're perfectly quaffable. A decent one to look out for is Montecarlo Bianco.

The Duomo, one of Florence's classic sights

© Steenie Harvey

Where to rent in Tuscany? If art and architecture top your list of interests, go straight to the birthplace of the Renaissance: Florence. The town of Michelangelo and Leonardo da Vinci, it was here that Dante wrote *The Divine Comedy*, Boccaccio *The Decameron*, Botticelli painted *The Birth of Venus* and *Primavera*, and the Medicis schemed and plotted against their rivals.

My advice is to rent an apartment outside July and August. Those legendary museums and galleries aren't as crowded and even the best *trattorie* won't demand reservations. Unlike in summer, many of the top designer boutiques have *sconti* (sales) signs pasted on the windows and storekeepers have lots more time for those who want to linger over the choice of an exquisitely bound book, a lacquered antique cabinet, or majolica-work plates.

Florence can be an expensive lady, and a three-course meal with wine in all but the most basic restaurants is likely to set you back at least $35. (More like $145 if you wander into the 15th-century setting of Enoteca Pinchiorri on Via Ghibellina, widely considered to be Florence's best restaurant.) However, you don't have to dine out every night, and some of the city's most memorable pleasures can be had for free. It costs nothing to stroll over the Ponte Vecchio, browse amongst the stalls of San Lorenzo market, or lose yourself in the maze of historic backstreets. My own favorite spot in this incredibly magical city is the Boboli Gardens, a statue-filled park behind the Pitti Palace.

Florentines call their city Firenze and you could go into a passionate f(i)renzy by moving into a 16th-century Renaissance palace on Piazza Santa Croce. Mostly rented out to foreigners, apartments in Palazzo Antellessi are furnished with a mix of modern and antique furniture. Tear yourself away from the palace's Renaissance rose garden and you can still tune into this century and the news from back home. Apartment TV sets all carry CNN. Priced in dollars, monthly rents start at $4,000, though 10 percent discounts kick in if you're staying longer than a single month.

Manfredi Piccolomini, 215 West 98th St., 12E, New York, NY 10025, tel. 212/932-3480, fax 212/932-9039, email: ciaomanfredi@aol.com.

Thankfully not all rents in Florence are quite so stratospheric. If you don't mind being outside the historic center, the average studio apartment rents for approximately $585 monthly. Florence House agency has English speakers in their office and offers both short- and long-term rentals in Florence and the Chianti region of the Tuscan countryside. Prices start at

The perfect setting for pageantry: June's Ferie delle Messe festival in San Gimignano re-creates medieval traditions and honors the town's patron saint, Santa Fina.

© Steenie Harvey

around $590 monthly for an efficiency to suit an unfussy student. Or go upmarket and rent a one-bedroom furnished flat (living room, kitchenette with washing machine, bathroom, central heating, and telephone) on Piazza Tasso for $836 monthly.

Florence House, Via de' Pucci 4, Firenze 50122, tel. 39/055-289-947, fax 39/055-219-191, email: info@florencehouse.it.

Americans looking for a long stay may want to contact Milligan & Milligan. The agency is run by Americans who have been living in Florence for more than 20 years. They'll help you with the bureaucracy of rental contracts, police forms, and explain how utility bills are calculated. They offer short-term (one week to one month) rentals, long-term rentals, and a choice of homes in both Florence and the Tuscan countryside. Weekly lets in Florence tend to be very expensive—a sample price is $760 weekly for a vacation flat sleeping two or three people in the Santa Croce area. However, if you're seeking something long-term, a 3rd-floor duplex apartment near Brunelleschi's fabulously domed Duomo (cathedral) rents for $1,178 per month. Properties are fully furnished, with a kitchen and bathroom or shower. The price of short-term rentals includes electricity, water, and agency fee. Long-term rentals are only inclusive of rent and agency fee, so obviously you'll need to budget for utility bills. You also have to provide a refundable "damage deposit": currently $162 for vacation rentals, $540 for long-term rentals.

Florence, a city of sunlight and statues

© Steenie Harvey

Milligan & Milligan, Via Alfani 68, Firenze 50121, tel. 39/055-268-256, fax 39/055-268-260, email: milligan@dada.it.

This agency also has rural Tuscan farmhouses available for rent. Some have been divided into vacation apartments, others you can rent for private use, and many come with manicured gardens and swimming pools. However, in most cases you'll need a car—these properties often tend to be fairly isolated, located far away from bus routes. You may also be quite a

AGRITURISMO—
RURAL IDYLL IN SAN GIMIGNANO

The best way of experiencing the rustic Tuscan lifestyle is to rent an *agriturismo* property from an on-site farm-owner. That's what we did when we stayed in a farmhouse apartment at Casanova di Pescille, within view of the towers of San Gimignano. If you enjoy walking, it's feasible to get around here without a car—the farmhouse is only 2 km (1.24 mi) from town. And don't let the fact that there are no trains to San Gimignano put you off. Plenty of buses make the hour-long journey between San Gimignano and the art-treasure town of Siena, which is on the railway.

The initial concept of *agriturismo* (rural tourism) was to let visitors stay on real Italian farms, and many farmers received EU grants to renovate their agricultural buildings. Perhaps inevitably, many farming families realized that paying guests were likely to be far more lucrative than olive-oil production. After installing a small swimming pool, they partitioned their old barns, sheds, and watermills into lots of tiny apartments. In some *agriturismo* places there's barely any sign of farming—and you can find yourself jostling for space around the pool with 20 other families. Whether it's through a rental agency or from the owner, be sure to check how many other visitors the property rents to.

You certainly won't feel overcrowded at Casanova di Pescille, where Roberto and Monica Fanciullini have more strings to their bow than just tourism. They still produce honey, olive oil, saffron, and wine on their small holding, and sell products from the farm shop. And although the property has a decent-sized swimming pool, this isn't a huge tourism complex. Along with five double bed-and-breakfast rooms, the Fanciullini's have only one apartment available. In dollar terms, the rental cost is around $100 per day. It's not the cheapest place in Tuscany, but for sheer beauty and tranquillity, it's worth every last cent. And, come nightfall, you can see the twinkly lights of glow-worms in the dark.

Roberto Fanciullini, Casanova di Pescille, Loc Pescille, San Gimignano, Tuscany, tel./fax 39/0577-941902, email: pescille@casanovadipescille.com.

Good websites for finding *agriturismo* rentals are www.chianti.it and www.emmeti.it. If you want to be in the Siena-San Gimignano area, also check out www.sienaol.it.

distance from the nearest village. If you're nervous about tangling with Italian roads and maniac drivers, you'll probably be happier in town rather than at a rural retreat. If, though, you're a confident driver, there are lots of properties to make your mouth water. Be warned, though—farmhouses and villas for private use rent for astronomical price tags. In the heart of the Chianti region, famous for its vineyards, Milligan's has a number of furnished apartments and houses. Depending on the season, apartments sleeping two rent for $275 to $456 weekly. Apartments sleeping four start at $405 rising to $914 in high summer; larger properties from $736 to $1,682.

Homes around Siena, San Gimignano, and many other locations throughout Tuscany and neighboring Umbria can also be had through Tuscan Enterprises, a licensed real estate agency with its own vacation rental department. They deal with many nationalities, so ask for a brochure in English as prices are given in dollars. Cozy homes for two around San

Gimignano of the dreamy towers rent for between $535 and $580 weekly. If you're feeling generous, you could rent a villa for yourself and 10 house-guests—but you'd probably need to be very wealthy. It costs a whopping $3,505–5,620 per week! For most properties, you have to provide a damage deposit of around $270 and the company can arrange maid service for around $10 per hour.

Tuscan Enterprises Srl, via delle Mura 22/24, 53011 Castellina in Chianti, Siena, Italy, tel. 39/0577-740623, fax 39/0577-740950, email: tuscan@si.tdnet.it.

You can also rent by the week or longer term through a U.S.-based company, **Rentvillas.com**. Vacation apartments for two in restored farm-houses in the hills above Florence cost between $372 and $1,164 weekly; apartments for four cost $748 to $1,370. Other properties include a restored farmhouse annexe, 3 km (2 m) from Florence. This rents out at between $2,314 and $2,625 weekly, with electricity costs extra. Near San Gimignano, apartments in a country house rent from between $706 to $1,004 weekly.

Rentvillas, 700 E. Main Street, Ventura, CA 93001, 800/726-6702 or 805/987-5278, fax 805/641-1630, email: mail@rentvillas.com.

If you were thinking of a longer stay, you may prefer a town that isn't quite so tourist-oriented as Florence. One of the nicest—and most afford-able—of the region's smaller walled towns is Lucca, the birthplace of Puc-cini. Its medieval center is Tuscan to the core—beautifully preserved, and brimming over with churches, palaces, and bell towers. Here you could rent a *mini appartamento* for $425 or a four-room apartment for around $735 monthly.

Essegi Immobiliare, Viale Pacini 15, Lucca 55100, tel. 39/0583-492-604.

For more information on Tuscany, contact the regional tourist office at **Azienda Promozione Turistica,** Via Cavour 1, 50122 Florence, tel. 39/055-290832, or contact www.tuscany.net.

Venice

Water, water, everywhere. Venice is like nowhere else on earth, a watery labyrinth of islands, bridges, canals, and medieval alleyways that rightfully belongs to another age. Here Main Street is the Grand Canal, lined with ornate 14th-century palazzos and candy-striped landing stages where you can hop on a water bus or *vaporetto*. Divided into six main areas, or *sestieri*, the traffic-free city is only about two miles long by one mile wide. Even so, it packs an entire world of wonders into an impossibly compact area.

You'll want to see the showpiece sights, but remember that one advan-tage of renting a property is being able to shop in local stores and markets.

Despite surface indications, this is also a city where ordinary people live and work. The average Venetian isn't buying $6 cups of coffee in one of the tourist traps around Piazza San Marco, lounging back on squashy cushions in a gondola, or downing Bellini cocktails in Harry's Bar. (By the way, when Hemingway drank here the place wasn't packed to the rafters with camera-toting American and Japanese day-trippers.) Never mind the guidebook recommendations for dining out—they all list Florian's and Quadri's—so consequently there are too many visitors piling into the same old places. And then they moan and groan about how expensive it is.

And no, you don't have to go to McDonald's for cheap eats. Doesn't it baffle you how so many people lose their sense of culinary adventure once they've left home territory? This is Italy, for heaven's sake, not some back-of-the-beyond hellhole where the natives snack on grubs and beetles. Even if you don't intend on cooking dinner for yourself, you **can** eat out in Venice without negotiating a mortgage first. Avoid the hordes and save lots of money by taking a delve into the web of backstreets where unpretentious *trattorie* serve delicious three-course meals for $18 to $26 a head.

A 15-minute stroll from San Marco, the Doges Palace, and Bridge of Sighs, you'll find a blessed escape from the razzmatazz: the Cannareggio *sestiere* is an unfrenetic backwater where you can still soak up atmosphere aplenty. A place of uncharted corners and dead-end *calle*, this is where many ordinary Venetians live, hanging out their laundry and caged song-birds from wrought-iron balconies. Crisscrossed with myriad veins and arteries of water, the Cannareggio Canal links the Grand Canal to the mist-ily mysterious Lagoon and its islands. This is one of the likeliest places to find an affordable apartment or studio, especially if you want to watch gondolas floating past the window.

Venetian Apartments is one of a number of agencies offering apartments in authentic medieval palaces and costs aren't as expensive as you may fear. For example, a studio apartment for two in Palazetto San Lio (in Castello *sestiere*) rents for approximately $730, apartments sleeping four for $1,452 weekly. Close to Campo Santa Maria Formosa, all this palazetto's properties have canal views and are furnished in 18th-century style with silk-covered walls, Murano chandeliers, and antique furniture. Kitchens are equipped with gas *hobs* (rings), fridges, cutlery, and crockery, and prices are inclusive of gas, electricity, and bed and bath linens. Based in the U.K., the company has been renting private apartments in Venice for 11 years. Some properties can be rented by the month (a top floor apartment in Campo Arsenale costs $2,800 monthly), others attract discounts for longer stays, though in some apartments you have to pay a heating supplement over winter.

VeniceRentals is based in the United States and has studios and one-, two-, and three-bedroom apartments throughout all the city's districts. They often have last-minute deals—in early spring for example, a two-person studio in the Accademia district was available for $128 nightly, $800 weekly.

Venetian Apartments, 408 Parkway House, Sheen Lane, London SW14 8LS, tel. 44/0-20-8878-1130, fax 44/0-20-8878-0982, www.venice-rentals.com, email: enquiries@venice-rentals.com.

VeniceRentals, P.O. Box 8711, Boston, MA 02114, tel. 617/472-5392, email: mail@venicerentals.com.

You can also rent apartments through the U.S. company, Rentvillas, address on page 162 in Florence/Tuscany section. Sleeping 2–4, apartments in an 18th-century building, just 100 meters from Piazza San Marco, rent for between $1,113 and $1,224 weekly. Ten minutes from the Rialto Bridge, a top-floor palazetto apartment sleeping four or five rents for between $1,213 and $1,466 weekly.

For a two- or three-night stay, various apartments are available in an elegant palazzo with antique furnishings overlooking one of the Castello *sestiere's* canals. Depending on the season, two-person apartments cost approximately $235 per day; a six-person apartment from $424 per day. **Residence San Giorgio degli Schiavoni,** Castello 3288, Venezia 30124, tel. 39/041-241-1275, fax 39/041-241-4490.

Immobiliare Cera rents properties by the month, week, or just for weekends. Listings include a two-bedroom apartment on the 4th floor of a Venetian palazzo, five minutes from St. Mark's Square. Depending on the season, weekly rent is from $474 to $735. In Canareggio, an apartment for two on the 2nd floor of an old palace rents for between $450 and $620 weekly. **Immobilare Cera,** Campo S. Stefano 2956, Venezia 30124, tel. 39/041-5220601, email: a.cera@venice-cera.it.

Venice Real Estate's properties for long-term rentals on yearly contracts include a luxury furnished apartment in the San Marco quarter, near Sant Angelo *vaporetto* stop. Renting for $2,970 monthly, the fourth-floor apartment has one bedroom, one bathroom, fully equipped kitchen, and a sitting room overlooking the Grand Canal. Less expensive rentals include a two-bedroom apartment on Giudecca Island for $1,380 monthly. **Venice Real Estate,** San Marco 1130, Venezia 30124, tel. 39/041-5210634, www.venicerealestate.it.

Venice isn't just a city—it's a province too. One way to dramatically reduce costs is by staying beside the turquoise Adriatic in seaside Venezia, and then making forays into La Serennissima by public transport—bus and *vaporetto* boat. Between September and May, you'll only pay around $147 per week for a furnished apartment sleeping two, $196 for something larger for four. Of course, Italians like sea and sun vacations too, so prices take a hike during high summer: In July and August expect to pay an average $390 and $505 weekly for the same properties. Al Portesin has a good selection of rentals along the Venice Lido and in Adriatic seaside villages.

Al Portesin Agenzia Immobiliare, Corso Venezia 158, Porto S. Margerita Caorle, Venezia, tel. 39/0421-260100, fax 39/0421-260150.

The Romance of Rome

There's a saying in Italy: *non basta una vita Roma* (one lifetime isn't enough for Rome). Unlike many old adages, this one has some truth in it—a single lifetime probably isn't enough to fully appreciate all the Eternal City's glories. Believe me, you can wear yourself down to a shadow trying to see everything this ancient capital has to offer: It's impossible to cover the Rome of the Caesars, the Rome of the Borgias, and the Rome of Fellini on just a week long vacation trip.

Even if you're only here for a brief visit, life is more enjoyable if you pace yourself. Divide your time between cherry-picking some of the major sights and taking it easy, sampling *la dolce vita* in one of the local neighborhoods. Stop at a café, sip a glass of Frascati wine, and let your imagination journey back through all that history. And don't bother hiring a car—all roads really do lead to Rome, traffic jams are horrendous, and you'll need at least three lifetimes to find a parking space. There are plenty of buses, cabs, and an underground train system for getting around. Tickets can be purchased from tobacconists and newspaper kiosks.

Across the Tiber—the river which divides the main bulk of the city from the Vatican—is romantic *Vecchia Roma* (Old Rome), where laundry flaps from the balconies of tall, ochre-colored buildings and narrow alleyways wind around ornate *piazzas*. The heart of this congested medieval district is Piazza Navona and its celebrated Fontana dei Fiumi (Fountain of the Four Rivers). If you rent an apartment near here, the Campo dei Fiori street market is the place to shop for olives from the barrel, juicy plum tomatoes, and bright bouquets of fresh flowers. (If you're like me and mad for markets, shun the swish stores of Via Condotti and browse for cheap shoes, lurid glassware, and other Roman bargains at the Sunday morning flea market at Porta Portese, near Trastevere underground station.)

If you don't want to cook, eating out doesn't have to be expensive. The trick is to avoid those places with umbrella-shaded tables on the pavement—go for somewhere that resembles grandpa's cellar instead. Away from the main squares, and especially in the Trastevere district, you'll find plenty of small *trattorie* lurking below street level—simple, bistro-like restaurants where a carafe of house wine and a three-course meal costs less than $45 for two. Two classic Roman dishes to try are *spaghetti all'amatriciana* (pasta with bacon, white wine, tomatoes, and pecorino cheese) and *saltimbocca alla romana* (veal scallops with ham and sage).

The easy way to find accommodations is through an agency. Originally a department within Roma University, Roman Homes now rents short- and long-term properties to vacationers as well as foreign students and academics. The cost of holiday and short-term rentals (1–3 months) include the agency commission and an allowance for gas and electricity. The only extra is likely to be for outgoing phone calls. Expect to pay around $755 monthly for a studio apartment in beyond-the-Tiber districts such as Trastevere. If you lease for six months, a larger two-bedroom apartment in a residential quarter near the Vatican costs around $1,545 per month.

Vecchia Roma? On Via della Vetrina, a quiet side street off Piazza Navona, you could rent a vacation apartment that sleeps two in a 15th-century palazzo. The corridors have beamed wooden ceilings, the courtyard has a mosaic tiled floor, but the apartments themselves are fully equipped, right down to TVs and CD players. Weekly price equates to around $840 low season, $896 high season.

Roman Homes, Via Stefano Bredo 30, Rome 00133, tel. 39/06-935-2216, email: info@romanhomes.com. Phones are always busy so they recommend that you contact them initially by email.

Another bilingual agency is Roman Reference. Their apartments, all in central locations, average $500 per week for a budget option, $655 to $820 for moderate, and $820 to $1,475 for a deluxe-class home. If you want to make your stay something really special, they can also arrange lessons in opera singing, lacquer work, mural painting, and much else besides.

Roman Reference, Via de Capocci 94, Rome 00184, tel. 39/06-489-03612, email: info@romanreference.com.

Italy's Lakes

Sapphire-blue looking glasses reflecting an alpine backdrop—the Italian lakes have inspired numerous poets, writers, and composers down through the ages. Edging north towards the mountain peaks of Switzerland and Austria, the lakes are one of the more tranquil areas of Italy, though the resort towns can get very busy in summer. As in all popular places, vacation rentals aren't cheap and prices rise as the season heats up. Typical weekly costs (all-inclusive) for fully equipped and furnished studio apartments sleeping two are $295 to $475, rising to around $770 during July and August.

Swagged by blazing bushes of bougainvilleas and oleanders, the Big Four are Lake Maggiore, Lake Lugano, Lake Como, and Lake Garda. Each lake has its own charms and its own clique of fans. Both Italians and non-Italians return year after year to while away the summer, taking leisurely lakeside rambles and hiking into the hills, listening to the sound of a Vivaldi concerto, or just messing about in boats. Spring through fall is the

VERONA—VIVA LA DIVA

Magic moments don't get any better. As twilight turns to velvety darkness, an expectant hush falls over the audience: the orchestra are entering the arena and taking their seats. It's the signal for the occupants of the stone *gradinata* tiers to light up the candles they have been given to read their *libretti* by. Thousands upon thousands of candles flicker away like fireflies in the blackness of this ancient Roman amphitheater. It sets the scene for the drama that's about to unfold.

Be warned—Verona is apt to turn you into a complete opera addict. Before you know it, you'll be thirsting for *Der Ring*, Wagner's 15-hour marathon of Valkyries and Volsungs, Nibelungs and Norns. I had my very first operatic experience at Verona, weeping like a waterfall at the tragic fate of Bizet's feisty gypsy heroine, *Carmen*. (It's a fact of operatic life that nobody on stage ever seems to have a nice day.) Italians adore seeing their heroines die from the effects of nasty diseases, funeral pyres, and assassins' daggers. Poor *Tosca* chucks herself over a balcony into a river, *Lucia di Lammermuir* goes stark raving mad. The heroes don't fare much better—if they're not committing suicide, it's usually a toss-up between the torture chamber, firing squad, or murder by a jealous rival.

Seating 16,000 people, the Arena di Verona is remarkably well preserved for a 2,000-year-old edifice. Although part of its outer colonnade fell down in a 12th-century earthquake, the bulk of the amphitheater is virtually intact—only Rome's Coliseum can dwarf it. It was mind-blowing to contemplate that if I'd been around in the 1st century A.D., I'd probably have been watching one of those "Lions 10—Christians 0" events.

The first opera to make a Triumphal March across this remarkable stage was *Aida* in 1913. Performed most years, Verdi's Egyptian extravaganza is Verona's favorite opera and it's a real showpiece with horses, the occasional herd of trum-

peting elephants, and a cast of thousands. Does it have a happy ending? Don't be silly—Aida and her lover are buried alive inside a tomb.

The opera festival runs from the end of June until late August. Alongside *Aida*, three or four other operas are staged each summer—usually some of the repertoire's better-known evergreens. *Tosca, Nabucco, Carmen, Turandot,* and *Madame Butterfly* have all been performed in recent years. And it doesn't have to be an expensive night out. Although many foreign tourists pay hundreds of dollars for seats at ground level in the *poltrona* and *poltronissima* sections, the locals pile into unnumbered *gradinata* seats in the vast stone tiers of the amphitheater. However, if you opt for a cheap seat, do as the Veronese do and rent cushions. Operas start (or are supposed to start) at 9:15 P.M. and if *Aida* is scheduled, it's going to be a long haul. Midnight comes and goes whilst you're still sitting there on your achingly hard stone seat.

As well as the cushion, the other essential item is the picnic. I kid you not, Italian families attend the opera armed with bread, wine, and salamis poking out of plastic bags. (Try doing **that** at Covent Garden or the New York Met!) If you're the least bit snobby or pretentious, the *gradinata* seats probably aren't for you. *Bambini* wail and fidget and crawl about underfoot, drinks get spilled, and everybody gossips away to friends and neighbors.

To be certain of a seat, particularly for *Aida*, buy tickets the day before or on the morning of a performance. However, it's usually possible to get tickets even at the last minute. That's if you're prepared to pay a premium and buy from touts instead of the box office. Tickets from official sources cost from $22 for the *gradinata* experience to $154 for top seats.

Arena di Verona, Via Dietro Anfiteatro 6b, 37121 Verona, tel. 39/045-8005151, fax 39/045-8013287, www.arena.it, email: ticket@arena.it.

best time to come—despite the proximity of the Alps and the ski resorts, winter on the lakes can be gray and rainy. You may actually find it quite difficult to get a place outside the season, as many locals in the apartment rental business head off to the cities between mid-October and late March.

Overlooked by the eternal snowcaps of the Alps, Maggiore can be reached by direct train from Milan. Its main town is Stresa and from here you can take boat trips out to the three Borromean Islands: Isole Bella, Isole Madre, and Isole dei Pescatori. If you're into botany, Isole Madre is particularly enticing for it's truly a garden island, blooming with more than 20,000 species of plants. Lake Como is ringed with harbor villages, all well connected to one another by boat. Perching at the southern end, the largest lakeside resort is Como, more town than village, and full of quaint cobbled streets. Its smaller sister lake, Lugano, is shared by both Italy and Switzerland but my own choice would be Lake Garda. It has all the right credentials: pretty little terracotta-roofed towns like Desenzano, Riva, Limone, Malcesine, Garda, and Sirmione, wooded mountain trails to wander, and fabulous views of the Trentino Mountains. On balmy summer evenings you can often sit at a lakeside bar, watching a fireworks display or listening to a free classical music concert. That's what we did one time in Riva, the most northerly lakeside village, built around a 12th-century fortress and a Venetian watchtower.

You can find vacation rental properties through tourist offices. Riva's APT office is at Giardini di Porta Orientale 8, Riva Del Garda 38066 TN, tel. 39/0464-554444, fax 39/0464-520308, email: aptgarda@anthesi.com. Sample rentals (both with communal swimming pool) include:

Residence Monica, Via Longa 18, Riva Del Garda 38066 TN, tel. 39/0464-551156, fax 39/0464-551502, email: Monica@Rivadelgarda.com. Two-bedroom apartments for $265 per week during low season, $729 in July and August.

Residence Filanda, Via S Alessandro 51, Riva Del Garda 38066 TN, tel. 39/0464-554734, fax 39/0464-557159, email: ResidenceFilanda@Rivadelgarda .com. Apartments for 2–4 $270 low season, $520 July and August.

If you're contemplating a long-term rental and looking for addresses of *immobiliari* on the FIAIP website, this area comes under the Trentino region. Another reason for coming to Lake Garda is that it's less than an hour from Verona—catch the train from the lakeside town of Desenzano. The pink marbled city of Shakespeare's Romeo and Juliet stages the most famous of Italy's outdoor opera festivals, and the extraordinary setting is a wonderful place to gain an introduction to a world of throbbing, raw emotions. It's an incomparable experience to see and hear opera performed in the incredible setting of a Roman arena, so don't miss it.

9 Greece, Cyprus, and Malta

GREECE

Along with the Olympic Games, Greece gave us the alphabet, medicine, democracy, and philosophy. Crammed with archaeological sites, it's the cradle of what we call "Western civilization." Although Athens is something of a polluted nightmare nowadays, away from the capital it still feels as if you're wandering through an antique land of gods and heroes.

The sound of goat bells, the smell of incense in a country chapel, bleached buildings with cornflower-blue shutters ... for me, Greece's best part is its islands. There are over 2,000 of them, and 166 are inhabited. They range from hectic holiday isles like Mykonos, Rhodes, and Crete, which have their own airports, to the artist's paradise of Hydra, a car-free hideaway where the only way to get your luggage up the hillsides is by donkey.

Although most travelers stick to one island group such as the Cyclades or Dodecanese, moving from one archipelago to another is a great way to spend a summer. Part of the Cyclades chain, Naxos is my own favorite island hideaway. Blessed with cloudless summer skies, its seas glint with jewel-like colors: lapis lazuli, jade, and turquoise. Come nightfall, the summer moon hangs in the sky like a giant lantern, turning paths to ghostly threads of silver. Cicadas chirp in the olive groves, slinky cats flit past like shadows, and the air is heady with the scent of thyme, sage, and jasmine.

Alternative places to look for rentals include the traditional villages of the Pelion, the Haldikidi peninsula, and the Peloponnese, birthplace of much of Greece's mythology. For more ideas contact the tourist office.

Greek National Tourist Office, Olympic Tower, 645 5th Ave., New York, NY 10022, 212/421-5777.

Greek National Tourist Office, 1300 Bay St., Toronto, Ontario M5R 3K8, 416/968-2220.

Legalities

North Americans don't need visas. You can stay for 90 days without getting entangled in bureaucracy. If you decide to linger, you'll need a residency permit from the Alien's Bureau in Athens. Apply at least 20 days before the end of your initial three-month stay. Permission to stay depends on various criteria— the most important being the ability to show that you have sufficient means of support.

Aliens Bureau, 173 Alexandras Ave., 11522 Athens, tel. 30/0-1-770-5711.

Embassy of Greece, 2221 Massachusetts Ave. NW, Washington, DC 20008, 202/939-5800.

Embassy of Greece, 80 MacLaren St., Ottawa, Ontario K2P 0K6, 613/238-6271.

The Language

Ancient Greek doesn't much resemble its modern counterpart. Even if you can translate the works of Socrates, your erudition is unlikely to make much impact on the average apartment owner. Thankfully it's not essential to know Greek to enjoy a holiday here. A basic phrase book will do for most situations—no matter how much you mangle the language, locals love your attempts.

Things get trickier outside mainstream tourist areas, though many people speak English because of time spent working in the United States, Australia, and Britain. Plus, English is now a compulsory school subject, and most children are willing interpreters if you find yourself muttering "it's all Greek to me."

Naturally there are opportunities to learn modern Greek. Athens has the most options: a 10-week basic course (two days a week, three hours a day) at the Athens Centre costs around $525. The company can arrange accommodations, including apartment rentals, and they also run summer schools on Spetses Island.

Kifissia is a northern suburb of Athens with bus and metro links to the center. Here Greek House offers language courses as well as seminars on subjects such as Greek cooking, mythology, and Byzantine music. Costs for language courses (60 hours) start at $520.

Athens Centre, 48 Archimidous St., 11636 Athens, tel. 30/0-1-7012268, fax 30/0-1-70186013, email: info@athenscentre.gr.

Greek House, Georganta 11, 14562 Kifissia, Athens, tel. 30/0-1-8085185/86, fax 30/0-1-808555184, email: mail@greekhouse.gr.

Vacation Rentals

There's simply no way to lay out a blueprint for Greece—it's one of those places where you take things as you find them. Rental prices vary between each island archipelago and are dependent upon time of year. Low season is April, May, and October; midseason is June and September; high season is July and August.

On islands, the easy way to find accommodation is to let it find you. Many locals have built speculative little developments of rooms and studios, rarely fancy, but invariably spotlessly clean. An eager crowd of prospective landlords and their progeny throng the quayside when a ferryboat puts into port. Competition to gobble up visitors is fierce. You're leapt upon by men, women, and kids holding up notices reading "DHOMATIA," "ROOMS," or "ZIMMER" (the islands are very popular with German visitors). Simple twin-bedded rooms with leaky showers cost around $15 per night, though there's little available for under $35 on fashionable islands such as Mykonos and Hydra. After agreeing on a price, you and your luggage will be crammed into a 30-year-old rattletrap car. You're whisked away before you have a chance to change your mind.

It's vital to pinpoint where the proposed accommodation is, and what you'll be getting for your money. The cheapest accommodations are basic

USEFUL HOUSING TERMS

Enikiazete—to rent   *Dhomatia*—room to rent rooms—no air-conditioning, no kitchen, just a couple of beds, use of a shower and, if you're lucky, a fridge. With prices starting at as little as $15 a day, they're okay for short stays, but not if you're looking for home comforts.

Next on the ladder comes studios. Priced by unit, these generally have twin beds, a minuscule corner kitchenette, and separate shower and toilet. Prices average $35 to $50 a day, but you'll pay more for classier studios in a specially designed complex with swimming pool and gardens. Outside the main season, you can rent by the day, but many owners only accept weekly bookings during July and August. Prices are often negotiable. Outside the main season, you should be able to bargain a 20 percent discount if you're staying for more than just a few days.

The same goes for apartments, which usually consist of a living room with open-plan kitchen, one or two bedrooms, and shower. Depending on luxury level, island, and time of year, expect to pay anything from $290 to $690 and upwards weekly for apartments sleeping between two and four people. Larger properties are quite hard to come by and incredibly expensive too. You'll be competing with wealthy Athenians who are quite willing to pay $2,200 a week for two-bedroom villas with pools. During peak season, houses and villas usually rent by the month, not the week.

Most properties include bed linens and towels. But no matter how much you pay, you're unlikely to be impressed by the quality of Greek bathrooms. First thing you'll wonder is "Why the huge supply of blue plastic bags?" Well, there's no avoiding the fact that Greek island toilet facilities are nastily primitive. The plumbing system is so antiquated that visitors are implored not to put toilet paper in the obvious place—the toilet. This

Greek island hopping: Ferries are the classic way to get around.

causes blockages and you're supposed to put **all** paper in the plastic bags provided. If you're in an apartment that includes cleaning services, the maid takes it away. Otherwise you grimace, pick up your plastic bag, and deposit it in an outside garbage can.

Power showers? Forget it—thanks to the peevish gods of the plumbing pantheon, water shortages occur with monotonous regularity. If the gods are smiling, a thin warm trickle may eventually appear, but don't hold your breath waiting. Shower curtains aren't the norm either, so don't go thinking your bathroom is worse than any other.

If you're traveling wherever the breeze takes you, the safest bet is to go to the tourist office (if there is one), or an accommodation office. They'll have descriptions and prices of properties, and you'll know if the location is suitable. Room-finding services often double as travel agencies, and there's at least one in the main port towns of popular islands. Although you'll pay around a third more than if making a private arrangement with an owner, you may feel it's worth it for peace of mind. Open all year, the Mykonos Accommodation Center is worth noting. The staff speak English, and they can also book you accommodations on most other Cycladean islands. Their office is at the end of Matoyianni, the main street in Mykonos town.

Mykonos Accommodation Center, P.O. Box 58, 84600 Mykonos, Greece, tel. 30/289-23160/23408, fax 30/289-24137, email: mac@ mykonos-accomodation.com.

If you want to arrange accommodations in advance, some owners of upscale apartments advertise on the Internet. Unfortunately you won't find a myriad options this way—the Web is still in the infancy stage in Greece.

Long-Term Rentals

Many visitors dream of what it must be like to live on a Greek island. Wouldn't it be fantastic to start every sun-drenched day by waking to the distant peal of monastery bells and breakfasting on a terrace swagged by pink bougainvillea blossoms? And think of the sublime view—distant islands, blue-domed churches, bright fishing boats bobbing in that wonderfully colored ocean....Yet the majority of Greek islands aren't awash with long-term foreign residents. The main reason is the climate. Despite those enticing images, the Aegean doesn't enjoy endless summer. Come mid-November, many islanders set sail for Athens and other mainland cities. Those who haven't are battening down the hatches and preparing for four months of miserable weather.

November ushers in the season of storms and disrupted ferry schedules, so think carefully before opting to stay on. Entertainment is almost nonexistent and there's very little to do except develop a solitary ouzo habit. Corfu, Rhodes, and Crete stay alive year-round, but on many islands you could find yourself starved for company. And although the Cycladean island of Mykonos always draws a small core of hikers, artists, and writers even out of season, it's not a typical Greek outpost.

The majority of tavernas get shuttered up and all those countless communities that bustled with life in summer change into ghost towns. It can be cold too. Homeowners who only use their houses as tourist lets in the blistering Greek summer don't usually bother to install costly central heating. Whether you've rented a villa, an apartment, or a traditional village house, dreary December may result in damp clothes, damp bedding, and damp spirits too!

To find long-term accommodations, the best bet is to go spend a vacation visit island-hopping and see which island feels right for you. Talk to locals, drive around looking for rental signs, or ask at the local holiday accommodation bureau or tourist office. If there's a realtor's office, they may have rental properties too. Corfu has a sizeable expatriate community and is one of the likeliest places to find long-term rentals. For example, apartments in Corfu town rent for between $345 and $810 monthly, or you could opt for a two-bedroom semi-detached maisonette in the countryside for $245 monthly.

For mainland accommodations, again check with local realtors or in newspapers. The Greek sign for "to rent" is *Enikiazete*, and newspaper advertisements usually come under the heading of *Enikiassis Akiniton*. Cyberspace isn't a great help, though you'll find some rentals on

The old town of Rethymnon, in Crete is a jumbled warren of narrow streets and curiosity shops.

© Steenie Harvey

www.greekreg.com. The *Athens News* is an English-language newspaper with listings, but many people still find their accommodations through word-of-mouth.

Rental Agreements

Unless a property comes under the description of "summer house" or "furnished apartments for temporary stay," the standard lease term is two or three years. Rent is normally paid in advance, and you may be asked to provide an amount equivalent to one or two months' rent as a security deposit.

Once You're There

Regarding health care, although Greece has some excellent private hospitals as well as clinics in tourist resorts, state sector facilities are not at the top of the European tree. To be honest, a Greek national health service hospital isn't somewhere I would want to go. Make sure your medical insurance covers you for private hospital treatment. Patients in the state sector (80 percent of the population) aren't coddled; it's still fairly common for friends and family to provide nursing duties such as changing bed linens and emptying bedpans.

While state hospitals and doctors provide free treatment, medicines have to be paid for and many people simply visit a pharmacy for nonemergency medical advice. The French medical organization, SOS-Doctors, has round-the-clock private doctors in the Athens area. They'll come out to your residence. Including initial treatment, fees are $46 weekdays and $57 nighttime and weekends. Phone 1016 in the Athens area.

Some Costs: 500 g (17.5 oz) loaf of bread $0.48, 1 liter (1.76 pt) milk $0.34, 2 liters bottled water $0.68. A week's car rental, economy model, starts at around $141. Living costs throughout Greece are far cheaper than in most western European countries. You can eat well in unfussy tavernas for under $12 a head, buy liters of quaffable wine from the grocery store for $3, and travel from village to town for $0.70.

Banking hours are generally 8 A.M.–2 P.M. Mondays to Thursdays and 8 A.M.–1:30 P.M. Fridays. Not all island towns have banks, though there are always some kind of exchange facilities available. Citibank and American Express have offices in Athens, but if you're living elsewhere for a lengthy period, it may make more sense to open a savings and checking account with a Greek bank. With offices all over Greece, the largest are National Bank of Greece and Alpha Credit Bank.

Athens

Yes, Athens is traffic-jammed, noisy, and unbearably hot in summertime, but it does have the Parthenon, the Theseon, the Temple of Zeus, Hadrian's Arch, the Tower of the Winds, and countless other ancient monuments. If you've got any sense of history, how can you resist walking amongst the very same places as Plato and Aristotle?

The worst time to visit is in July or August when the smog is at its thickest, so plan a visit for spring or fall. Start early, break the day with a long siesta, dine like the locals around 10 P.M., and you'll find the city much easier to cope with. The apocalyptic gridlock problem should get easier with the new underground system and if it all gets to be too much, there's plenty of escapes. Places within day trip range include sites such as Delphi and Mycanae and the islands of Aegina and Hydra.

On the slopes of the Acropolis, Athens's leafy old quarter is known as the Plaka. With its secret courtyards, meandering streets, and restored neo-classical mansions, it teems with bars and restaurants. It's the favorite neighborhood of arty Athenians as well as many foreigners. Other districts to consider include Pangrati, a 10-minute walk from the center and Syntagma Square. It has more of an authentic local atmosphere, with hole-in-the-wall shops selling medicinal herbs, shady little squares called *plateias*, and some excellent tavernas where you can feast on delights such as *papoutsaki*—"little shoes" of halved eggplant bulging with minced lamb and cheese.

Kolonaki is a fashionable quarter below Mount Lycabettus, one of the city's best vantage points. At dusk, ride the funicular railway up its steeply wooded slopes for spectacular views over the Acropolis. During Holy Week, when midnight strikes and Saturday turns to Sunday, a candlelit procession winds its way down the mount from St. George's church. The Exarkhia neighborhood is popular with the young, cool, and funky, while the old proletarian quarter around Kermakos cemetery is only just starting to show signs of gentrification. Mets is another attractive residential district girdling the 1896 Olympic stadium. An easy bus or metro-ride away, the suburbs include the "Athenian Riviera" resorts of Vouliagmeni and Glyfada.

If you're looking for a vacation rental, the Delice and Perli apartment-residences are both in the city center. In Glyfada, the Oasis complex has 70 apartments, all with fully equipped kitchens. Twenty minutes from central Athens, and perfect for shucking off the heat and dust, the residence is set in large gardens with a swimming pool, and only a short stroll from a sandy beach and Glyfada yacht marina. Depending on the season, one-bedroom apartments rent for $123 to $155 daily; two-bedroom apartments from $152 to $224.

Delice Apart-Hotel, 3 Vassileos Alexandrou St., Athens, tel./fax 30/0-1-7238311.

Perli Apartments, 4 Arnis St., Ilissia, Athens, tel. 30/0-1-7248794, fax 30/0-1-7248797.

Oasis Apartments, 27 Poseidonos Ave., Glyfada, 16674 Athens, tel. 30/0-1-8941662, fax 30/0-1-894-1724, email: astra@travelling.gr.

One way for non-Greek speakers to find long-term apartments is through the classified ads of *Athens News*, an English-language paper. Advertisements are placed by both individuals and agencies. In Athens and its suburbs, small furnished apartments (living room, one bedroom, kitchen, and bathroom) rent for between $680 and $1,000 monthly, though you'll pay substantially more for top locations. Rentals through www.rocorem.com recently included a two-bedroom apartment in the "mountain suburb" of Drossia for $836 monthly, and three-bedroom furnished units in Kifissia and Anixi for $2,090 and $950, respectively. Prices in Ekali reflect its desirability—here you'll pay around $1,140 for furnished studios. Realtors often handle rentals as well as sales; Arnacao and Helen's are two agencies advertising rentals in *Athens News*.

Armaco Real Estate, tel. 30/1-8981622/8980267, fax 30/0-1-8941391.

Helen's Real Estate, tel. 30/1-7790783/7796536, fax 30/0-1-7790138.

Orfanides Real Estate, 19 Irodotoy St., Kolonaki, 10674 Athens, tel. 30/0-1-7220386, fax 30/0-17248516.

Rocorem, G. Lambrakie, 43B, 14565 Drossia, Athens, tel. 30/1-622-8822, fax 30/1-813-3243, email: realinfo@rocorem.de.

Infocasa, 70, Dionysou St., 14563 Kifissia, tel. 30/10-623-3945, fax 30/10-623-4025.

The Cyclades Islands

It's hard choosing between island groups, but there's nothing to stop you moving from place to place until you find a haven where you fancy dropping anchor. I recommend starting a discovery tour in that magical wheel of outposts in the Aegean called the Cyclades. Linked by ferries and hydrofoils, 24 of the 39 Cycladean islands are inhabited and most are only an hour or two's boat-ride from a neighbor.

It's a great place to indulge in some serious island-hopping, but choose carefully. Ios, the so-called "party" island, is one I'd avoid—package tourism and all-night discos have ruined it. Reclusive types should check out islands such as Milos, Sifnos, Kythnos, Syros, and Folegandros where locals still depend on the sea for their income and life is lived at a donkey's pace.

For sheer drama, Santorini takes the biggest accolades. Sometimes also called *Thira* or *Fira*, this crescent-shaped isle of black-sand beaches, hot springs, and blood-red sunsets was formed when a volcano erupted around

1500 B.C. The volcano destroyed Crete's Minoan civilization and—if you believe the myths—caused the waves to close over Atlantis, the "lost continent" of legend. You can find houses and apartments through Santorama Travel, which also operates as an accommodation-booking agency.

In the island's capital, Fira, Kykladonisia is one of the few Santorini apartment complexes open year-round. All rooms are fully furnished and equipped with kitchen, TVs, and air-conditioning. Facilities include a swimming pool and bar. Apartments sleeping two people cost an equivalent of $505 weekly during winter and low season, $600 midseason, and $705 during July and August.

Santorama Travel, Fira Tourist Office, 84700 Santorini, Greece, tel. 30/286-23177/23180, fax 30/286-23177/22120, email: santorama@otenet.gr.

Kykladonisia Apartments, 84700 Fira-Santorini, Greece, tel. 30/2860-22458, fax 30/2860-25184, email: info@kykladonisia.gr.

With its thatched windmills and dazzling cubist houses painted in the azure and white colors of the Greek flag, Mykonos is chock-full of visual appeal. But—and it's a big but—Europe's holiday crowds descend on the island like locusts. It hums even in May, and I wondered what things must be like in July and August, when temperatures hit the 90s and as many as 80,000 visitors are on the prowl. Mykonos surrendered its soul to tourism decades ago, and trades on its reputation as a hedonistic gay paradise. With its nude beaches, pricey restaurants, and designer boutiques, it's not the real Greece. That said, it might appeal to those who prefer a cosmopolitan lifestyle. If your idea of bliss is to go clubbing until daybreak, you'll undoubtedly love it. If not, the best way to experience Mykonos is on a day trip from one of its more sedate neighbors.

The Mykonos Accommodation Center has plenty of options. Or try Costa Ilios, a small "village" built and furnished in traditional island style. All apartments and houses are equipped with the essentials for home-away-from-home living. Each also has its own courtyard and mini-garden and residents have the use of a swimming pool and private beach. Depending on the season, weekly rents for an apartment sleeping two people cost from an equivalent $307 to $580. You'll also be required to provide a damage deposit of $200.

Mykonos Accommodation Center, P.O. Box 58, 84600 Mykonos, Greece, tel. 30/2890-23160/23408, fax 30/2890-24137, email: mac@mykonos-accomodation.com.

Costa Ilios, Mykonos, tel. 30/2890-24522/26966, fax 30/2890-24522 (Athens number 30/1-4175988/4175949), Lemacim@attglobal.net.

Tínos is best suited to adventurers, as you'll probably have to negotiate for accommodations at the port. Although we carried no luggage, we were swarmed upon by locals offering rooms for around $16 a night. One of the quieter Cycladean islands, Tínos is for traditionalists. Mass tourism is unknown and the island only gets busy on Orthodox religious holidays. Although only an hour from Mykonos by ferry, the contrast between the two islands is almost surreal. If you tried nude bathing, you'd probably be lynched by a posse of fierce-looking, black-clad grannies. No beach parties and no glamour boys wearing spangly thongs here!

The port and hub of island activity is Tínos town, where scores of good-value tavernas line the backstreets. Often tagged "the Greek Lourdes," Tínos has been declared a sacred island by the Greek Orthodox Church. The island's big day is August 15th, when thousands of pilgrims journey on their hands and knees to the huge Church of the Annunciation. The object of such devotion is an icon of the Virgin Mary, reputed to have healing powers.

The sound of Tínos isn't that of the latest summer dance hits, but the rhythmic click of worry beads. Retired farmers and fishermen, not tourists, congregate at the shady little café-bars known as *kafenions*. Playing backgammon, sipping small cups of strong black coffee and glasses of ouzo, these weatherbeaten old-timers epitomize the simplistic face of Greece. Strolling around the port, we saw squid being hung out to dry on makeshift washing lines and were often greeted with a polite "*Kalimera*." Unlike Mykonos, where everybody seems to speak English, this is an island where a phrase book would be useful.

Both Mykonos and Tínos are ideal bases from which to visit the uninhabited isle of Delos. Now home only to mosaic-floored ruins and scurrying lizards, Delos once shimmered at the very center of the Hellenic world of gods and goddesses. Myths tell that Poseidon (ruler of the oceans) anchored the island to the seabed with chains of diamonds.

Hot, hot, hot: Birds seeking a shady hideaway from Greece's fierce summer sun.

© Steenie Harvey

From Mykonos, head south on a "Flying Dolphin" (a hydrofoil) to mountainous Naxos. Tickets for the 50 minute journey cost approximately $12. The largest of the Cyclades archipelago, Naxos is greener and more fertile than its neighbors. It has just about everything you could want from a Greek island holiday: sandy beaches, crystal-clear waters, and a labyrinthine old town. More legends too: it's said that the heroic Theseus honeymooned here with Ariadne after killing the Cretan Minotaur.

Although tourists are well cared for, Naxos is nowhere near as overdeveloped as Mykonos. Away from the bustle of Naxos town, village life goes on much as it has for centuries. Late spring or fall is a perfect time to come—the meadows are a vivid carpet of wildflowers and gardens are lushly producing beans, zucchini, and pomegranates. Best of all, it's not too hot to meander the many ancient drovers' tracks that people have been using since Homer's day. Linking tiny Byzantine chapels to untouristy mountain villages, these age-old tracks form a spiderweb across the island's hilly interior. One village to visit is atmospheric Filoti, clinging to the foothills of Mount Zas, the highest peak in the Cyclades. It takes around two hours to climb to the 1,000-m (3,280-ft) summit, where you'll see the islands of Páros and Antiparos.

Crowned by a castle or "Kastro" built by Venetian invaders, higgledy-piggledy Naxos town is one of the prettiest Cycladean towns. Just to confuse visitors—especially those using the local bus services which ply to and from the beaches and into the mountains—it's also often called "Hora," "Chora," or "Khora." This name is given to all of the main towns on Greece's islands. On Naxos, the khora's tangled lanes are flanked with stone-built houses, and flowers spill from just about every balcony and vaulted archway.

With balmy nights and plenty of inexpensive waterside restaurants, there's no excuse for not sitting out under the stars and enjoying the local cuisine. Including a bottle of local red or white "Portora" wine, dinner shouldn't cost much more than $13 to $18 a head in most tavernas. My favorite Greek meal is this: a plate of feta cheese and fat green olives with fresh crusty bread, followed up by squid (kalamaria), salad, and fries. And, if I can manage it, a wickedly sticky honey and nut pastry (baklava) and a glass of Metaxa brandy. If you like liqueurs, look out for Kitron, a lemon liqueur made on Naxos.

You shouldn't have problems finding accommodations on Naxos. If you're wary about negotiating with locals at the port, there are a few places where you can book in advance. Despite the quaint-sounding name, the Summerland complex of studios and apartments is very upmarket. In the island's southwest (where the best beaches are), it's 17 km (10.5 m) from Naxos town and has been built on the principles of a traditional Cycladean village. Added attractions include swimming pool, tennis courts, and on-site car and bike rentals. Depending on the season, studios range from $46 to $80; apartments from $69 to $113 nightly.

In summer, contact Summerland, Kastraki, 84300 Naxos, tel. 30/285-75461/62, fax 30/285-75399. It closes over winter but you can book through their Athens office at Spetson 37, 15232 Chalandri, Athens, tel./fax 30/1-6847638, email: summerland@forthnet.gr.

Stella Studios, Plaka Beach, 84302 Naxos, tel. 30/285-42526/23166, fax 30/285-42526. Rooms and studios from $29 to $65; apartments from $34 to $81 nightly.

Nikolas Studios, Mikri Vigla, 84303 Naxos, tel. 30/285-75465, fax 30/285-23789. Studios for two from $40 nightly.

An hour's hop west of Naxos, Páros (not to be confused with Poros, a Saronic Island) is the Cyclades crossroads isle. It has some of the archipelago's best boat links—almost every ferry docks here at some stage during their Aegean odysseys. Páros gets busy in summer, especially around the main port of Parikía and expanding seaside village of Naoussa, which was sacked in 1537 by the red-bearded pirate Barbarossa. For goats, olive groves, and seclusion, look to inland villages such as Marpissa and Lefkes, which are still very traditional. On our last trip we toyed with the idea of exploring its hidden landscape of windmills and farming communities, but the sky was a perfect azure blue and the sun was blazing. It was impossible to resist the temptation of lazing on Piso Livadi's beach, floating in the turquoise sea, and sipping cold beer in a taverna. That's the beauty of the Cyclades—you can do a lot, a little, or nothing at all. If Páros sounds like your kind of island, the Mykonos Accommodation Center (address on page 178) rents places here.

Crete

Sitting in splendid isolation, Crete has an entire cornucopia of charms. The largest of Greece's islands, it has the distinct feel of a world apart. I once spent two lazy-day weeks here, beside the Libyan Sea, renting an apartment in Plakias, a small southwest seaside resort with simple tavernas and a wonderful beach fringed by shady tamarisk trees.

Basically there are two Cretes—east and west. The main tourist resorts throng the island's east where you'll also meet up with the Cretan capital, Heraklion, and the Minoan Palace of Knossos. For wild mountain gorges, small resorts, and more traditional lifestyles, look to western Crete. Anywhere around Chania, an old harbor-town below the White Mountains, would be a good bet.

Within a 20-minute drive of sandy beaches, elegant Chania was built by the Venetians and it's where the farm-folk of the west come to sell their produce in an appealing covered market, shaped like a Greek cross. You can buy everything from hand-tooled leather boots to octopus, bunches of oregano, and carnival masks. Exploring the backstreets behind the port, my husband recklessly ducked into a hole-in-the-wall barbershop for a haircut. He got rather more than he bargained for. The barber (who bore an uncanny resemblance to Anthony Quinn in *Zorba the Greek*) insisted on smothering him in talc, pomade, and highly scented aftershave. He emerged smelling like an escapee from a harem.

Set in picturesque locations and traditional villages, there are around 130 homes to rent through **Kalamaki Travel,** 73100 Chania, Crete, tel. 30/821-31459/32184, fax 30/821-32245, email: info@smart-holidays.com.gr.

More Islands

The green and bosky Saronic Islands are one of the most expensive places to rent homes, as they're the nearest islands to Athens. Property here changes hands for shipping magnate prices and the islands can get very busy with weekend trippers. Hydra, with its artists' studios and 18th-century houses surrounding a horseshoe-shaped harbor, is the prettiest, but Aegina has the best choice of accommodations.

A drowsy summer afternoon in Rethymnon

© Steenie Harvey

Pipinis Agency, 2 Kanari St., 18010 Aegina Island, Saronic Islands, tel. 30/297-28780, fax 30/297-28779, email: info@ pipinis-travel.com.

The Ionian Islands, off Greece's west coast, include Corfu, Zakynthos, and Kefalonia, where much of the best-seller *Captain Corelli's Mandolin* was set. Green and mountainous Corfu is popular with the British so you'll find quite a large English-speaking community of expatriates. If you're seeking a holiday rental, Oniro Villas are a small complex of traditional ter-raced houses, set around a swimming pool and with views over the Ionian. Ten miles south of Corfu town, apartments sleep up to four and rent for between $72 and $123 daily.

Corfu Property Agency is one source of long-term rentals. In the resort of Milia, a one-bedroom apartment with central heating rents for $225 monthly. In Corfu town, a four-room apartment rents for $680 monthly.

Oniro Villas Corfu, Ai Yannis, Peristeron, Corfu, tel./fax 30/0-661-72500.

Corfu Property Agency, Kapodistriou 19, Kerkyra, Corfu Town, Corfu, tel. 30/0-661-28141, fax 30/0-661-46663, email: office@cpacorfu.com.

The Dodecanese chain takes in Patmos, where St. John had his vision of the Apocalypse, and Rhodes, home to the Colossus, one of the seven wonders of the ancient world, and a castle of the crusader knights of St. John.

The nearest islands to neighboring Turkey are those of the northeast Aegean—they take in Sámos (which gave the world Pythagoras and his wretched mathematical theorem) and also Lesvos, birthplace of Sappho. In the Sporades Islands, Skiathos is a popular tourist hangout, but Skopelos, Alónnisos, and Skyros have maintained a more traditional feel.

On Skopelos Island, you can find accommodations through www .skopelos.net. George Pachis has 14 studios and apartments near Stafilos beach. Near Skopelos town, studios of his rent for $24 daily in the low season; $51 in July/August. Two-room apartments rent for between $28 and $57 daily; three-room units for between $34 and $72.

George Pachis, Skopelos Island 37003 North Sporades, tel. 30/0-424-23125, fax 30/0-424-22219.

CYPRUS

The third largest island in the Mediterranean, Cyprus has many of the same attractions as Greece. Unlike Greece's Aegean Islands, Cyprus enjoys warm winter sunshine. Open for business year-round, it draws many of the over-50 set between November and March. Although best-known for its coastal resorts, this lovely island has some stunning landscapes. Studded with Byzantine churches, the Troodos Mountains offer up cedar forests, trout restaurants, and wine-growing villages where ways of life are pleasingly traditional.

The lemon-scented "Island of Aphrodite," Cyprus has a population of around 730,000 and is a country in its own right. Despite the tavernas and bouzouki music, it's somewhat misleading to describe it as another, larger Greek island. One major difference is that Britain was the island's colonial master until 1960 and almost everybody speaks English as a second language. However, although it's geographically closer to Syria than Athens, southern Cyprus does effectively operate as a Greek colony.

Turkey occupied the north of the island in 1974. Now Cyprus is split by the so-called "Green Line," and though trouble hasn't brewed up for decades, there's a U.N. military presence. Recognized only by Turkey, Northern Cyprus is something of an international pariah and most foreign visitors holiday in the south, on the Greek-Cypriot side of the dividing line.

Cyprus Tourism Organization, 13 E. 40th St., New York, NY 10016, 212/683-5280, www.cyprustourism.org.

Legalities

North American citizens don't need a visa for a stay of up to 90 days; if you plan on staying longer, apply on arrival for a special visa, which allows stays of up to a year. Although travel between the Republic of Cyprus (the south) and the Turkish Republic of Cyprus (the north) is restricted, there are plenty of options for exotic short trips from the island—travel agents offer three- and four-day trips to Syria, Egypt, and Israel. Some expatriates even make regular weekend shopping trips to Lebanon.

Embassy of the Republic of Cyprus, 2211 R St. NW, Washington, DC 20008, 202/462-5772 or 202/462-0873.

There is no embassy in Canada, only a consulate. **Consulate General of the Republic of Cyprus,** 365 Bloor Street East, Suite 1010, Toronto, Ontario M4W 3L4, 416/944-0998.

Accommodations

Short- and long-term rental accommodations are always available. Vacationers should start by requesting the tourist office's accommodation guide, which has sections on villas, modern holiday flats, and apartments in traditional village houses. Prices for basic seaside studios begin at $26 daily; villas run between $69 and $138 daily.

Southern Cyprus's main resort towns are Paphos, Larnaca, Limassol, and Ayia Napa. If you're seeking a slower rhythm try the Akamas peninsula. Here the wildlife includes vultures and bee-eaters as well as turtles, which come to lay their eggs in the peninsula's sandy expanse of beaches. Seaside Pissouri, midway between archaeologically rich Paphos and bustling Limassol, is also a good place to recharge your batteries. Its flower-bedecked square is traffic-free and the mainstays of village life remain intact: church, bakery, little post office, and, of course, a handful of family-run tavernas. Paths through the vine terraces lead to the white sands and cliffs of Pissouri Beach.

The majority of Cypriot realtors also operate as rental agencies, both for holidays and the long term. Undoubtedly it's to entice you to buy a home here, but many of their rental properties are luxurious affairs, set in brand-new developments with swimming pools, tennis courts, and private walkways to the coast. Apartments and villas are invariably well furnished, and there's heating and air-conditioning too. Cyprus is definitely not a typical Greek island—here kitchens come with washing machines not plastic buckets, large family-size stoves instead of two-ringed toys, and refrigerators that hold more than two bottles of beer.

"Holiday rentals" are for periods of up to three weeks and are usually all-inclusive except for any telephone charges. For a classy apartment sleeping two people in the Limassol area, expect to pay around $240 weekly in winter, $535 weekly in July and August. If you can do without a swimming pool, sea view, and on-site bar and restaurant, you'll find cheaper studio and apartment options in Limassol and Larnaca for $170 weekly/$520 monthly.

Historic Paphos is the prettiest of the larger resort towns and rentals are generally higher than elsewhere. Through Benacon, a month's stay in a top-notch apartment costs approximately $785 in winter, $1,180 in April/May. On a two-month rental, the total rent would be $1,357 in winter, $2,120 in April/May. Furnished village houses in the olive groves start at monthly rents of around $1,470. When renting by the month, tenants are usually billed separately for electricity costs. The company offers to plug new arrivals into the island's expatriate social whirl—you could take lessons in icon-painting, join rambling and bird-watching clubs, go horseback riding, scuba diving, or sign up for aerobics classes.

Chris Michael Estates offers both holiday and long-term rentals. River Beach Shop No. 1, Potamos Yermasoyias, Limassol, Cyprus, tel. 357/0-5-321130 or -311201, fax 357/0-5-311666, email: info@chris-michael.com.cy.

Benacon, 75 Archbishop Makarios Ave., P.O. Box 560, Paphos, Cyprus, tel. 357/6-241543, email: benacon@cytanet.com.cy.

MALTA

Malta is another popular winter retreat for retirees. A sizable enclave of foreigners live full time or maintain holiday homes on Malta, and just about everybody—around 95 percent of the population—speaks English as well as Malti. Basking in a year-round golden glow, this Mediterranean island lies between Sicily and North Africa. According to legend, it was on Malta that the goddess-nymph Calypso seduced Ulysses. Tagged by the tourist office as "the island of sunshine and history," this outpost of just 350,000 people can certainly justify claims to both. Along with its smaller satellite islands of Gozo and Comino, Malta has been colonized by an entire litany of ancient powers: Greeks, Phoenicians, Byzantines, Romans, and many more besides.

Sights to see include megalithic temples dating back to 3000 B.C., Roman catacombs, and medieval Mdina. Known as "the silent city," this intriguing town of high-walled houses and twisting, secretive streets was Malta's capital until the 16th-century Crusader Knights of St. John built the present-day capital, Valletta. The island's most famous historic visitor was St. Paul the Apostle who was cast ashore here in A.D. 60. Islanders commemorate the event with the colorful festival of "St. Paul Shipwrecked" every February. Even the church towers tell a story—most have two clocks: one real, the other a painted fake. Apparently the reason is to confuse the Devil!

Baking the landscape to a golden crisp, the sun beams down for almost 11 hours per day in summer and for six in the depths of winter. Even in late October, sea temperatures still remain above 20°C and the crystal-clear waters are ideal for snorkeling and diving. If you enjoy walking, winter is the best time to appreciate the island as the hot dry summers can be energy sapping. Harvest-time comes early, at the end of June, and is celebrated by night-long picnics where gargantuan amounts of stewed *fenek* (rabbit) are consumed. Harvest festivities also include fireworks, folk-singing, and bareback horseracing through the streets. Just like at an Italian *Palio*, the prizes are brocaded banners, which the winners donate to their village church.

In North America, contact **Malta National Tourist Office,** 65 Broadway, Suite 823, NY 10006, 212/430-3799, www.visitmalta.com.

Legalities

North Americans don't need visas to spend up to 90 days as a tourist in Malta. Providing you can support yourself, it's possible to stay on longer by obtaining a Temporary Resident visa through the Principal Immigration Officer in Valletta.

Embassy of Malta, 2017 Connecticut Ave. NW, Washington, DC 20008, 202/462-3611/3612, fax 202/387-5470.

Accommodations

Sliema and St. Julian's are the liveliest spots on the Maltese coastline, but older expatriates favor the Mellieha and St. Paul's Bay areas. For vacation rentals, expect to pay $115 to $140 per week for a standard apartment sleeping two. Most properties are fully furnished and equipped, but during a long-term stay, it's usual to pay extra for electricity and maid service. Long-term rental apartments begin at around $220 per month for something small, with houses starting at the $530 mark. Luxury three-bedroom seafront apartments rent for between $820 to $1,310 monthly; villas with private swimming pools start at around $1,450.

For both short- and long-term rentals, try **Cassar & Cooper,** St. Anne's Court, Tigne Sea Front, Sliema SLM 15, Malta, tel. 356/343730, fax 356/334374, email: sliema@cassar-cooper.com.

Recently, Sara Grech's agency was offering a 500-year-old mill house in Zebbug village. Costing $1,200 monthly, the restored house has three bedrooms and a central courtyard with swimming pool. A monthly rent of $290 will get you a two-bedroom penthouse apartment with sea views in M'Scala.

Sara Grech Ltd., 169 Tower Road, Sliema SLM 12, Malta, tel. 356/315205, fax 356/338061, email: saragrech@saragrech.com.

PART VI

Spain and Portugal

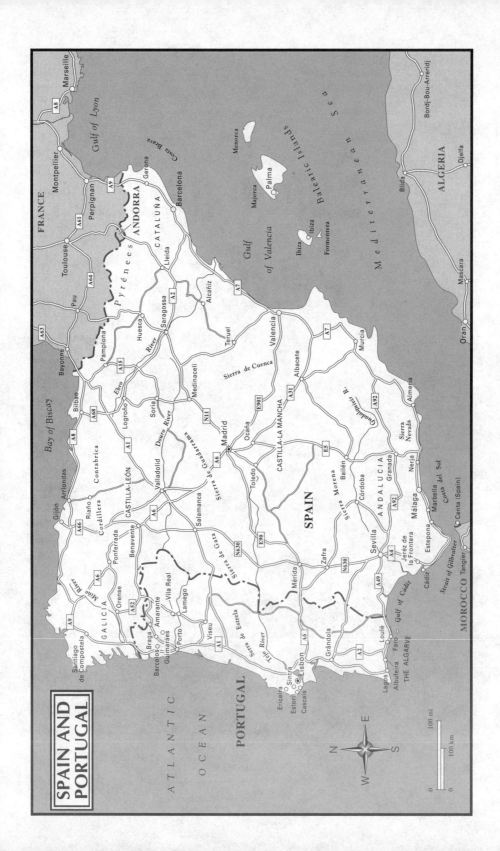

SPAIN AND PORTUGAL

FRANCE

Marseille
A8
Montpellier
Gulf of Lyon
Toulouse
A61
Pau
A64
Bayonne
A63
Perpignan
A9
Gerona
Costa Brava
Barcelona
CATALUÑA
ANDORRA
Pyrénees
Pamplona
Lleida
A2
Alcañiz
A7
Huesca
Saragossa
River
Ebro
Teruel
Valencia
A15
Logroño
Soria
Medinaceli
Sierra de Cuenca
Bilbao
A68
Cantabrica
A1
Donro River
N11
Madrid
E901
Albacete
A31
Murcia
A7
Bay of Biscay
A8
Valladolid
A6
Ocaña
CASTILLA-LA MANCHA
Almería
A92
Gijón
Arriondas
Cordillera
Riaño
CASTILLA-LEÓN
Sierra de Guadarrama
Toledo
E5
Granada
Sierra Nevada
Nerja
A66
Ponferrada
A6
Benavente
Salamanca
Sierra de Gata
Sierra Morena
Bailén
Córdoba
ANDALUCIA
A92
Málaga
Costa (Spain)
Centa (Spain)
Orense
A52
Amarante
Vila Real
N630
E90
Zafra
Mérida
N630
Sevilla
A4
Marbella del Sol
Marbella
Estepona
Santiago de Compostela
A9
GALICIA
Miño River
A6
Braga
Barcelos
Guimarães
Porto
Lamego
Viseu
A1
Serra de Estrela
Grândola
A6
Jeréz de la Frontera
A49
Cádiz
Gulf of Cádiz
Strait of Gibraltar
Tangier
Ericeira
Estoril
Cascais
Sintra
Lisbon
PORTUGAL
Tejo River
Loulé
A2
Faro
Lagos
Albufeira
THE ALGARVE
MOROCCO

SPAIN

Guadalquivir R.
Guadiana

Mediterranean Sea

Gulf of Valencia
Menorca
Majorca
Palma
Ibiza
Formentera
Balearic Islands

ALGERIA
Bordj-Bou-Arrerid
Djelfa
Blida
Mascara
Oran

ATLANTIC OCEAN

N
W   E
S

100 mi
100 km
0
0

10 Spain

Put Rodrigo's *Concierto de Aranjuez* on the CD player, close your eyes, and let that seductive guitar music waft you to sun-kissed Spain. One of Europe's most visited countries, it is at the same time one of its most mysterious. Although relatively few foreigners ever stray from the southern coastline, Spain has lots more than just sun, sea, and sangria.

From green and mysterious Galicia to the sizzling Andalucian frying pan, this vast country of around 40 million inhabitants breaks down into distinctive regions, each stamped with a varied culture and history. Wherever you go, you're almost sure to encounter a fiesta: Spain is said to have more than anywhere else in the world. For an overview of different regions, contact:

Tourist Office of Spain, 666 5th Ave., 35th Fl., New York, NY 10103, 212/265-8822, www.okspain.org.

Tourist Office of Spain, 2 Bloor St. W, Toronto, Ontario M4W 3E2, 416/961-3131.

Legalities

North Americans can remain for three months without *Residencia* permits. If you're a retiree, or don't need to work for a living, obtaining permission to stay shouldn't be difficult. Note though, that the wait for documentation could be as long as eight months. While the red tape is being untangled, you're issued a receipt, which should be carried with you at all times.

Requirements for obtaining residency permits are proof of income or pension, a "good conduct" certificate issued by your local police, proof of private medical insurance, a temporary *Residencia* visa from a Spanish consulate, a certificate that you're registered with your home embassy in Spain, and a rental contract. Any English-language documents must be translated into Spanish.

Embassy of Spain, 2375 Pennsylvania Ave. NW, Washington, DC 20037, 202/728-2330, www.spainemb.org.

Embassy of Spain, 122-74 Stanley Ave., Ottawa, Ontario K1M 1P4, 613/741-8399.

The Language

If the prospect of finding a home by phrase book seems daunting, head for Andalucia's Costa del Sol or the neighboring Costa Blanca. The accents will be different, but this is where you'll find the greatest concentration of British expatriates. As relatively few expats speak Spanish, most realtors, lawyers, and leasing agents have English-speaking staff.

Although English is more widely spoken nowadays, away from the coast it's difficult to get by without knowing any Spanish. Every sizable town has at least one language school and you'll always be able to find someone giving private lessons. One option is Gadir school in Cadiz, a historic port town in western Andalucia. Private lessons are around $19 a session; intensive two- or three-week courses start at $125 weekly. Longer language and culture courses are available and you could even opt for a flamenco-dancing course ($76 weekly). The school can arrange accommodations in shared apartments with Spaniards or other foreign students. Prices are $52 daily for singles, $40 per person for doubles, with reductions for longer stays.

If the Moorish city of Granada appeals, try Sociedad Hispano Mundial. Fees for one-week courses (15 hours) start at $128. A four-week course (25 hours of lessons each week) costs $712. Madrid's language schools include

Elemadrid, which can also arrange apartment stays. A two-week course (40 hours) starts at $160; a two-week apartment stay starts at $500.

Gadir Escuela Internacional de Español, C/Pergolas 5, P.O. Box 31, 11007 Cadiz, Andalucia, tel./fax 34/956-260-557, email: info@gadir.net.

Sociedad Hispano Mundial, Ribera de Genil, 6–1 planta, 18005 Granada, tel. 34/958-010-172, fax 34/958-101-173, email: info@shm.edu.

Elemadrid, Serrano 4, 28001 Madrid, tel. 34/914-324-540, fax 34/914-324-541, email: hola@elemadrid.com.

Vacation Rentals

Southern Spain and its islands have long been Europe's most popular summer holiday destination. For a stay on the coast around Easter, Whitsun (early May), or in July or August, I wouldn't advise leaving things until the last minute. You will usually have to book a property for a minimum of a week (generally Friday to Friday or Saturday to Saturday) at this time of year, too. Outside of those times, I've never had a problem renting a place for three days and then moving on.

If you aim to spend Easter in the city of Seville, famous for its Holy Week processions, you will need to be very quick off the mark to find holiday accommodations. During late July, it may also be quite hard to find a property in the Galician countryside around Santiago de Compostela. Saint James (Sant Iago) is Spain's patron saint, and the city seethes with pilgrims and revelers on his feast day, July 25th, and also the day before. Consequently, rural properties within striking distance of the city are a big attraction for families who want to join in the celebrations and have a holiday at the same time. Again, book as far in advance as you can.

A pilgrim with blistered feet being given a helping hand in Santiago di Compostela to complete the journey.

© Steenie Harvey

USEFUL HOUSING TERMS

agriturismo—rural vacation properties
alquilar—to rent
alquileres—property rentals
ambiente—the club scene

cuenta de no-residente—nonresident bank account
cuenta de residente—resident bank account
inmobiliaria—rental agencies
pueblos blancos—Andalucia's white villages

Thousands of holiday properties string the coastline and many owners only use them in high summer. The rest of the year, they are available for rental, either by the week or the month. Often they are available by the day, although owners typically prefer to rent properties for at least three days. Many properties are now advertised through Internet sites. For example, vacation rentals through www.spainonecall.com include a villa in the lovely Andalucian village of Nerja that rents for $740 in the low season and $1,110 during high season.

Lingering longer won't break the bank. Low-season monthly rates for studios and apartments in popular resorts average $670 to $950. Every seaside town abounds with rental agencies, most offering 10 to 20 percent discounts for long winter rentals. Holiday properties aren't usually inclusive of tax, unless listings state otherwise, so allow an additional 7 percent.

Long-Term Rentals

Most property rentals, or *alquileres,* are handled through authorized agencies. Many have the word *inmobiliaria* in their title. The tenant pays commission fees: usually the equivalent of one month's rent or 10 percent of the first year's rent.

No problem if you're looking for an unfurnished rental, but away from the Mediterranean coastline, there's something of a shortage of furnished city rentals. Only 15 percent of Spain's housing stock makes up the rental market. Although Barcelona apartments can be had for under $550 monthly, you'll probably have to pay between $1,150 to $2,300 for a decent property in Madrid. The situation is even more chronic if you're looking for a detached house rather than an apartment. Furnished city houses for long-term rental are rarities.

Spaniards tend to rent unfurnished properties and this normally means very little in the way of fixtures and fittings. No curtain rails, no light fixtures, and no towel racks. However, a kitchen is usually considered an immovable object so chances are an unfurnished apartment will have some kitchen cabinets and a stove.

Few rental agencies have websites, but a number do list available properties in the *pisos y locales* section of www.alquiler.com. In addition,

Re/Max (www.remax.es) has recently entered the market here. A number of Spanish agents have franchises, though the rental properties listed on the site to date are mostly in Madrid and Andalucia.

Rental Agreements

Within cities, lease terms are invariably for a six-month minimum term, though things are more flexible in holiday areas. Deposits are usually the equivalent of a month's rent, but can be more for quality properties. This is refundable at the end of the lease term providing you haven't caused any damage beyond normal wear and tear.

Although the landlord is responsible for property-related taxes and any necessary structural maintenance, you should check whether the monthly rental covers community charges. Although long-term tenants of luxury detached homes and villas usually have to arrange for the upkeep of their own garden and pool, apartments and town houses along the coast also often have communal recreational facilities. Community charges fund such things as lighting and cleaning of communal areas, upkeep of gardens, and pool maintenance. Within some of the older city apartment houses, the community charge sometimes includes heating and hot water too. However, tenants generally pay for metered utilities such as gas, electricity, water, and telephone.

Old ways in an old country: a backstreet market in Santiago di Compostela.

© Steenie Harvey

Once You're There

Long-term residents electing to take out health insurance with a Spanish provider pay around $33 to $92 per month, per individual. Charges for consultations with general practitioners are generally in the region of $23 to $40; specialists' fees may be closer to $60.

Some Costs: 1 kg (2.2 lb) bananas $1.16, 1 kg (2.2 lb) strawberries $1.90, 0.5 kg (1.1 lb) pistachio nuts $4.50, 1 kg (2.2 lb) tomatoes $0.70, 1 liter (1.76 pt) milk $0.69, bread $0.37, large chicken $6.30, dozen eggs $1.50, 500 g (17.5 oz) coffee $4.16, 1 kg (2.2 lb) steak $10–18. Markets are the best place to buy fruit and vegetables. Depending on the type of heating and cooking facilities, and whether an apartment has air-conditioning, utility bills will probably work out to somewhere between $100 and $200 per month. During the winter months, heating will certainly be necessary in inland cities like Madrid, whose citizens wrap up in overcoats in December and January. If you want to rent a car, economy models start at $157 weekly.

Bank hours vary, but the norm is 8:30 A.M. to 2:00 P.M. Monday to Friday and Saturday mornings during winter. Nonresidents can open a *cuenta de no-residente* bank account, but once you have a resident's permit, you must change your account to a *cuenta de residente*. Credit cards (Visa more so than MasterCard) are widely accepted.

Madrid

As capital cities go, for some reason Madrid never has been a must-see European heavyweight. Although Old Madrid still carries echoes of grandiose imperialism and steel-helmeted conquistadores, a bustling commercial metropolis now encircles it. If you're in Spain purely for pleasure, you may prefer the intimacy and dreamy romanticism of Andalucia, cosmopolitan Barcelona, or Santiago de Compostela, a timeworn pilgrimage city in the northwest.

Of course, not everyone has the luxury of choice when sent on overseas assignments. As far as the business world is concerned, Madrid is the happening place. And there's plenty to linger for if you enjoy shops, strolling in parks, and poking around museums. The Prado is one of the world's finest art galleries—paintings by Titian, El Greco, Velázquez, and Goya are only a fraction of its massive collection.

Spaniards are notoriously late eaters and Madrileños eat even later than most. Lunch hour is around 3 P.M. so if you want to dine out at night with the locals, have a pre-dinner siesta and set your alarm clock for 10 P.M. The city seems much more magical and mysterious by night, with spotlights dancing across the imperial palaces and fountains transformed into cascades of silver. The Salamanca quarter is the place for *tapas* bars, and there's a slew of traditional restaurants in the main shopping area between Gran Via and Puerto Del Sol.

If you want to experience the city's exhausting weekend nightlife (which roisters on until dawn), the club scene, or *ambiente,* swirls around the

Chueca, Latina, and Santa Ana neighborhoods, the latter an old Hemingway haunt. Start with a drink in Los Gabrieles, a 19th-century bar whose jam-packed rooms are covered in exquisite ceramic tiles. One memorable club is the Palacio de Gaviria, an authentic palace complete with marble statues, gilded mirrors, and painted ceilings where you can salsa off any remaining energy. Both places are within easy staggering distance of Plaza Santa Ana.

Madrid is an apartment city and rentals can seem punishingly expensive. Most Madrileños are owner-occupiers rather than tenants and only around 15 percent of properties are available for rental. The most sought-after districts are Jeronimos, Chamberi, and Salamanca—two-bedroom apartments here rent out for at least $1,710 per month and you could pay as much as $4,600 for a three-bedroom dwelling. However, prices are more affordable in the suburbs. Re/Max Nova agency quoted $684 monthly for a three-bedroom furnished apartment in Fuencarral el Pardo. Through "Rent-and-Buy," $1,056 monthly rents a four-room furnished apartment in Arturio Soria, which has good bus and metro links into the city center.

Re/Max Nova, Calle Santiago APostal 3, Alcobendas, Madrid 28100, tel. 34/91-658-6255, fax 34/91-654-8649.

Agentes Inmobiliarios Rent-and-Buy, Lopez Aranda 22, 28027 Madrid, tel. 34/91-320-32-25, fax 34/91-320-89-61, email: e-mail@ryb.es.

For somewhere more central, Apartamentos Tribunal has apartments with kitchens that could suit either a short- or long-term stay. Near the Museo Nacional, and with plenty of local grocery stores, one-bedroom apartments rent for $60 daily, $320 weekly. Two-bedroom apartments go for $137 daily, $750 weekly.

If you're only in Madrid for a couple of days, it often works out cheaper to rent from Friday to Sunday. Prices are higher during the work week when businesspeople are looking for short-term serviced apartments. At the Eurobuilding complex, for example, daily rates for a two-person apartment are $137 on weekends, but $174 daily from Monday to Thursday. Again, discounts apply for monthly stays.

Apartamentos Tribunal, San Vincente Ferrer 1, c/v a Fuencarrol 79, 28004 Madrid, tel. 34/91-522-1455, fax 34/91-523-4240, email: info@hotel-tribunal.com.

Edificio Eurobuilding 2, Orense 69, 28020 Madrid, tel. 34/90-222-2227, fax 34/91-570-2567, email: info@eurobuilding-2.com.

Apartamentos Plaza de Espana, Plaza de Espana 7, 28008 Madrid, tel. 34/91-542-8585, fax 34/91-548-4380.

Apartamentos Gran Via, Gran Via 65, 28013 Madrid, tel. 34/91-541-3170, fax 34/91-541-7328.

Apartohotel Galeon, C/Francisco Medrano 4, 28020 Madrid, tel. 34/91-571-2120, fax 34/91-570-9496.

The Costa del Sol

"The Andalucian sun starts singing a fire song and all creation trembles at the sound," said the Spanish poet Lorca. If it's sun you want, look no further than Spain's deep south. Recreation facilities are excellent, accommodations are affordably priced, and the *sol* blazes down for more than 300 days of the year. Along with its well-known coastline, the Andalucia region also encompasses the beautiful old Moorish cities of Seville, Granada, and Cordoba. This part of Spain was under Arab rule from A.D. 711 to 1492. If you're on the Web, www.andalucia.com is an excellent English-language site that gives a taster of its towns and cities as well as lots of practical information.

Made up of eight provinces and fringed by the Costa Del Sol, Andalucia is Europe's top spot for winter holidays and golfing vacations. The coast stretches for 300 km (186 m), from Motril in the east to Gibraltar in the west. You'll need to be very choosy about where you go—parts are probably going to seem much grimmer than what you expected. Lax planning regulations in the 1960s and 1970s led to whole stretches of coastline being brutalized by high-rise hotels and holiday-apartment ghettos. Many wouldn't look out of place in the old Eastern bloc countries.

Beating the drum for the Feast of St. James in Santiago di Compostela.

© Steenie Harvey

Despite the jet-set image of Marbella, and elegant marinas like Puerto Banus where million-dollar yachts anchor under jewel-blue skies, some depressingly tacky places blight the Costa Del Sol's seascape. Resorts like Torremolinos and Benalmadena mostly cater to young, package-tour vacationers who aren't really interested in experiencing Spanish culture. Avoid such places like the plague. That's unless your idea of the perfect vacation involves English pubs and Irish bars, all-day breakfasts of greasy bacon, eggs, and sausage, and what the brochures describe as "legendary nightlife." "Legendary" is the vacation industry's code word for the relentless thump of wall-to-wall discos. Crowds of 18-year-olds to 30-somethings stagger from bar to disco, out of their skulls on Ecstasy tablets and cheap wine.

Thankfully not all of the coast is an abomination. Although Marbella is definitely a resort city rather than a fishing town, like neighboring Puerto Banus it has stacks of charm. Don't think you'll have it to yourself, however. The permanent population is just over 100,000 but during most winter weeks there's an extra 60,000 visitors. During the summer, the figure swells to 400,000.

To dissuade the riff-raff, Marbella can be horrifyingly expensive. A three-bedroom garden apartment in a luxury seafront development easily rents for $1,070 weekly in the low season. Prices drop a little if you rent for a month, but for similar properties some well-heeled visitors will pay around $3,500 monthly in the low season and a massive $9,500 during high summer. If your heart is set on luxurious Marbella, Artola agency has a wide choice of properties for both short- and long-term rentals.

Cheaper options exist if you can do without sea views or the privacy of a swanky villa. Marbella Habitat lists a selection of reasonably priced properties in Marbella itself, and in nearby resorts such as Estepona. Many properties are in small complexes of apartments, set around gardens and a communal swimming pool. Except in August, when the minimum rental period is two weeks, you can rent weekly or monthly. A stroll from Marbella beach, the Alhambra Del Mar complex has apartments which sleep up to four people. Weekly rents range from $855 to $970. Monthly rents start at $1,378 low season, rising to $3,325 during July and August.

La Mairena is a development of white wedding cake apartments and villas in private parkland overlooking Marbella. Views stretch to the Sierra Nevada mountains and to Gibraltar. If you don't fancy the beach, you can laze around a couple of swimming pools. Two golf courses are only a five-minute drive away, and there's 28 more within a 50-km (31-m) radius. Depending on the season, two-bedroom apartments rent for between $785 to $1,120 weekly.

In Andalucia's far west, Cadiz province remains unblighted by the onslaught of tourism. Great bird-watching and walking country, this corner of Spain is one of the prime bird migration routes to and from Africa. You may spot eagles, vultures, and honey buzzards soaring on the thermals. Cadiz town itself was founded by Phoenician merchants in 1100 B.C.—it's a real layer cake of a port with medieval walls built on Roman foundations. Its splendid belfries and church towers were paid for with the gold and silver spoils that the conquistadores grabbed from the New World.

Cadiz province is where you'll find some of southern Spain's most affordable rental properties. A small furnished apartment in the low season can cost as little as $410–520 monthly if taken for a three-month period. However, long-term prices don't usually include gas or electricity.

Inmobiliaria Artola, Ricardo Soriano 12, Edif, Marqués de Salamanca, 29600 Marbella, tel. 34/952-86-50-91, fax 34/952-86-70-43, email: iartola@ctv.es.

Marbella Habitat, Centro Comercial "Marbella 6," Local 19, Avda Miguel Cano 6, 29600 Marbella, tel. 34/952-86-68-91, fax 34/952-86-28-86, email: marhabit@ctv.es.

La Mairena, POB 2059, 29600 Marbella, tel. 34/952-83-60-92, fax 34/952-83-62-23, email: mairena@mairena.com.

VIP Rentals, Apartado 35, 11310 Sotogrande (Cadiz), tel. 34/956-79-45-71, fax 34/956-79-45-23, email: vip@vnet.es.

Rural Andalucia

Away from the Costa del Sol's busy resorts and golf course developments is a secret Andalucia that few package vacationers ever see. An escape from the tourist hordes, this is a bewitching world where scores of deeply white-washed villages cling like limpets to the hillsides. Known as *pueblos blancos*, many of these "white villages" have been here since the time of the Moorish invasion and, only a century ago, this was bandit country! Think donkey-width passageways, old-fashioned saddlery shops, and shady plazas where bright bouquets of flowers spill from wrought-iron balconies. Here pavement cafés are the haunt of grizzled old grandpas enjoying a session of cards along with carafes of local wine.

No mass tourism, no high-rise hotels, just a timeless landscape of orange groves and avocado plantations where mules and oxen remain in daily use. One magical place to rent a property is in or around one of the 31 towns and villages of the mountainous Axarquia district, high in the sierras between Malaga and Nerja. To encourage visitors to explore the lesser-known parts of Andalucia, the regional government has set up *villa turisticas* in each of Andalucia's eight provinces (Malaga, Granada, Seville, Cadiz, Huelva, Cordoba, Jaen, and Almeria). Malaga's *villa turistica* is in the Axarquia.

Built in the local architectural style, accommodations range from studio rooms to villas. Most "villages" have pools, tennis courts, and other sports facilities, and offer a range of activities including horseback riding, mountain biking, and guided hikes. Priced by the day, studios for two start at around $62, with two-bedroom villas for four at around $105. If you're traveling with kids, rates for them are reduced 50 percent during the week and 30 percent on weekends.

Overlooking the glittering Mediterranean, Nerja is the Axarquia district's best-known town. Famous for its caves and the cliff-top Balcon de Europa, it receives a fair amount of the more upmarket type of summer tourists. A popular area with expats, many realtors here have departments dealing in rental properties (*alquileres*). Village houses in Andalucia's *pueblos blancos* are popular buys with Europeans and are often available for holiday rentals or the longer term. Language shouldn't be a problem as most agencies have English-speaking staff. Outside July/August there's a great choice of homes for monthly rents of $470 to $830.

Nerja's pretty satellite villages include Frigiliana. The last place in Spain to be abandoned by the Moors, its streets bear wall plaques picturing the Moorish conquest. With winding steps, mysterious cobblestoned alleyways, and stupendous views down a valley toward the sea, it's a dream village. You'll probably want to stay forever.

You can find websites where you can rent directly from the owners. For example, www.1001-villa-holidaylets.com lists a Nerja apartment sleeping four people just a five-minute stroll from the beach. In a residential complex with swimming pool, it rents for between $230–518 weekly depending on the season.

The mountains beyond Granada are another possibility. Casa Paquita, a cottage in Chite village with views of the Sierra Nevada mountains, rents for approximately $948 monthly (through Rustic Blue). And though you probably wouldn't fancy it long-term, www.costaholidays.com arranges rentals in one of the numerous troglodyte caves that abound in this region of wooded sierras and Moorish castles. Prices start at $230 for a one-week cave rental.

Villa Turistica de La Axarquia, Carril Del Cortijo Blanco, 29710 Periana, Malaga Province, Andalucia, tel./fax 34/95-253-6222.

SEDUCTIVE SEVILLE

Fifty miles from the coast, Seville is the quintessential southern Spanish city, famous for its Spring Fair and Holy Week processions. The historic core of this ancient Moorish stronghold is the Barrio de Santa Cruz, an engaging labyrinth of *tapas* bars and alleyways so narrow that many of the whitewashed houses almost seem to touch. It's a neighborhood of shady squares, pattering fountains, and balconies cascading over with geraniums.

Want an insider's view? Rentals include Apartamentos Murillo, at the heart of the Santa Cruz district and within strolling distance of the flamboyant Alacazar Palace, the Giralda Tower, and many of the Andalucian capital's other highlights. Apartments are fully equipped and sleep either 2–3, or 4–5 people. Depending on season, small apartments range between $65 and $106

daily, larger apartments $106 to $124. Long-term rates apply for monthly rentals: $1,064 for smaller apartments, $1,615 monthly for larger properties.

With a three-day minimum stay, Apartamentos Centro-Sevilla also offers studios and apartments sleeping up to six people in Barrio de Santa Cruz. Again, rates are seasonal, with prices for two-person studios starting at $26, and apartments sleeping four at $43 nightly.

Apartamentos Murillo, Reinoso 6, Barrio de Santa Cruz, Sevilla, tel. 34/95-421-09-59, fax 34/95-421-96-16, email: apartamentos@hotelmurillo.com.

Apartamentos Centro-Sevilla, C/Adolfo Rodriguez Jurado, 6 Atico B, 41001 Sevilla, tel. 34/95-450-02-06, email: info@centrosevilla.com

James Perez Real Estate, C/Cristo 62, 29780 Nerja, (Malaga), tel. 34/952-525763, email: jp@nerjaholiday.com.

Inmobiliaria Ruiz Montero, C/Pintado 35, 29780 Nerja (Malaga), tel. 34/952-526723, fax 34/952-526626.

Millennium Vacations, C/Granada 31, 29780 Nerja (Malaga), tel. 34/952-523608, fax 34/952-523486, email: millem@spa.es.

Rustic Blue SL, Barrio La Ermita, 18412 Bubion, (Granada), tel. 34/958-763381.

Homage to Catalonia: Barcelona and the Costa Brava

Overlooked by the Pyrenees, the province of Catalonia, or *Catalunya*, sweeps south from the French border. Although part of Spain, the region was independent in the 9th century and still has a strong sense of being a separate country. Catalans first, Spaniards second, the people have their own customs and a notoriously difficult language which General Franco unsuccessfully attempted to outlaw. And while Catalan remains the language of the streets, everybody speaks Spanish too.

Catalonia's two principal cities are Gerona and cosmopolitan Barcelona. An energetic seaport city, Barcelona combines artiness and earthiness in equal measure. Don't be surprised if you turn into a *ramblista*—a rambling addict. A feast for all the senses, the aptly named *La Rambla* is one of the world's most beguiling promenades. Shaded by plane

Gigantes wander the streets of Santiago di Compostela during the feast of Saint James.

© Steenie Harvey

trees, this is Barcelona's wide central thoroughfare, a splendid 1.5-mile-long walkway between the Port and Placa de Catalunya. Here, on Sunday mornings, you may chance upon troupes of *castellers* building human pyramids. They've been holding *casteller* contests on the square since the 1880s. The most acrobatic can achieve nine layers of these people structures.

Day or night, *La Rambla* heaves with people. Barcelona is a city that doesn't know what sleep is. Here are bookstalls, buskers, and transvestite flamenco performers; glorious art nouveau cafés like Café de l'Opera with its aproned waiters and marble-topped tables; flower sellers, fire-eaters, and gypsy fortune-tellers; shops where you can buy rosary beads or an authentic Spanish guitar; the bird market's orchestra of caged canaries singing their tiny hearts out. The best time to shop for provisions is early morning—just take a detour into the world of La Boqueria, a 19th-century food market of chickens, fish, and colorful displays of fruit and vegetables. If it all gets to be too much, dive into one of the old-style bodegas and drink *cava*, a quaffable Catalan version of champagne.

Beckoning from the east side of *La Rambla* is the *Bario Gotic*, or Gothic quarter. Its focal point is the cathedral, where geese roam under the palms and magnolias of the cloister gardens. Full of curiosity shops, it's as densely tangled a medieval warren as you could wish for. Getting lost is all part of the fun and you might as well just chuck away your map and wander the labyrinth at will.

Then there's the museum and art trail—the only word for Barcelona's architecture is stunning. Pablo Picasso was an adopted son and the fabulous monuments of *Modernista* architect Antoni Gaudí are scattered across the city. A number are in the Eixample district, a late-19th-century neighborhood north of Placa de Catalunya.

Salvador Dalí described Gaudí's works as "demented" but maybe he had been bitten by the old green-eyed monster. With its towering pinnacles glittering with a colorful mosaic of broken pottery and glassware, the highlight is the Sagrada Família temple, Gaudí's surreal fantasy version of a Gothic cathedral. It's still unfinished after more than a century. Apparently he lavished so much care on the decoration of the towers because he believed that the angels would see them. Another gem is Parc Güell. Designed by Gaudí to be a residential area, it ended up as a people's park of rippling tiled terraces, rainbow frogs made from mosaic, and little fairy-tale homes built around walkways supported on concrete palm trees.

The Internet is useful for tracking down properties for short-term stays. Accommodations are listed on local sites such as www.barcelona-on-line.es, www.costabrava.org, and www.dlleure.com. Depending on property size, expect to pay $62 to $240 per day with good discounts for long-term winter stays. For example, a studio sleeping one or two near the old part of the city rents for between $72 and $90 daily, depending on season. A one-bedroom apartment near the Picasso Museum rents for $100 nightly.

As most apartment-hotels and residences have kitchen facilities, they're worth considering for both short- and long-term stays. In Aparthotel Silver, studios for two cost $64 per night or $1,270 monthly. In the Eixample district, near Rocafort metro, studios for two in Apartments Calabria start at $99 nightly.

If you prefer to be at the heart of the downtown action, the French group Citadines has a residence on *La Rambla* itself. For stays of up to a week, a studio sleeping one or two costs between $120 and $138 nightly. Stay for a month or longer and the rate falls to $108–124 nightly. An apartment for four costs between $180 and $205 nightly for short stays; $162–185 nightly if you've booked a month or more.

Aparthotel Silver, C/Breton de los Herreros 26, 08012 Barcelona, tel. 34/93-2189100, fax 34/93-4161447, email: reservations@hotelsilver.com.

Apartments Calabria, Calabria 129, Barcelona 08015, tel. 34/93-4264228, fax 34/93-4267640.

Citadines Barcelona, La Rambla 122, 08002 Barcelona, 34/93-270-1111, email: info@citadines.com.

Barcelona is an apartment city. Although its old quarters are aesthetically appealing, not all residences have air-conditioning and can often be quite ramshackle from the outside. The sought-after residential districts are a metro-ride to the west: neighborhoods such as Pedralses, Bonanova, Tres Torres, Sarria, and Sant Just.

Long-term rentals are generally for six months minimum. Unfurnished properties start at around $215 monthly for studios in old Barcelona but you could pay as much as $2,150 for a classy five-bedroom residence in Tres Torres. Furnished properties start at $410 monthly for studios and $565 to $980 for two- and three-bedroom apartments. *Barcelona Metropolitan*, an English-language monthly, carries listings as does *La Vanguardia*, a local newspaper. There are plenty of Barcelona rental agencies on the www.alquiler.com website; listings include furnished apartments in good areas starting at $685 monthly.

Fincas Sacristan, C/Balmes 23, 08007 Barcelona, tel. 34/93-302-7253.

Bergua, Bailen 92/94, Barcelona 08009, tel. 34/93-246-6565.

Fincas Castan, Josep Tarradellas 84, tel. 34/93-430-8381.

Sprinkled with picturesque villages and hilltop monasteries, Catalonia province is hemmed by the pine-covered cliffs of the Costa Brava, the Wild Coast. Sadly not as wild as in the days before developers discovered its charms, it nonetheless has some appealing hideaways where you can escape Barcelona's frenetic city life for sun, sand, and the sapphire-blue Med. Don't go to tacky Lloret de Mar—look instead to small resorts and fishing villages such as Tamariu, Calella de Palafrugell, and Llafranc. Lovely inland villages include hilltop Begur with its 16th-century castle,

Palafrugell which has a bustling Sunday market, and car-free Pals whose narrow medieval alleyways are little changed since the 10th century.

The coastal villages have a handful of provision stores, though most locals go inland to Palafrugell for their main shopping. If you don't want to do more than prepare breakfast, there's a good selection of restaurants where you can try paella, octopus rings fried in batter, and traditional Catalan dishes. Sailing boats, windsurfers, and kayaks can be rented from many beach resorts, and Tamariu has a diving center. Other activities include walking the coastal paths, playing beach volleyball, or snorkeling in the crystal-clear waters.

Nightlife in these small Costa Brava villages is very low-key and no wall-to-wall nightclubs spoil the tranquillity. During summer, Tamariu stages weekly performances of the *sardana*, the traditional Catalan folk-dance that General Franco attempted to ban. Visitor participation is encouraged and there's often more impromptu dancing on Saturday nights when musicians play along the seafront.

Outside July and August, locating self-catering accommodations shouldn't be problematic if you simply turn up and ask around. You'll find plenty of listings on the websites www.costabrava.org, www.dlleure.com, or by contacting Tourism Catalonia's Barcelona office, tel. 34/93-268-1855, email: tourism@catalonia.net.

Finques Frigola rents properties by the day, week, or month in tranquil seaside villages such as Tamariu and Llafranc. Weekly prices start at $270 in the low season and can go up to $2,300 for the monthly rental of a house in Calella de Palafrugell. Rosas is a livelier Costa Brava resort; here Aparta-mentos La Solana has various sized properties. Depending on season, studios for two rent for $122 and $296 weekly; apartments sleeping 4–6 rent for between $179 and $447.

Finques Frigola, Calella de Palafrugell, Costa Brava, tel. 34/972-615-336.

Apartamentos La Solana, Port de Reig 17, Rosas, Costa Brava, tel./fax 34/972-256-545, email: lasolana@lasolana.com.

Galicia and Santiago de Compostela

Pounded by Atlantic breakers, remote Galicia is a green and surprisingly rainy region with an intriguing Celtic past. With Portugal to the south and the Picos Europa mountains to the east, it lies in Spain's northwest, a place of fjord-like sea inlets called *rias* and workaday fishing villages.

No flamenco dancers, no sun-drenched coasts, yet Galicia manages to entice thousands of wayfarers every year. Most come to visit Santiago de Compostela, which takes its name from *Sant Iago* (St. James), the country's patron saint. If you're renting a vacation property in Galicia, do try and visit this fabled city on July 25th, St. James' Day.

Throughout the Middle Ages, Santiago de Compostela was regarded as one of the three Holy Cities of Christendom (the others were Jerusalem and Rome) and medieval pilgrims from all over Europe undertook arduous journeys to get here. Since the 9th century it has guarded what many believe to be the bones of St. James the Apostle.

Much may have changed but timeworn Compostela remains mysteriously magnetic. Not only does the city honor the saint with holy processions, it seethes with fairs, carnival pageantry, and the salsa beat too. What you won't find is silence—not unless you shut yourself away inside one of the solemnly splendid churches. St. James Eve is marked by a barrage of firecrackers and unsuspecting travelers must think they've entered a city under siege.

A university city, many of Compostela's 30,000 students come out to sing for their supper, meandering from bar to bodega, wrapped in black cloaks festooned with rainbows of ribbons. The medieval maze hides dozens of inexpensive restaurants and *tapas* bars: the more unsophisticated a place looks, the better it's likely to be. Local wines from the barrel are served in jugs and usually come with a tiny slice of tortilla, half a dozen green olives, or a fat black mussel on a crust of bread. Shortly before midnight on the 24th, everyone abandons the drinking dens to watch a firework extravaganza, the spectacular *Fuego Del Apostol*.

Day and night, Galician bagpipers stroll the porticoed streets and indulge in mournful wailing, but one of the most peculiar sights around town are the *gigantes*. Representing pilgrims of all nations, these swaying giants on skirted stilts roam Compostela's ancient labyrinth of rain-washed squares. Just as thrilling for the hordes of big-eyed Spanish toddlers are the enormous-headed *cabezudo* figures who perform unwieldy dances wherever there's room.

For a thousand years and more, travelers have been plodding westwards along the *Camino*. Arrowing in from France, this lengthy pilgrim path marches for more than 200 miles across northern Spain. Pilgrims still trudge the ancient route but nowadays few are seeking miracle cures or remission from an expected sentence in Purgatory. The weary wayfarers are more likely to be raising money for charity or have traveled the *Camino* for a sense of spiritual satisfaction. Scallop shells are a reminder of the ancient pilgrimages. These pilgrim badges are everywhere: garlanding hucksters' stalls, swinging from necks and staffs, and tied to bicycles and backpacks.

Residents call Compostela *la ciudad de ensueno,* the city of dreams, and it really does seem to belong in the shadowlands that border sleep. Early evening is a perfect time to absorb the atmosphere. The alchemy of sunset transmutes lichen-covered stones into glowing pomegranates; granite-gray churches, palaces, and bell towers melt down to warm shades of honey; terracotta roofs turn amber and the ornate fountains cascade into pools shot with garnet and topaz fire.

Beckoning across the vast Plaza Del Obradoiro are the shimmering spires of Compostela's magnificent shrine to St. James, the 11th-century Romanesque Cathedral. Inside its main door is the Gloria Portal: a masterwork of the medieval stonemasons' craft depicting almost 200 biblical figures. Under the statue of St. James, pilgrims place a hand on a pillar and whisper a prayer. Over the centuries, their fingers have burrowed out five holes in the solid marble.

More ritual happens behind the Cathedral's High Altar. Pilgrims form long queues to embrace another statue of St. James and then descend into a tiny crypt where the legendary bones lie in a silver casket. If you're wondering how the Apostle materialized in Spain, tradition tells that his remains arrived from the Holy Land in a marble boat. Buried in a field, they were discovered in the 9th century by a shepherd, led to the grave by a supernatural light. In medieval writings, the shrine was called *Campus Stellae* (the starry field).

During morning Mass on St. James' Day, the Cathedral's *Botafumeiro* swings into action. An incense burner of mammoth proportions, this "smoking barrel" weighs over 70 pounds. Six brawny vergers in scarlet habits suspend the lethal silver missile on ropes, then launch it up and down the nave like a pendulum. Way back when, plenty of incense was needed to mask the stench of malodorous pilgrims. Best not to ask why the tradition continues!

St. James' Day in Santiago di Compostela, and the Cathedral's **Botafumeiro** *(smoking barrel) swings into action.*

© Steenie Harvey

A U.S.-based company, Villas International, has Galician rentals. One-bedroom properties start at $690 in peak season and go up to $1,750 for a villa sleeping eight. Most are in and around coastal villages, but they also have cottages and farmhouses inland. Don't expect the architecture to be the blindingly white sugar cubes of southern Spain. Houses here are built of dark brickwork and stone, often beside peculiar-looking stilted barns that are indigenous to the region.

Also look at Galicia's own

website at www.galinor.es. Its rural tourism section has farmhouse-style properties close to Santiago de Compostela. One is the three-bedroom Finca San Lorenzo, which rents for $143 per day. A 10-minute drive from Santiago, in Cacheiras village, a villa sleeping five or six people is listed on the www.1001-villa-holidaylets.com site. This rents for between $800 and $1,000 weekly.

If you're seeking a long-term rental, Baixolar's properties start at $210 monthly for very basic unfurnished studios. For $508 monthly you could rent what's described as a furnished "chalet of dreams."

Villas International, 4340 Redwood Highway, Suite D309, San Rafael, California 94903, 415/499-9490, fax 415/499-9491, email: villas@villas.intl.com.

Finca San Lorenzo, Corredorio dos Muinos 24, 15705 Santiago de Compostela (La Coruña), tel./fax 34/981-593572, email: agatur@feriagalicia.com.

Baixolar, C/Sto Domingo 38-3, 32003 Ourense, Galicia, tel./fax 34/988-392014, email: baixolar@baixolar.com.

Spain's Holiday Isles

Anchored off Spain's coast, 132 miles from Barcelona, are the *Iles Balears*: Mallorca, Menorca, Ibiza, and its tiny satellite Formentera. Some visitors arrive with strange preconceptions, fondly imagining the Balearics to be the hangout of artists, writers, and the rich and famous. Maybe the islands were like that half a century ago, but not any more. Only if you go to the northern tip of Mallorca will you find dream locations that haven't been blighted by tourism's worst excesses.

There's a saying that "Mallorca looks to Spain, Ibiza to Africa, and Menorca to France," but the truth is that little distinguishes them. Although relatively secret pockets of exclusivity still exist, many resorts seem a byword for "pile it high, and sell it cheap." The large concrete-block resorts have Irish bars, British pubs, German bierkellers, and fast food joints. Shops brim with tourist debris: castanets made in Taiwan, plastercast donkeys wearing sombreros, key rings with bullfighters dangling on the end.

Although Ibiza is almost beyond redemption, Menorca is still relatively sleepy. Its 170 miles of coastline is blessed with around 100 beaches, from deserted coves to broad sandy bays. The island's southern half is the most developed, though even here you can escape the crowds by plunging into the green ravines called *barancas*. Menorca is fine if you simply want a relaxing holiday, but don't expect to get much insight into Spanish culture.

If you're the sporty type, consider Club Ciudadela. In Menorca's southwest corner, beside Son Xoriguer beach, it's an upmarket complex of self-catered apartments set around attractive gardens and a swimming pool.

The weekly rental price ($755–1,150 for couples; $965–1,490 for a family of four) includes use of surfboards, sailing boats, kayaks, and mountain bikes. Although Mahon is now the island's capital, the title used to be held by Ciudadela. Frequent buses cover the six-mile journey to this old Moorish town of cobbled, medieval streets.

Mallorca is the largest of the islands. To be fair, it isn't entirely charmless, and Palma City, the island capital, feels recognizably Spanish. Stretching for several miles around a bay, it's a mix of old and new—the preserved old districts are surrounded by fairly luxurious residential developments. If you're interested in a short- or long-term rental here, Portal's portfolio of south coast options includes a two-bedroom Palma duplex for $745 monthly. However, like Ibiza, Mallorca has its hellhole resorts and "nights of complete abandon." Stringing the south coast, Santa Ponsa, Palma Nova, Magalluf, and El Arenal are the most notorious.

The disco-maniac crowd tends to stay away from Mallorca's northwest. It remains unspoiled, a place of mountains, pine forests, and villages that descend in terraces to the coastline. Deya, the village where the poet Robert Graves made his home, is a gem. Other attractive inland villages for walking or bird-watching holidays include Soller and Bañalbufar. To glimpse Mallorca as it used to be, look to seaside villages like Formentor, Puerto Soller, Cala San Vicente, and Pollensa, where Mallorcan architecture has been influenced by the former Arab and Roman invaders.

Based in Pollensa, Sol Inmobiliaria covers northern Mallorca. Holiday rentals start at around $460 weekly—one lovely property, not far from the town center, sleeps five and rents for between $575 and $760 weekly. Reflecting the exclusivity of the region, some stone-built Mallorcan farmhouses built around garden courtyards can achieve rents of between $5,000 and $6,000 monthly. If you're looking for more than a short vacation rental, Insular Immobilien handles countryside properties as well as seaside apartments.

On Mallorca's eastern coastline, Cala d'Or resort is popular with families. Although built for resort purposes, the town's architecture is Moorish-style, with palm trees and pavement cafés gracing its pedestrian-friendly center. The scenery varies from dramatic pine-covered headlands to sharply indented coves and sandy beaches. Apartamentos Las Rocas is an attractive complex with large gardens and the requisite sun terraces, tennis courts, and swimming pools. Studios rent for $45 daily in April and $105 in August; an apartment for four costs from $62 to $133 daily.

If the Balearics appeal, one useful website is www.baleares.com. Look under the *Cliente* section for local businesses—property rental agencies come under *I* for *Inmobiliarios*. Rural vacation properties come under *A* for *Agriturismo* and there's a central reservation facility.

Club Ciudadela, Apartado de Correos 257, Urbanization Son Xoriguer,

07760 Ciudadela de Menorca, Menorca, tel. 34/971-387086, fax 34/971-387081, email: Club@surfsailmenorca.com.

Portals Immobiliaria, Carretera Andratx 43, 07181 Portals Nous, Mallorca, tel. 34/971-677000, fax 34/971-677001, email: portals@portals.es.

Sol Inmobiliaria, Via Pollentia 17, 07460 Pollensa, Mallorca, tel. 34/971-535045, fax 34/971-535081, email: enquiries@pollencaproperties-sol.co.uk.

Apartamentos Las Rocas, Avda Es Fonti 107, 07660 Cala d'Or, Mallorca, tel. 34/971-643615, fax 34/971-643576, email: lasrocas@roc-hotels.com.

Insular Immobilien, Balear SL Carrer de Can Bordoi, No 3 Bajos, 07012 Palma de Mallorca, tel. 34/971-715457, fax 34/971-712846, email: iib@immobilienbalar.com.

11 *Portugal*

ollow the trade winds to Portugal, where the old and new coexist side
by side. Spain's next-door neighbor, this small country of just over 10
million people packs a big punch. It's hard to believe now, but during its
16th-century heyday, Portugal was a world power, controlling an empire
stretching from Africa, through Asia and into South America.

The pine-clad hills and mountains of the north, swathed in mist and
terraced with vineyards, give way to a central plain of sun-baked grass-
lands, fairy-tale towns like Sintra, and the charming capital, Lisbon. Further
south lies snowbird country, the delectable beaches and manicured golf
courses of the Algarve. Now a favorite European retirement haven, it's also
a prime holiday area. Nicknamed "Sportugal," the Algarve is the country's
vacation playground. Although overdeveloped in parts, vignettes of authentic village life still remain: scenic old buildings faded from the sun, fishermen's nets hanging on the docks, and brightly colored fishing boats
bobbing in the harbor. To discover more, contact:

Portuguese National Tourist Office, 590 5th Ave., 4th Fl., New York,
NY 10036, 212/719-3985.

Portuguese Trade & Tourism Commission, 60 Bloor St. W, Ste. 1005,
Toronto, Ontario M4W 3B8, 416/921-4925.

Legalities

Only those who intend on staying less than 90 days can escape the flurry of forms and applications. Otherwise you'll need to apply to the Portuguese embassy for either a student visa or a "Type 1" residence visa. These are initially valid for a period of 180 days. If you want to further extend

your stay, you'll then need to contact the nearest office of the immigration authorities (*Serviço de Estrangeiros e Fronteras*) and apply for a residency permit.

Embassy of Portugal, 2125 Kalorama Rd. NW, Washington, DC 20008, 202/328-8610, email: embportwash@mindspring.com.

Embassy of Portugal, 645 Island Park Dr., Ottawa, Ontario K1Y 0B8, 613/729-0883.

The Language

The fiendishly difficult Portuguese language is spoken by more than 180 million people worldwide. In the Algarve, Portugal's prime tourist area, virtually all the people you'll come into contact with speak some English, though things are more tricky throughout the rest of the country. However, even in tourist areas, a few words of Portuguese such as a simple "Obrigado" (thank you) are always appreciated.

There are plenty of language schools, particularly in Lisbon, Porto, and the Algarve. If you have Web access, the most useful site is www.aeple.pt. AEPLE stands for Associção de Escolas de Português Lingua Estrangeira— the association of Portuguese language schools for foreigners. Costs depend on the type and length of course. Here are some sample prices from Lisbon's Centro Europeu school: Including walks around Lisbon and a day trip to Sintra, a month-long "beginners course" of 40 hours costs $385 for group tuition, $583 for the same course but with one-on-one tuition. If you can't access the AEPLE website, Cial and Inlingua have schools in Lisbon and Porto. Write or phone for more details.

Centro EuroPeu de Linguas, Ave. Padre Manuel da Nóbrega 3A, 1000-222 Lisbon, tel. 351/218-407-425, fax 351/218-487-915, email: centroeuroling1@mail.telepac.pt.

CIAL-Centro de Linguas, Rua Passos Manuel 222-5, 4000 Porto, tel. 351/22-302-0269, fax 351/22-208-3907.

Inlingua, Rua Sá da Bandeira 605-1, 4000-437 Porto, tel. 351/22-339-44-00, fax 351/22-339-44-09.

Vacation Rentals

This is how I found a holiday apartment during our last visit. First, I sat down at a shady outdoor café where I could stack the luggage whilst sipping a drink. Next, I gave my husband the phrase book and instructions to not come back until he'd found suitable accommodations. Third, I waited for 10 whole minutes.... Honestly, it really was as simple as that, and our trip was in high-season July. We had washed up in Praia Ancora, a little Atlantic seaside town on the Costa Verde, near Porto in the north of Portugal. It was chock-full of apartment rentals—no fuss, no deposit, and no problem about extending our stay to six days rather than the initial two.

Of course, many people prefer not to leave things to chance. I would suggest that you make advance bookings for the Algarve between Easter and September, and especially during July and August. This is the most popular area of Portugal for summer vacations, and at this time of year most bookings will be for a week minimum, probably starting on a weekend—either Friday or Saturday. The Algarve is strung with resorts, and I have no doubt that you'll find a rental property of some kind if you simply turn up in high summer. However, what you'll be left with are the properties that nobody else wants.

Local tourist offices will send out lists of rental properties, you can locate numerous rental companies and umbrella groups on the Internet, and you'll find specific agencies and contact addresses within this chapter. Many realtors manage vacation rentals as well as sales and long-term rentals. One good site for locating holiday properties throughout the whole of Portugal is www.portugalvirtual.pt. Others worth checking out are www.vacationvillas.net and www.1001-villa-holidaylets.com.

For the widest choice, look to the Algarve. Costs start at around $150–200 weekly for one-bedroom apartments, but properties come in many different shapes and sizes—much depends on location, season, facilities, etc. For example, if your dream is Algarve golf and white sandy beaches

USEFUL HOUSING TERMS

alugam-se—homes to rent	*não mobilado*—unfurnished rentals
arrendamento—rentals	*numero contribuinte*—tax number
Obrigado—thank you	*Serviço de Estrangeiros e Fronteras*—
mobilidad—furnished rental	immigration authorities

on the doorstep, Villas & Vacations have two-bedroom/two-bathroom villas overlooking the famous Quinta do Lago golf course. Other on-site facilities in this "village" complex include three swimming pools and tennis courts, and arrangements can be made for horseback riding and water sports. Renting a villa for a week costs $745 low season, $1,590 high season.

Villas & Vacations, Apartado 3498, 8135-906 Almancil, Algarve, Portugal, tel. 351/289-390501, fax 351/289-390511, email: rentals@villas-vacations.com.

VACATION RENTAL AGREEMENTS

When booking through an agency, you'll often have to pay around 25 percent on confirmation of booking and the remainder 60 days before you arrive. The rental price normally includes gas, electricity, a weekly cleaning, and a change of linen and towels. You may also have to provide a security deposit of around $175. This, however, is only general; it's not a hard and fast rule. We weren't asked for a security deposit for our Praia Ancora apartment, but ours was a private arrangement—and we'd simply turned up out of the blue. Many places require advance payment to cover the possibility of no-shows.

The northern town of Barcelos holds one of Portugal's largest open-air markets.

© Steenie Harvey

Long-Term Rentals

Leaving aside the Algarve, there's a general shortfall of rental accommodations within most cities. Most people live in apartments and condos; city houses are expensive and hard to come by, particularly if you're looking for a furnished rental. Portugal has one of the EU's lowest per capita incomes and rents are extortionately high for people on local wages. Within Lisbon and Porto, the average monthly rent for a 100-sq-m (1,080-sq-ft) apartment is put at $820 and $765, respectively. These figures relate to unfurnished rentals (*não mobilado*) and you can easily pay $1,100 to $1,365 for a more upmarket home in a modern apartment block within a city center. Furnished rentals cost even more.

In popular expat areas—the Algarve and Lisbon coastal resorts such as Cascais and Estoril—you can't really say there's such a thing as "the average rent." Most three-bedroom apartments in Cascais cost between $820 and $1,100, while in Estoril a similar-sized property can reach a staggering $4,350 depending on luxury level and whether there's a sea view. The Algarve tends to be cheaper: typically $490 monthly for a three-bedroom apartment in the interior, $770 in the tourist resorts.

Plenty of agencies and newspapers advertise homes to rent (*alugamse*). English-language publications include *Algarve Property News*, which you can pick up in most resort towns. If you're looking for somewhere other than the Algarve, the *Anglo-Portuguese News* is probably your best bet for tracking down a furnished rental, a *mobilidad*. One way of finding suitable accommodations is to search through the web database (Associados Section) of APEMI, the Portugal Real Estate Agents Association, at www.apemi.pt.

The Internet turns up endless possibilities, though don't expect it all to be in English. Rentals through both private individuals and agencies can be found at www.ocasiao.pt. Mercado Imobiliario is the section you'll want, then *arrendamento* leads into rentals as opposed to property sales. Recent snips included a furnished three-room apartment in Lisbon available for a monthly rent of $665. If you're scouring websites, the notations T1, T2, T3, etc. may baffle you. Well, the "T" indicates an apartment and the following number refers to the number of bedrooms.

The greatest choice of properties is on the sunny Algarvian coast where northern Europeans own many homes. Although some apartments and villas have been bought solely for investment purposes, most are holiday homes—and usually only used for summer vacations until the owners manage to fulfill their cherished dream of retiring to Portugal. Often rented by the week, Algarve properties can command high rents during summer and a two- or three-month stay could work out to be very expensive if you take the first home that's offered.

It's much more affordable during the mid-October to March period. Then properties are often rented by the month at discounted rates. Take an apartment that rents at around $255 per week during the off-season. Rent it for a month or longer, and you should easily be able to shave somewhere between 10 and 20 percent off of the listed rate.

Many properties are rented out by management agencies. You can also find rentals through online English-speaking magazines and residents' groups. Two worth looking at are www.algarveresident.com and www.carvoeiro.com. Available on a six-month lease, a four bedroom in the eastern Algarve was recently available for $1,800 monthly.

APEMI (Associacao Portuguesa das Empresas de Mediacao Imobiliaria), R.D.Luis de Noronha 4, 1069-165 Lisboa, tel. 351/21-792-8770, fax 351/21-795-8815, email: apemi@mail.telepac.pt.

LONG-TERM RENTAL AGREEMENTS

Once you've decided on a property, a lease agreement between you and the landlord is drawn up by a notary. The agreement will state the amount of rent and when it is to be paid, the contents of the property, length of contract, etc. The minimum period for a long-term rental is generally a year, but in well-known holiday areas you can often negotiate a three- or six-month lease.

Rents are payable in advance, either by the month or quarterly. Contracts usually include a requirement that you pay a security deposit—generally one month's rent—to cover any possible damage. If you plan on renting for a year or more, the annual rent increase shouldn't be higher than the official percentage set by the government at the end of each year. This percentage is linked to the official rate of inflation.

In most instances, the landlord is normally responsible for paying the annual property taxes; tenants are liable for utility bills. In some apartments, there are quarterly charges to cover maintenance and concierge fees. The rent may or may not cover these fees, though the contract should state whether the landlord or tenant is liable for these charges.

Once You're There

Health care throughout Portugal has improved tremendously over the past few years. Larger villages have a *Centro de Saude*, or National Health Center, where you can avail of outpatient facilities. Away from large cities such as Lisbon and Oporto, the Algarve is best suited to offering the standard of service that many foreign visitors are used to. Faro, Portimão, and Lagos have large, state-run hospitals, and numerous foreign private doctors. Consultations with general practitioners cost between $26 and $52, but bills can quickly mount up. Private medical insurance is vital.

Some Costs: A week's car hire, economy model, from $96 weekly. Train ticket, Lisbon to Cascais, $1.10. As you can still get simple three-course meals for around $13, you may not want to spend much time cooking, but fruit and vegetables are astoundingly cheap. Most main towns have a permanent municipal market that sells fresh produce daily.

The most widely accepted credit cards are Eurocard, Visa, American Express, and MasterCard. Obtaining cash is rarely a problem as all banks participate in the ATM network known here as *Multibanco*. However, you can only open a bank account if you've obtained a tax number (*numero contribuinte*) and produced necessary identification papers. As anyone receiving any kind of remuneration or financial benefits is liable to the Portuguese tax system, you may not want to linger too long.

Lisbon

Portugal's capital gives its visitors an authentic taste of the rich and golden past. Anchored to the ocean, its seven hills gaze towards the Tagus estuary, one of the largest harbors on the Atlantic. During the 15th- and 16th-century Age of Discoveries, it was from here that Portuguese explorers such as Magellan, Vasco da Gama, and Henry the Navigator set sail to conquer new lands. Lisbonites found themselves at the hub of an expanding colonial empire and the trade of gold, spices, and slaves made Lisbon into one of Europe's wealthiest cities.

Although plenty of convents and churches still shimmer with Brazilian gold, five short minutes turned much of this capital city's riches into ruins. The 1755 earthquake caused massive devastation but what rose from the rubble is today's downtown Baixa district: a planned city center of black and white mosaicked pavements confined in an orderly grid system, tree-lined avenues, spacious parks, and fountained squares. Even though some of the buildings now seem a bit grimy and dilapidated, it's a very agreeable quarter, complete with a moving picture-show of smoky chestnut braziers and flower stalls, rickety trams, and shoeshine boys.

Bring comfy walking shoes, the city is built on seven hills.

© Steenie Harvey

Although the Baixa's heyday is undoubtedly over, there's still a raddled allure to this neighborhood. Its heart beats around four adjoining squares—Figueira, Dom Pedro, the Rossio, and Restauradores where outdoor cafés make great spots for soaking up the streetlife. Like most port cities,

Lisbon mixes a rich palette of styles and cultures and this could easily be a crossroads where Europe meets Brazil, Africa, and the Orient.

The small, dark squares of Bairro Alto are known as "the high neighborhood." Restaurants are thick on the ground, and it's where many Lisbonites come for a night out. The funicular Gloria elevator whisks foot-weary revelers up and down from the Restauradores square.

Away to the east, the exotically appealing Alfama neighborhood is Lisbon's old Moorish quarter and many dim alleys and stairways still have Arabic names. The 18th-century planners who tried to create order from its almighty chaos made a total pig's ear of it with terrace upon terrace of narrow pastel-washed tenements teetering above the river in a precarious house of cards. Cobblestoned twists and turns stumble into what appears to be a sprawling open-air laundry or even a North African souk, women still collect water from communal fountains, chickens flap underfoot, and washing lines are strung between almost every paint-peeled building. The atmosphere is spellbinding. Oblivious to the trams wheezing uphill, old men snooze the afternoons away in sun-dappled courtyards. Deep in the labyrinth, outdoor barbers work through a hubbub of passionate domino games and urchins playing hopscotch. Competing to waylay you are scores of amazingly cheap restaurants where melancholy fado music often wails out into the night. Here it's not so much tourist gimmick, but more of a lament sung by and for the Alfama's inhabitants.

Trams and trolley buses are the easy way to travel between the city's neighborhoods.

© Steenie Harvey

The street maze is horrendously perpendicular but eventually you reach Portas do Sol. These "Gates of the Sun" open onto a magnificent panorama— below the hotchpotch of terracotta-tiled roofs are waving palm trees and the twin-towered cathedral, ships bound for sea, and the immense white statue of Christ the King in the distance. Crowning everything is Castelo Sao Jorge, where views from the ramparts are even more spectacular. Flower gardens and the pandemonium of peacocks make the castle grounds a favorite Sunday haunt for local families.

Back down the hill, the place to head on Tuesdays and Saturdays is Campo Santa Clara, site of the Alfama's *feira da ladra* or "thieves market." Stalls crammed with all that's weird and wonderful stretch into infinity— new clothes, old clothes, African carvings, potteryware, antiques, and enough army surplus to give a crazy colonel big ideas. Those without stalls simply arrange their dubious treasures over the grass. Want some secondhand dentures, a dressmaker's dummy, scratched Suzi Quatro records or a battered copy of Captain Hornblower in Portuguese? You'll find it all here. But even if you've no intention of haggling over piles of spectacle frames or dancing toy crocodiles, do go along. For sheer entertainment value it's terrific.

Lisbon's best-known coastal suburb is Belem, where pride of place is given to the 16th-century Jeronimos Monastery. Looking like an exquisite white wedding cake, it guards the tomb of Vasco da Gama. This is the place to see the manic style of what the Portuguese call "Manueline" architecture at its most flamboyant. The monastery cloisters are a turbulent tidal wave of ships and shells and sea monsters, all elaborately carved from stone. Afterwards go take a look at the gigantic Monument to the Discoveries. Forever facing the sea, it's what Lisbon is all about.

Lisbon is actually one of the trickiest European capitals for foreigners to find long-term rental accommodations. The city currently has a shortfall of around 150,000 homes and many of its inhabitants have been forced out of the central area into the spectacularly ugly high-rise apartment blocks of surrounding municipal districts. In addition, the urban decay of some areas has resulted in the spread of shantytowns, occupied by people on the margins of society. Those who can afford to tend to live along the Lisbon coast and commute into the city.

That's not to say that it's impossible to find accommodations in central Lisbon. The Europe-wide chain of realtors and rental agents, ERA, have Lisbon offices. Agents with rental listings on the APEMI site include Villa Palace and Cobertura. Unfurnished rentals start at around $640 for a two-room apartment in the suburbs, but you'll pay more in the center. For apartments around the prime residential areas flanking Avenida Liberdade, expect to pay an average monthly rent of $820 for a T1, $1,100 for a T2, $1,210 for a T3, and $1,356 for a T4. In the higgledy-piggledy Alfama quarter, a T1 averages $675, a T2 $715, and a T3 $1,075.

Serviced apartments are popular with businesspeople but casual travelers and families can rent them too. In the heart of the Baixa district, the Orion Eden Apartments features include a private terraced bar and swimming pool; the apartments have fully equipped kitchens, en-suite bathrooms, satellite TV, and private telephone. Depending on apartment size, prices range from around $171 nightly, with 10 percent reductions for stays of over seven days. At the far end of the city's central artery, Avenida Liberdade, the Altis Apartments are similarly luxurious. They have single studios at $157 to $167 per night, apartments for two from $157 to $167, and triples from $180 to $190.

You can also find vacation rentals in the historic center through companies such as www.holiday-rentals.com. In Graca, a few streets away from the Alfama, a three-bedroom apartment with views of the castle of Sao Jorge rents from between $158 and $237 nightly.

ERA Carnaxide, Rua Joáo das Regras 3A, 2795-519 Carnaxide, tel. 351/21-424-1260, fax 351/21-424-1269, email: carnaxide@eraportugal.com.

Villa Palace Imobiliaria, Rue Infantaria 16—NO55, 1350–161 Lisbon, tel. 351/21-384-40-45, fax 351/21-384-40-47, email: villapalace@mail.telepac.pt.

Cobertura Imobiliaria, Rua Salitre 122E, 1250 Lisbon, tel. 351/21-388-24-00, email: cobertura@mail.telepac.pt.

Aparthotel VIP Eden, 18-24 Praca dos Restauradores, 1250 Lisbon, tel. 351/21-321-6600, fax 351/21-321-6666, email: aparthoteleden@viphotels.com.

Altis Apartments, R. Castilho 11, 1250 Lisbon, tel./fax 351/21-319-1400.

FADO AND FADISTAS

Whoever said that there's music for every occasion was right. Fado is perfect for those times when you feel like jumping off a high building and ending it all! A traditional *fadista* singer is a ruby-nailed, ruby-lipped creature of despair, plumbing the musical depths with her tormented songs of grief and nostalgia. If ever there was evidence that Portugal is not Spain, it is in their music. Fado, a word that means fate, bears little resemblance to the hot fire of flamenco.

Often described as the most tragic music in the world, fado is Portugal's version of the blues, seemingly designed for souls who have lost the will to live. The spirit that gave birth to it is called *saudade*, one of those untranslatable words which shakes up a tearful cocktail of love betrayed, the anguish of parting, and above all a kind of nostalgia for all that was, is, and might have been. In fado songs, everything turns to ashes—home, hope, and happiness. The

fadista's world is a bleak winter landscape in which everything has been lost forever.

The likeliest place to hear authentic fado music is in the steep midnight streets of Lisbon's Bairro Alto and Alfama districts. The fado singer works within a strict agenda, and so does the audience, who will not tolerate any interruption of a good performance. Unless the singer is dire (in which case it's permitted to jeer), the rule is to sit in absolute silence. There's plenty of opportunity to give voice at the end when the room erupts in a cacophony of table-banging, whistling, and much stomping of feet. The best performances produce shouts of *"fadista!"* which in this context means more than "singer of fado." In the 19th century the word described dissolute Lisbon low-lifers who wore black caps, carried knives, and didn't give a hoot for bourgeois morality. The first great musical *fadista* was Maria Severa, whose passionate affair with the Comte de Vimioso scandalized Lisbon in the 1830s.

Lisbon's Coast

Glorious beach resorts such as Estoril, Cascais, and Ericeira are little more than half an hour's bus or train ride from the capital. The *Costa de Lisboa* is a good place to try water sports—conditions are usually perfect for windsurfing—though most visitors are content to get out on one of the numerous golf courses or rent a big shady umbrella and lounge for the day. With its palm-lined promenade, casino, and a holiday home owned by the Monaco royals, Estoril has a reputation for sophistication and elegance—and high prices. Neighboring Cascais is cheaper, but it is on the European package-holiday map and there are some rather unattractive apartment high-rises. If you're not bothered by nonstop nightlife, Ericeira is a lovely place. It still has the feel of a sleepy fishing town and its origins date back to 1229.

How much you'll pay for a vacation property depends on the time of year. Like most places throughout Europe, July and August are always the months for premium prices. On the www.vacationvillas.net website, which lists private rentals, there's a pretty bleached white traditional-style villa at Ericeira sleeping four. This rents for $341 weekly during the low season, but costs $624 in August. On the www.portugalvirtual.pt site, a studio for two at Cascais rents for $240 weekly in winter, $392 from June to September. Estoril is right at the top end of the price scale. Through Feriasol, an apartment for two with Atlantic views at the classy Estoril Eden rents for $638 to $905 weekly. Expensive, but the facilities include three swimming pools and guests get reductions at local golf courses and tennis courts.

A little way inland, fairy-tale Sintra once served as a kind of summer capital for the Portuguese royal family, and its misty hills still provide a retreat for wealthy Lisbonites who come here to escape the heat of the city. Full of Gothic palaces, mysterious gargoyles, and mossy grottos, the town's romantic aura has inspired artists, writers, and poets for centuries. "Glorious Eden" gushed one of its most famous visitors, Lord Byron, who recorded that the place was filled with "Beauties of every description, natural and artificial. Palaces and gardens rising in the midst of rocks, cataracts and precipices; convents on stupendous heights, a distant view of the sea and the Tagus." Sintra's charms evidently had an inspired effect, for this was where Byron penned his epic poem, *Childe Harold's Pilgrimage*. Byron's Sintra is still recognizable, and although the area has been developed, it hasn't been spoiled.

Along with their coastal properties, Feriasol has three-bedroom bungalows in a residential complex on the outskirts of Sintra. Depending on the season, weekly prices are between $385 and $565. If you prefer to be near the beach, the same agents have cottages and apartments on the Vila Bicuda estate, near Cascais. Properties sleep up to four people and rent for between $658 and $1,064 weekly, depending on the season.

Or, for a treat, stay in a cottage on the grounds of a luxurious restored manor house, the Quinta da Capela. In the Sintra hills, this was the 16th-century home of the Duke of Cadaval. With views of the Atlantic and Sintra's Moorish castle, the grounds include a chapel dedicated to Nossa Senhora da Piedade, covered in 18th-century *azulejos* tiles. These porcelain picture books often depict biblical stories and the chapel's *azulejos* retell the life of Christ. A public midday Mass is still held here on Sundays. The Quinta da Capela's cottages have one or two bedrooms and all come with a terrace, private garden, and access to a small swimming pool. Definitely in the spoil-yourself-rotten category, weekly prices range from $998 for double rooms to $1,230 for one-bedroom cottages; $2,413 for larger ones.

If you're looking to rent for the longer term, Portugal Real Estate has properties in the Ericeira vicinity. Monthly rents for a condo just 200 meters from the beach are $532 between October and May, $605 in June and September, $1,060 in July, and $1,690 in August. RentaVila has luxury villas in the Cascais area from $1,250 monthly.

Feriasol, Av Gonçal Velho Cabral 194-7, 2750 Cascais, tel. 351/21-486-1574, fax 351/21-483-0783.

Manor Houses of Portugal, Apartado 596, Viana do Castleo 4900, tel. 351/258-835-065, fax 351/258-811-491, email: lumby@nortenet.pt. Check out more idyllic hideaways at www.manorhouses.com.

Portugal Real Estate, Rua do Ericeira 23-2, 2655-172 Ericeira, tel. 351/261-869071, fax 351/261-869073, email: cite@cite.pt.

RentaVila, Quinta da Marinha Vila 130, 2750 Cascais, tel. 351/21-482-7075, fax 351/21-482-7095, email: rentavila@portugal-info.pt.

The Algarve

The name "Algarve" was bequeathed by the Moors who called Portugal's sunny, southernmost region *al Gharb*. It means "the land beyond" and it's one of Europe's favorite destinations for a family holiday. The turquoise-blue sea is crystal clear and safe for toddlers to splash about in. Stretches of silver sand run for miles, broken here and there by secret coves, spectacular brick-red rock formations, and craggy cliffs, often honeycombed with caves and tunnels. A kind of expat heaven for northern Europeans, it's estimated that around 20,000 Britons, 10,000 Germans, and 4,000 Dutch have taken up permanent residency here. For anyone looking for an idyllic rural hideaway, or a scenic seaside location, it's a place with lots to offer—including a climate that gives over 3,000 hours of annual sunshine.

Algarve summers are hot enough, but the cooling Atlantic breezes ensure that the heat isn't of the same intensity as the frying-pan temperatures of southern Spain. Winters are mild, with the temperatures ranging from 18° to 25°C. The first signs of spring appear in early February, when the almond trees are laden with pale blossoms. Outdoor activities take place year-round—not just golf, but tennis, pony-trekking, sailing, surfing, biking, and hiking.

It must be said right away that some parts of the Algarve are just **too** overdeveloped. The worst excesses are to be found around the central part of the province, in particular resorts close to Faro city. (Faro is the Algarve's transport hub and home to the regional airport.) The big resort towns of Quarteira and Albufeira are quite truly and spectacularly horrible. Nothing wrong with their beaches, but I guess you aren't coming to Portugal to see joyless acres of high-rise concrete. You could easily believe that these towns were designed by planners from the Stalin era of the old Soviet Union. Of course, if your heart leaps at the prospect of holing up in a concrete jungle, stay here by all means. Some of the Algarve's cheapest rentals are in these towns and their satellite coastal villages.

No? Well, anybody else in search of a seaside vacation should head towards the far east or west of the province. The good news is that around half of the Algarve's 150-km (93-m) stretch of coastline remains pretty much unsullied. East of Faro city, Tavira remains practically untouched by development, a seaside town of monasteries, cloisters, and medieval arcades. In the wilder landscapes of the western Algarve, look around Sagres and Lagos (pronounced Lah-gosh).

With its broad esplanades and shady traffic-free precincts, Lagos is one of the Algarve's classiest coastal towns. Complete with towering cliffs and dramatic rock formations, some of the province's best beaches stretch westwards from here towards Praia de Luz. There are all kinds of water sports available at the beach or you can walk the cliff-top paths that meander through an aromatic carpet of summer growth: poppies, wild thyme, lavender, and purple-headed sage. This is definitely still holiday villa and apartment country, but developments are low rise and certainly not the kind of brutalist blots on the landscape that Algarve central specializes in. In the Lagos/Luz Bay area, most little villas are highly picturesque. Many have their own private swimming pools and are set in wonderfully secluded gardens of bougainvillea, hibiscus, and arum lilies.

There are plenty of agents specializing in furnished rentals in the western Algarve. To give a few samples of prices, $265 to $470 weekly rents a studio in a historic building within Lagos's walls. The price includes access to a communal swimming pool. Depending on the season, one-bedroom apartments in pretty "holiday villages" average $260 to $610, with two-bedroom properties commanding around $810 in July and August. Detached villas with private swimming pools start at around $465 weekly, though a two-bedroom villa will cost around $1,070 weekly or more in high summer. The larger a property, the more you'll pay.

You can often negotiate reductions for long-term winter stays. According to Algarve Gold agency, the monthly rent for a furnished apartment for two people averages around $590 between October and May. When renting on a monthly basis, you'll usually pay extra for gas, water, and electricity but it really is peanuts—a mere $30 a month.

Although the Algarve is regarded as Portugal's holiday playground, there's more to the province than just a strip of coastline. Beyond the fringe of red-cliff beaches, old ways still survive. You'll stumble across white-washed villages of higgledy-piggledy houses and pretty little churches, often decorated with 18th-century *azulejos* tiles depicting Bible stories. This is another world entirely: a rustic land of goatherds, cork forests, and old-fashioned farmhouses surrounded by groves of almonds and oranges.

Head northwest from Faro and you'll come to one of the Algarve's most attractive inland towns: historic Loulé. The town has a fabulous Saturday market and it takes a resolute will to resist the allure of bargain hunting. So much competes to catch the eye—bunches of dried oregano, jars of wild local honey, and boxes of toothsome almond and marzipan sweets for under $2 apiece. One stall had linen tablecloths with exquisite drawn threadwork starting at around $25—and they came with half a dozen matching napkins. Terra-cotta bowls and pots were an unbelievable $5 to $7. Loulé is only a short distance from the ocean, and it also has an indoor covered market where resident shoppers can choose from a glittering array of seafood: sardines, swordfish, red mullet, and an entire cornucopia of shellfish. If you don't fancy cooking, two people can feast on a three-course fish dinner with wine for less than $30.

Although there isn't the same pick of rental accommodations as on the coast, you can find furnished cottages and villas around Loulé and throughout other corners of the rural Algarve. Through Jordan & Nunn for example, a three-bedroom villa with private swimming pool near Loulé rents for between $474 and $1,185 weekly, depending on season. In the hills above Lagos, Algarve Gold's properties include Quinta Oliveira, a farmhouse property near the ancient market town of Vila do Bispo. Converted into self-contained apartments, the quinta is set in a garden of orange, lèmon, carob, and fig trees. Two-person apartments rent for $380–500 weekly; four-person apartments for $500–560; six-person apartments for $620–680.

Algarve Gold Imobiliaria, Largo de Santa Maria de Graça 12–14, Lagos, 8600–518, tel./fax 351/282-770640 or 351/282-768319, email: info@algarve-gold.com.

JNB Villa Management & Property Rentals, CC Viasul, Loja 9, Rua da Praia, Praia da Luz, 8600 Lagos, tel./fax 351/282-788622.

Royol Property Management and Rentals, Cerro do Convento, Lote 7–2c, 8600–644 Lagos, email: info@royol.com.

Jordan & Nunn, Av Duarte Pacheco 226, 8135 Almanail, tel. 351/289-399943, fax 351/289-395249, email: jordan.nunn@mail.telepac.pt.

Into the North

For a different vacation, northern Portugal takes some beating. A sense of enchantment lies everywhere and I can't understand why travelers neglect this region. Ribboned by the river Douro and its tributaries, it's a place where mountains are green, traditions are ancient, and vineyards stretch further than your eyes can see.

Chances are you'll start or end a Douro journey in Porto (Oporto), Portugal's second city. Plentifully blessed with monuments and museums, it's famed for its port wine lodges. Many famous merchant shippers such as Sandeman and Crofts have "caves" here. Most offer free tours and the hospitality includes generous tastings. Outside the lodges, you can take pleasure cruises or simply watch the little wooden riverboats bobbing about. Once used for transporting wine, their square sails now advertise numerous brands of port.

Not for the faint-hearted driver, Portugal's second city, Porto, is a place of switch-back streets and narrow passageways.

Overlooked by the Torre dos Clerigos, Portugal's highest bell-tower, the city's old Ribeira quarter tumbles down to the waterfront. Laundry billows from every paint-peeled tenement and wharfside tavern. Cozy eateries, *tascas,* exude mouthwatering aromas and three-course meals with wine can cost as little as $11. Try the bewildering array of seafood or indulge in Oporto's culinary specialty—tripe.

Along its Atlantic coastline, the Costa Verde, workaday harbors link a long silvery chain of beaches, and colorful inland towns are steeped in centuries of history. Portugal's first capital was in the north, at Guimarães. Straight out of the Middle Ages, it's a storybook town of stone

© Steenie Harvey

archways, Gothic spires, and great silence. Quieter still are the atmospheric hilltop villages, pale sentinels on a china-blue skyline.

Although we managed to get around on public transport, you probably need to rent a car to get the most from a self-catering vacation here. Trains and buses are slow and infrequent. Even so, you should certainly try one train ride just for the experience of white-knuckled panic. In the Douro Valley, the ramshackle trains are like something from the Wild West, scampering recklessly down hillsides and across yawning chasms. Although I spent most of it with my eyes closed, I'll never forget the train journey to Peso da Regua, a riverbank town where women use the Douro as their laundry, spreading washing out to dry on sunsplashed rocks.

Markets brim with country produce—home-cured hams, live chickens, cherries and almonds from surrounding orchards. The town of Barcelos has a marvelous market. Held every Thursday, it's a mammoth affair with much to tempt the farming community. Ox-carts? Not the easiest buy to ship home, and your money might be better spent on intricate lace work or some of the curious local black pottery that's baked not in ovens, but in the ground.

Lamego, an attractive small town in northern Portugal.

© Steenie Harvey

When September haze turns to October mist, villages erupt with harvest festivals. Vineyards have been here since Roman times and today there are around 100,000 of them. But any time of year there's certain to be a celebration somewhere in the region. Some of the best Holy Week processions are held in Braga, another treasure-chest town of shrines and churches.

You'll doubtless make your own discoveries but we found three inland towns, Vila Real, Amarante, and Lamego, well worth exploring. Vila Real slumbers on the cliffs of the river Corgo, circular white churches dotting its medieval shopping streets. Tall houses have shutters painted a deep forest green, and the pavements swirl with monochrome mosaics. As summer temperatures soar well above 30°C, I appreciated the chance to cool off at the town's outdoor swimming complex. Almost on its doorstep is the sumptuous Mateus Palace, a picture of which decorates every Mateus Rosé wine bottle. Visit the baroque splendor of the palace and gardens before sampling a glass for free at the Mateus estate.

Shadowed by the Serra Marao Mountains, the town of Amarante is how picture postcards should look. A timeworn bridge spans the river Tamega, overhung with leafy verandas and elegantly old-fashioned tearooms. Gatao, an appley-tasting *vinho verde* wine, comes from here so sit at a balcony, watch the river flow, and try some. Bottles are unmistakable: Puss in Boots strides across the label. On St. Bartholomew's Day, something more diabolical supposedly strides across Amarante's cobblestones—the Devil himself! Until 1870, the townsfolk appeased two shamelessly carved statues of Old Scratch with offerings. Shocked by this pagan practice, their archbishop castrated the statues and sold them off. Happily, the dismembered devils are now back, housed in a small museum.

A bus from Peso da Regua jolts you deeper into northern Portugal's countryside. Crowned by a dilapidated castle, Lamego really does seem locked in another age. Former palaces and some splendid old churches compete with watermills and open forges to catch your eye. In early September, expect to be embroiled in a "Battle of the Flowers" and pilgrimage processions, for Lamego is where many Portuguese penitents come to shrive their sins. More than 700 steps (we lost count) clamber towards the town's awesome Sanctuary of our Lady of Remedies. The entire way up this heavenly staircase, fountained terraces are embellished with decorative tiles, all blue and white and gold. Remedies? Well, you'll need them if you tackle the climb in the midday sun like we so foolishly did.

Manor Houses of Portugal have some lovely holiday properties in this area. For $428 weekly, you could rent a studio cottage in the village of Caminha. Not far from Minho, it's only a 10 minute walk from sandy beaches. Or how about a cottage in the grounds of the Casa das Paredes, a wine-growing estate in the Douro Valley? From the swimming pool, there are views over the terraces of vineyards to the river below. One-bedroom cottages cost $72 nightly; two-bedroom cottages $114 nightly. All are fitted with kitchenettes, have open fires in the living room, and are equipped with central heating for winter visits. Feriasol also offers cottages on a country estate at Paço D'Anha, 3 km from the Costa Verde beaches. Prices range from $74 to $157 nightly. The minimum stay is three nights.

Manor Houses of Portugal, Apartado 596, Viana do Castelo 4900, tel. 351/258-835-065, fax 351/258-811-491, email: lumby@nortenet.pt.

Feriasol, Av Gonçal Velho Cabral 194-7, 2750 Cascais, tel. 351/21-486-1574, fax 351/21-483-0783.

PART VII

Scandinavia

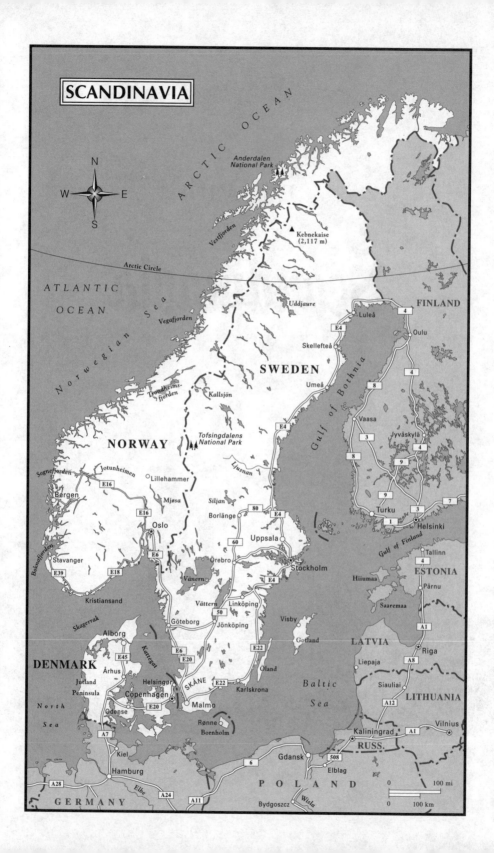

12 Scandinavia

*V*iking dragon ships, majestic fjords, and Hans Christian Andersen's fairy tales. Abba songs, smörgåsbords, and 45 million Lego bricks. Flaxen-haired blondes emerging from steamy saunas ... Scandinavia offers a kaleidoscope of images and experiences. Its great outdoors is a wilderness of lakes and forests where you can go white-water rafting, cross-country skiing, and maybe even see reindeer, all under a midnight sun. During winter, the eerie northern lights light up the Arctic sky with an incredible sweep of colors. To the ancients, the aurora borealis must have seemed frighteningly supernatural. It's hardly surprising they forged legends about giants, troll kings, and shield maidens carrying fallen warriors across the rainbow bridge to Valhalla.

Despite Scandinavia's splendors, high prices make it one of Europe's least-visited regions. Yet the Nordic countries featured here (Denmark, Sweden, and Norway) aren't unaffordable, not if you opt for a self-catering holiday. Many Scandinavians spend their own vacations canoeing on lakes, sailing around islands, and barbecuing fish in front of a little red-and-white wooden cottage.

Note that a similar immigration policy applies throughout Scandinavia. A stay in any Nordic country (Denmark, Norway, Sweden, Iceland, and Finland) within the previous six months counts towards the three-month time limit applying to North American tourists.

A single chapter can only provide a taster. To discover more about vacations here, Canadians and U.S. citizens should contact:

Scandinavian Tourist Board, P.O. Box 4649, Grand Central Station, New York, NY 10163-4649, 212/885-9700, fax 212/885-9710, www .goscandinavia.com.

DENMARK

Surrounded almost totally by water, Denmark is an island kingdom of 5.3 million people. Although the province of South Jutland is physically attached to Germany, most places are within 30 miles of the sea. Copenhagen, the capital, sits on Zealand (*Sjaelland*) Island, separated from the Jutland Peninsula by an almost circular island called Funen (*Fyn*).

Latticed with myriad channels and inland waterways, rural Denmark feels very wholesome, a patchwork of verdant farmland, toy-town villages, and ancient castles, hemmed in by the North Sea and Baltic coasts. If you fancy combining Copenhagen with a countryside holiday, the tourist board provides details of various regions and vacation home contacts.

Danish Tourist Board, 655 3rd Ave., 18th Fl., New York, NY 10017, 212/885-9700, email: info@goscandinavia.com.

Legalities

North Americans can only stay three months unless work and residence permits are obtained beforehand. Stringent immigration regulations means permits are rarely issued. Unless you have close relatives in Denmark, this effectively rules out long-term stays. Students and those working for multinationals aren't subject to the same restrictions, but contact the Danish Embassy for exact requirements.

Royal Danish Embassy, 3200 White-haven St. NW, Washington, DC 20008, 202/234-4300, fax 202/328-1470, www.denmarkemb.org.

Royal Danish Embassy, 47 Clarence St., Ste. 450, Ottawa, Ontario K1N 9K1, 613/562-1811, fax 613/562-1812, www .danish-embassy-canada.com.

The Language

English is widely understood and vacationers can get by with just a phrase book. However, Berlitz and other language schools offer Danish lessons. Most communities have social organizations like AOF (Arbejdernes OplysningsForbund), FOF (Folkeligt OplysningsForbund), and HOF (Hovedstadens OplysningsForbund), which provide adult language classes either free or at a nominal price.

Copenhagen University's annual eight-week intensive summer course is aimed at exchange students, but if places are available, it's open to individuals too. Along with learning the language, the course includes field trips and lectures about Danish life. This year's course costs $653.

Berlitz International Danmark AS, Klampenborgvej 232, Copenhagen DK 2800, tel. 45/70-21-50-30, fax 45/70-21-50-40.

International Office, University of Copenhagen, Fiolstraede 24, Copenhagen 1010, tel. 45/35-32-26-26, fax 45/35-32-32-39-00, email: inter@adm.ku.dk.

Vacation Rentals

Most Danish holiday homes take the form of privately owned cottages and cabins. *Feriehuse* are located throughout Denmark, some only 30 minutes from Copenhagen. Many can be rented year-round. If your idea of bliss is spending January in a back-to-nature hermit's cabin, you'll be able to rent one for less than $165 per week. Otherwise, weekly rentals mostly fall into the $430–1,100 range.

Most cottages are well furnished and equipped. Some luxury homes can accommodate up to 12 people and may have an indoor swimming pool, sauna, and solarium. Although most Danes take full advantage of the beach and woods, there's plenty of opportunity for excursions. From Jutland, you could explore Denmark's second city, Århus, and take the kids for a day at Legoland. Copenhagen is easily reachable from almost anywhere on Zealand.

USEFUL HOUSING TERMS

In Denmark ...
bolig—housing
Feriehuse—privately owned cottages and cabins
lejelejlighed—rented apartment
møbleret—furnished

In Sweden ...
Allemansrätt—right of public access
Vårdcentral—local health care clinic

In Norway ...
bolig—houses
hytter—chalets
til leie—to rent

Local tourist offices have lists of properties in their own area. It means doing some homework—for example, the North Zealand region beyond Copenhagen has 20 different offices. Each has their own cache of rentals. If you can access the Internet, the www.holiday.dk site has good links and you'll find private rentals on www.ferieboligweb.dk. A number of Danish companies facilitate vacation rentals. Dancenter, Novasol, and Dansommer are the biggest—the latter produces a 760-page catalog the size of a telephone directory. If a week seems too long, cottages can be rented for three to five days except in high summer. Sample price for a Zealand cottage for four at Dronningmølle Strand (near Helsingør/Elsinore and "Hamlet's Castle") is $245 to $573 weekly, depending on the season.

Dancenter, Lyngbyves 20, 2100 Copenhagen, tel. 45/70-13-16-16, fax 45/70-13-70-73, www.dancenter.com.

Dansommer, Voldbjergvej 16, 8240 Risskov, tel. 45/86-17-61-22, fax 45/86-17-68-55, email: booking@dansommer.dk.

Novasol, Fiskerbakken 7, DK-3250 Gilleleje, tel. 45/48-30-31-11, fax 45/48-30-31-09.

VACATION RENTAL AGREEMENTS

In July and August, most cottages are rented Saturday to Saturday. At other times they're usually available for shorter periods with arrival on any day. For advance bookings, you normally pay 33 percent after receiving the contract,

From April to October, visitors can cruise Copenhagen's harbor and canals and experience a unique view of the city's sights and history.

© Cees van Roeden

with the remainder payable 60 days prior to arrival. It's advisable to take out holiday insurance. A fee of 13 percent is charged if you cancel up to 60 days prior to the start of your holiday. Cancel within 60 days, and you won't usually get a refund if the house cannot be rented. If it's rented to somebody else, you're entitled to your money back, less an administration fee.

Electricity use is generally billed separately. With tourist office rentals, you settle up with them when taking back the key. (Large holiday rental companies all have service centers within the most popular localities.) Bed linen and towel rental is normally extra—around $9–13 per set. To ensure houses are left in a clean condition, you normally pay a security deposit on arrival—$105–240, depending on house size and whether it has a swimming pool. Final cleaning can be done on your behalf and charged at somewhere between $60 and $110.

Long-Term Rentals

The majority of Danes who aren't homeowners live in local authority and trades union housing. It's almost impossible for foreigners to find accommodations through these types of housing associations. For starters, the tenancy waiting list averages five years. Of course, there's the private rental sector, but options are fairly limited. Rents are sky-high compared to state sector housing.

The website www.alldenmark.dk offers relocation services and help in finding accommodations. If you don't want to use an agency, many newspapers carry rental advertisements. Naturally they're in Danish, and the place to look is in the *bolig* (housing) sections. As it carries free advertisements, a popular paper for both landlords and accommodation seekers is the *Blue Paper* (Blå Avis) which appears on Mondays and Thursdays. Key words to look for include *lejelejlighed* (rented apartment) and *møbleret* (furnished). However, if you're heading for the capital, try the weekly *Copenhagen Post,* an English-language paper. Another option is the Danish Embassy's website, which has a notice board for posting accommodation requirements.

www.alldenmark.dk, Strandvejen 203, DK 2900 Hellerup, Denmark, tel. 45/70-22-40-00, fax 45/70-22-60-00, email: info@alldenmark.dk.

LONG-TERM AGREEMENTS
Most Danish tenancy agreements run for a one-year minimum. The usual deposit is equivalent to three months' rent. All tenures in private rented dwellings are governed by the Rent Act, which carries a long series of provisions. One key principle is that landlords are prohibited from unilaterally terminating the tenancy agreement. The lessee, however, may terminate a tenancy agreement with three months' notice. Any dispute between landlord and tenant may be brought before a judicial housing court. At the end

of the lease term, tenants are usually liable to clean and decorate the interior of the property before moving out. If you're not a paint-and-brush type, landlords often accept a cash payment instead.

Once You're There

Denmark's medical service provides free health care to all citizens and residents. Although other Europeans qualify for immediate treatment, non-EU citizens who have obtained the necessary work and residency permits have a six-week waiting period before gaining access to the system. If you need treatment, you initially see a general practitioner who then refers you to a specialist if necessary.

Some Costs: dozen eggs $2.84, loaf of rye bread $1.43, 1 liter (1.76 pt) milk $0.80, 500 g (17.5 oz) coffee $4.78, bottle of French Bordeaux wine $4.10, 1 liter (1.76 pt) Coke $2.33, 500 g (17.5 oz) bacon $4.88, 2 kg (4.4 lb) sugar $1.99, 250 g (8.75 oz) butter $1.68. A week's car hire, economy model, from $289. The average yearly expenditure on heating and energy is $1,622.

Banking hours are 9:30 A.M. to 4 P.M. Monday to Friday, extended on Thursdays to 6 P.M.

Copenhagen

Copenhagen bills itself as Europe's greenest capital: over a sixth of the city is made up of grassy spaces. It's an extremely likeable place, and compact enough for many locals to travel from the residential districts to work by bicycle. Visitors can actually bike around for free. Bike depositories are scattered throughout Copenhagen—you deposit a coin in a slot and get the same amount back when returning the bike to one of the stands.

The famous Little Mermaid statue, the Tivoli Gardens with its merry-go-rounds and 100,000 tiny lights strung up everywhere, the paintbox-colored frieze of houses, and all-you-can-eat herring buffets of the Nyhavn waterfront—it all suggests the folksy world of Hans Christian Andersen. However, Copenhagen is also big on jazz festivals, art galleries, and design centers. Plus it has Stroget—what's claimed to be the longest pedestrian-only shopping street in the world. Handily placed side by side, Stroget's must-go-in stores include the Royal Copenhagen pottery shop (a hand-painted dinner plate takes an exact 1,197 brush strokes), Jensens's silverware store, and Illums Bolighus, a department store specializing in designer home wares. You'll want to rush out and rent an unfurnished apartment just so you can come back with an excuse for buying up the store.

Everywhere in Copenhagen is so ordered, the tiny neighborhood of Christiania comes as a shock. A former army barracks on the waterfront, about half a mile south of Nyhavn quayside, Christiania was colonized by Copenhagen's hippies in 1971. New-agers are still here, doggedly hanging on to their 80-acre enclave and independent lifestyle. Like the original squatters, Christiania's residents refuse to pay taxes, build whatever and wherever they want to, and run a kind of open-air market in soft drugs. Its main street—unofficially called "Pusherstreet"—is lined with booths where hash cakes and marijuana are openly traded. Pot is sold in bags, in packets, or as pre-rolled cigarettes. All attempts to clear Christiania have failed and the authorities seem happy to let it continue as a kind of social experiment. This being Denmark, it all feels very unthreatening. Along with carefully tended organic vegetable plots, there are cafés where people eat, drink, and try out their potty purchases.

If the Danish authorities allow you a residency permit, don't confuse Christiania with Christianshavn. Tagged "Little Amsterdam," Christianshavn is a quality residential neighborhood—the nickname comes from its canals and bridges rather than a propensity for indulging in druggy habits. Other desirable neighborhoods include Østenbro, Frederiksberg, and Amager. Just north of Copenhagen, with regular commuter trains, the woods, beaches, and sea views of Charlottenlkund make this another prized location.

Copenhagen's supply of good quality homes that foreign tenants can rent is limited—and unbelievably expensive. One-bedroom furnished apartments can be had for around $890 monthly, but you could pay as much as $2,700 for something similar in a classy neighborhood. A three-bedroom unfurnished apartment in Frederiksberg rents for $3,412 monthly; a three-bedroom unfurnished house in

An internationally acclaimed engineering masterpiece, the Great Belt Link is the largest suspension bridge in Europe, connecting Copenhagen and Odense by rail in just one and a half hours.

© Wonderful Copenhagen

Charlottenlkund costs $3,745 per month plus an additional $190 monthly for utilities. The cheapest area is Nørrebro, behind the railway station, where one-bedroom unfurnished apartments start at around $780 monthly.

One way of finding long-term accommodations is to place an advertisement in the weekly English language newspaper, the *Copenhagen Post*. Dansk Boligformidling always has a good selection of apartments. Sample furnished rentals include a 3rd-floor city center apartment near the Royal Palace and Marina. At just under 200 sq m (2,160 sq ft), it consists of kitchen, bathroom, sitting room, dining room, library, bedroom, and guestroom. Rent is $3,265 monthly plus $128 for utilities.

For vacations in Copenhagen, check out the www.ferieboligweb.dk website. Private rentals included an apartment sleeping 2–4 in the Frederiksberg neighborhood for between $215 and $410 weekly. There are also a couple of companies that can arrange short-term apartment stays. Citilet offers serviced apartments, fully fitted with modern kitchens. Sleeping between one and six people, these can be rented on a daily, weekly, or monthly basis. Daily rents are in the region of $139 to $247 with reductions for longer stays. For example, a one-bedroom apartment rents for $140 daily, $888 weekly.

The many parks and gardens in Copenhagen offer a peaceful refuge away from the bustle of city life.

If you can live without daily maid service and other luxuries, try the Hay4You agency. Studios sleeping two rent for $326 weekly, and $888 monthly. Apartments sleeping up to four are $588 weekly, and $1,632 monthly.

Copenhagen Post, Skt Peters Straede 27B, 1453 Copenhagen, tel. 45/33-36-33-00, email: info@cphpost.dk.

Dansk Boligformidling, Hellerupves 78, 2900 Hellerup, tel. 45/70-15-90-07, fax 45/70-15-67-07, email: email@ danskboligformidling.dk.

© Ireneusz Cyranek

Citilet Apartments, Fortunstraede 4, DK 1065 Copenhagen, tel. 45/33-25-21-29, fax 45/33-91-30-77, email: citilet@citilet.dk.

Hay4You/Scanhomes, Vimmelskaften 49, DK 1161 Copenhagen, tel. 45/33-33-08-05, fax 45/33-22-08-04, email: hay4you@cool.dk.

Woodlands, nature reserves, Stone Age burial sites, white cliffs, and wonderfully clean beaches. With good bus and rail links, parts of the scenic North Zealand (*Nordsjaelland*) region are only half an hour's journey from Copenhagen. You could be building sandcastles on the beach in the morning, and visiting royal castles in the afternoon. North Zealand's clutch of fortresses includes mighty Kronborg Castle at Helsingør, which dates back to the 1500s. Shakespeare turned it into Elsinore, the home of Hamlet, Prince of Denmark. In summertime, theater groups put on performances of the play.

One of the region's attractive little towns is Helsinge. At midsummer, on the Eve of Sankt Hansi (June 23rd), people still come here to drink from the waters of a sacred spring, believing it cures them of their ills. Helsinge's tourist office has cottages beside woods and lakes and also at the nearby beaches of Tisvildeleje. Average price is $353 to $682 per week, depending on the season. Nationwide holiday rental agencies also have plenty of North Zealand properties. The provincial Nordtour office is another source of information.

Helsinge Informationscentret, Gadekaervej 17, Postboks 174, DK 3200 Helsinge, tel. 45/48-79-51-66, fax 45/48-79-63-66, email: helsinge@hte.dk.

Interstudio is one of Copenhagen's exclusive furniture houses, featuring both Danish and international designs from streamlined modernism to cool kitsch.

© Wonderful Copenhagen

Nordtour Nordsjaelland, Biskop Svanes Vej 59, DK-3460 Birkerød, tel. 45/45-82-10-33, fax 45/45-82-56-33, www.nordtour.dk.

Århus and the East Jutland Coast

In the center of the Jutland Peninsula's eastern coastline, Århus is the country's second largest center of population. A winsome town with lots to do, it bills itself as "the smallest big city in Denmark." It's a good base for exploring the Peninsula and discovering a part of Denmark that's practically unknown to non-Scandinavian visitors. The surrounding countryside brims with castles and manor houses; the coastline is speckled with fishing villages and sugar-white strands that can get quite crowded in July and August.

Århus itself has a number of museums including *Den Gamle By*, where you can take an open-air walk through Danish history and see how families used to live. Open all year, the cobbled streets of the "Old Town" have 75 houses and buildings dating from the Renaissance to the early 20th century. During Danish school holidays there are special activities for kids. From late April to late August, you could also take youngsters to Århus's Tivoli Friheden, an old-fashioned amusement park with clowns and pink-knuckle rides.

The Øresund fixed link means Sweden's third largest city, Malmö, is only 35 minutes from Copenhagen.

© Wonderful Copenhagen

In Dansommer's holiday cottages brochure, this area comes under the Sydlige Østkyst section. Small properties rent from $230 to $545 depending on the season; a beautiful thatched-roof house on Loddenhoj strand sleeping eight rents for between $489 and $1,063 per week. Århus tourist office arranges stays in summerhouses too. Despite the name, Bed-and-Breakfast Århus agency also offers apart-

LEGOLAND

What could you do if you had 45 million Lego blocks and a big Danish park to put them in? For starters you could build a miniature model of the world. In Legoland's "Miniland" it only takes minutes to get from the Japanese temples of the Land of the Rising Sun to the Statue of Liberty, the Taj Mahal, and Copenhagen Harbor (complete with boats).

Legoland is in the center of the Jutland Peninsula, near the town of Billund. Best suited to the 3–11 age group, it offers the gentle side of the theme park experience, a world where little ones can zip around on dinky electric cars, build models in a playroom, and enjoy rides that won't make their stomachs perform somersaults.

The park's sections include Castleland,

where you can ride boats through Captain Roger's Pirate Caves, and Adventureland, with its Jungle Racers. One of the most popular areas is Duploland, site of the Lego Driving School. Kiddies drive little electric cars through a miniature town complete with pedestrian crossings, junctions, and stoplights—and they can take a test and get a driving license.

Buses go to Legoland from a number of Jutland Peninsula towns. There are also day trip excursions from Copenhagen. The park is open from early April to late October. Summer admission prices are $21 with reductions for children.

Legoland AS, DK 7190 Billund, tel. 45/75-33-13-33, fax 45/75-35-31-79.

ment stays. Apartments from $71 per day, or $45 daily if rented for a month or more.

Hold Ferie i Danmark, Tourist Århus, Radhuset, 8000 Århus, tel. 45/89-40-67-00, fax 45/86-12-95-90, email: info@visitaarhus.com.

Århus Bed and Breakfast, Inge & Svend Aage Andersen, Boegebjergvej 14, DK 8270 Hoejbjerg, tel. 45/86-27-51-30, fax 45/86-72-51-30.

SWEDEN

Sweden is a land of 96,000 lakes, over 51,000 islands, and quiet little towns where residents display the blue and yellow Swedish flag in their front gardens. Fringed by 4,800 miles of coastline, this is one of the cleanest, greenest, and safest countries in the world. Nobody dreams of dropping candy wrappers on the sidewalk or driving their Volvos above 20 mph.

Roughly 30 percent of Sweden's total population of 8.9 million live in Stockholm, Gothenburg, and Malmö. Beyond the southern half of the country (where 85 percent of Swedes live) lies some stunning countryside and wilderness regions. The gilded wheat fields and half-timbered farmhouses of south Sweden give way to a central lakeland district, then the vast wilderness of the far north—a world of wolves, reindeers, and nomadic Lapps.

Midsummer, between June 21st and 23rd, would be a good time to visit. This is the lightest time of year and the Swedish Midsummer is steeped in traditions originating in pagan times. Many revelers dress in national costume and most towns and villages raise a maypole that gets decorated with flowers and leafy branches. There's dancing, singing, and people bring along picnics of traditional food such as pickled herring, new potatoes, strawberries, beer, and schnapps. Another surviving tradition is that unwed girls pick seven kinds of wildflowers to place under their pillows at night. This bit of country magic supposedly brings dreams of their future husbands.

Providing you don't trample down crops, you can wander where you will, loading baskets with mushrooms and berries. Sweden's countryside is governed by a centuries-old tradition known as *Allemansrätt* (right of public access) which allows people to walk, ski, or ride through any fields or forests without being turned back by landowners.

Swedish Tourist Board, 655 Third Ave., New York, NY 10017-5617, 212/885-9700, fax 212/885-9764, www.gosweden.com.

Legalities

Although North American citizens don't need visas, they must obtain residence permits if wishing to stay for more than three months. These must be obtained beforehand, and are unlikely to be given without a job offer, a university place, or strong family ties.

Embassy of Sweden, 1501 M St. NW, Washington, DC 20005, 202/467-2600, www.swedish-embassy.org.

Embassy of Sweden, 377 Dalhousie St., Ottawa, Ontario K1N 9N8, 613/241-8553.

The Language

Nearly everybody speaks English, so vacationers shouldn't encounter linguistic problems. If you want to learn Swedish, there are plenty of opportunities, through language schools, "Folk" universities, evening classes, and private tutors.

Berlitz International, Apelbergsgatan 57, 111 37 Stockholm, tel. 46/8-412-1300, email: info@berlitz.se.

Vacation Rentals

Most local tourist offices within urban areas can fix you up with an apartment or a private room with kitchen facilities. However, the most popular types of vacation accommodations are log cabins or holiday chalets, usually in lake or seaside locations. Be warned, though. The least expensive cabins don't have luxuries such as hot water, inside toilets, and showers. Although Sweden has one of the world's highest living standards, something in the national character seems to think that vacations should be spent emulating the back-to-basics lifestyle of the ancestors.

Local tourist offices keep property lists—expect to pay around $430 for a traditional wooden chalet in June. If you can access the Internet, take a look at www.swedenhomerentals.se, which has hundreds of private rentals. There are also links to rental agencies in particular localities.

The Sälen area, 400 km (248 m) northwest of Stockholm, is a center for active vacations—skiing in winter, hiking, mountain biking, and horseback riding in summer. You can catch your own dinner in one of the surrounding lakes and for youngsters there are toboggans, go-karts, ponies, and water adventures. It's a splendid part of the country for seeing wildlife such as elk deer, foxes, grouse, and golden eagles. Sleeping six, you could book a fully equipped cabin in the Joängsbyn Sälen "holiday village." It rents for between $172 and $570 depending on the season.

Sven-Erik Sanden, Joängsbyn Sälen, Lummergången 54, 135-35 Tyresö, tel. 46/8-742-1313, fax 46/8-742-1434, email: s-e.sanden@telia.com.

VACATION RENTAL AGREEMENTS

Deposits are usually $60 or 20 percent of the rent, with the balance paid at least 60 days prior to arrival. If booking within 60 days, the entire rent is sought. To guard against 90 percent cancellation costs if you do cancel and the property cannot be rented to other vacationers, tourist offices can arrange insurance cancellation if you've booked through them. This amounts to $30 per property. Electricity is sometimes included in the rent, but not always. You usually have to pay a security deposit too—$60 to $120 depending on property size. Houses are expected to be left in spotless condition.

Long-Term Rentals

Nonprofit housing corporations own around 50 percent of Sweden's rental accommodations. Waiting lists are very lengthy for these properties but there's a slight possibility that an existing tenant may wish to sub-let—perhaps through being called up for military service or through spending time working or studying in another part of the country. Figures issued by the Swedish Institute put the average monthly rent (including heating) for an apartment with three rooms and bathroom at $470 and for four rooms and bathroom at $582. However, in blocks of flats built over the past five years, rents are about 20 percent higher than the average.

LONG-TERM AGREEMENTS

Rents are normally payable monthly in advance. A contract is drawn up between landlord and tenant specifying things such as the amount of rent and what it covers. Heating and water are usually inclusive and you'll sometimes find that electricity is too. The contract states the amount of notice you have to give before leaving, which shouldn't be any more than three months. In the case of furnished apartments there should also be a detailed inventory.

Once You're There

Unless you're a student who has obtained a one-year residency permit, you won't be able to take advantage of Sweden's national health care system, which is available at free or minimum cost to EU passport holders. Note that the general practitioner system doesn't apply in Sweden. If you need attention, either visit the nearest hospital or a *Vårdcentral*, a local health care clinic. Fees, which you should be able to claim back from your health insurance provider, average $21 ($35 for specialists), plus extra daily charges of approximately $20 for a hospital bed. However, much depends on what hospital treatment is required. Costs could mount up to as much as $280 per day.

Some Costs: 100 g (3.5 oz) coffee $3.43, 1 liter (1.76 pt) milk $1.28, 1.5 liter (2.64 pt) Coca-Cola $1.50, 1 kg (2.2 lb) bananas $1.46, bread $1.60–3.20, 1 kg (2.2 lb) bacon $8.80, 1 kg (2.2 lb) cheese $7–18, 1 kg (2.2 lb) pork $18.50, 1 kg (2.2 lb) lamb cutlets $9.20. Food prices vary, but one inexpensive supermarket chain is PrisXtra. A week's car rental, economy model, starts at $338.

Banking hours are 9:30 A.M. to 3 P.M. Monday to Friday, with extensions to 5:30 P.M. on Thursdays. All major credit cards are widely accepted.

Stockholm

Sweden's capital has more than royal palaces and the famous IKEA furniture store. Built on 14 islands—and surrounded by another 24,000 islands, rocks, and skerries in the Baltic Sea—this watery city of 1.6 million people sits on one of the world's biggest archipelagos. It's another Nordic capital that prides itself on environmental awareness. It's so clean, in fact, that you can go swimming and fishing for salmon and trout in the city center.

Begin explorations amongst the cluster of ancient buildings, copper-spired churches, and narrow cobbled alleyways of *Gamla Stam*, "the Old Town." Surrounded by water, but linked by bridges to other parts of the city, this little island was the original Stockholm. It's great fun simply wandering around its antique stores, cafés, and artisans' workshops. Another of the capital's highlights is Skansen, the world's first open-air museum. Historic buildings have been imported and resurrected from every corner of the country—wooden homes, a church, windmills, farms, and even a Lapp camp with reindeer. Along with handicraft workshops, Skansen also contains a zoo where you can see wolves, elk, and arctic foxes.

If you can negotiate the immigration restrictions, Bo Tjänst and Bostad are apartment and home renting agencies with English-speaking staff. Bo Tjänst specializes in sub-letting; Bostad maintains a database of local rental agents. Recent properties included three-room apartments for $470 and $740 monthly.

For vacationers looking for shorter stays, B & B Service Stockholm can locate apartments for periods from two days upwards. Sample properties include a two-person studio with kitchenette, 10 minutes' walk from the central station, for $86 daily. A one-bedroom apartment at Djursholm, a fashionable suburb 10 kilometers from Stockholm's center, rents for $660 monthly.

Bo Tjänst, Kungstensgatan 40, 11359 Stockholm, tel. 46/8-34-51-00, fax 46/8-34-52-00.

Bostad, Folkungagaten 72, South Stockholm, tel. 46/8-644-5820, fax 46/8-644-5860, www.bostadfordig.se.

B & B Service Stockholm, Sidenvägen 17, S17837, Stockholm, tel. 46/8-660-55-65, fax 46/8-663-38-22, www.bedbreakfast.a.se.

Many locals own weekend cottages in Skärgården, Stockholm's archipelago of 24,000 islands, which stretches out for 60 miles into the Baltic. During the summertime, fishing, messing about in canoes, building rafts, and preparing meals over barbecues are the order of the day. You can rent cottages and chalets on many islands, which are often chained fast to each other by bridges. Choose the right island (150 are inhabited year-round), and it's easy to cross back and forth to Stockholm by car, bike, or passenger ferry.

With several daily services to Stockholm, Vaxholm is a great location for anyone who wants to get a feel for the archipelago but not miss out on the capital. Complete with a castle and a clutch of galleries and restaurants, this typical maritime settlement acts as a hub for ferry services to outer islands. If you're interested in Viking history, don't miss Björkö Island. This is the site of Birka, Sweden's oldest town which came into existence around A.D. 750. An important trading center in the 9th century, it still has the remains of houses and a huge Viking cemetery.

For archipelago rentals, contact Stockholm Tourist Service or DESS. Sample properties include a cottage for four at Vaxholm that rents for between $372 and $460 weekly. Cottages in the archipelago near Stockholm rent for similar prices.

Stockholm Tourist Service, Kungsträdgården, Box 7542 S-10393 Stockholm, tel. 46/8-789-2400, fax 46/8-789-2450, www.stoinfo.se.

DESS - Destination Stockholm Skärgård AB, Lillström S-18497 Ljusterö, tel. 46/8-542-48100, fax 46/8-542-41400, www.dess.se.

Malmö and Skåne

Odds are you've never heard of Malmö, Sweden's third largest city—or of the southwestern province of Skåne. Until fairly recently, both were well-kept secrets. Separated from Denmark by a 10-mile strait, Skåne's rolling farmland and pretty coastal towns became much more accessible when the Øresund Bridge opened in July 2000. It's an excellent base for bagging two Scandinavian countries in one go. For road and rail travelers, Swedish Malmö is now only a half-hour journey from Danish Copenhagen. (The Swedish capital, Stockholm, is four hours from Malmö by train.)

Malmö is Skåne province's main center of population. Bounded by canals and woodlands, it's another waterfront city with an Old Town of green-copper domes and spires, a 15th-century castle, and half-timbered houses. Seven km (4.3 m) of sandy beaches are within walking distance.

Skåne has plenty to explore. Just 15 minutes away from Malmö by train, the university town of Lund seems trapped in an enchanted medieval web. It has some wonderful sights, such as an astronomical clock where mechanical figures come out to battle with swords and blow trumpets at noon and 3 P.M. Another gem from the Middle Ages is the coastal town of Ystad, which maintains one of the last night watches in Europe. A night watchman has been sounding a bugle from the main square's watchtower for the past three centuries. Originally to safeguard against fire, and reassure townsfolk that all is well, the call rings out every 15 minutes from 9:15 P.M. to 3 A.M. Until the mid-19th century, any watchman who fell asleep was rewarded with the death penalty!

The www.foteviken.se website carries a curious invitation: "All Vikings are welcome to participate and live here with the resident Vikings." If you do have Viking blood coursing through your veins, then Foteviken is one place you shouldn't miss. On the Naset Peninsula, below Malmö, Foteviken is no theme park, but a real community where people try to live the same Viking life as their forebears. Grains are sown, animals are tended, and a project is underway to build a Viking ship and sail on one of the old trading routes to China.

For Skåne vacation rentals, first contact the regional tourist office at Lund for listings and brochures. Bookings are then made through local offices. For example, the Ystad office's properties include a cross-timbered farm cottage on a working farm, three km (1.9 m) from the sea. Sleeping

AMBER—THE GOLD OF THE NORTH

Amber, fossilized tree resin, has been traded since Stone Age times. Regarded as a precious commodity for centuries, Baltic amber was known to the Phoenicians, Greeks, and Romans. In the Emperor Nero's day, the "Amber Games" were held in the gladiatorial arena. Valuable chunks of amber ornamented the protective netting separating combatants from spectators, and amber chips were strewn across the arena floor.

The sandy shores of Sweden's Skåne province are a particularly good place to pick up pieces for free. The best time to look is after a storm when pieces get caught up in hanks of seaweed or amongst the seashells. You should certainly be able to find amber pebbles, though chunks are rare. So too are "inclusions" which contain fossilized insects. (Remember the *Jurassic Park* movie where scientists extracted dinosaur DNA from the blood of mosquitoes trapped in amber?)

Nowadays amber is usually used in jewelry, but during the Middle Ages it served as a magic charm. In an age of superstition, tradition told that it could guard against snakebite and the powers of witchcraft and evil spirits. There was no possibility of a baby being stolen from its cradle to be replaced by a changeling—not if it was wearing a heart-shaped amber amulet around its neck. Amber was also credited with having healing properties. Worn as a necklace or carried in a bag, it was reputed to alleviate everything from rheumatism to sore throats and stomach disorders.

Between the 16th and 18th centuries it was also used to make buttons, boxes, chess sets, and watchcases. Perhaps its most unusual use was to be crafted into mouthpieces for expensive pipes. To see some rare samples, and discover the best Skåne beaches for finding amber, the Swedish Amber Museum is 20 km (12 m) south of Malmö, at Höllviken. Open daily from mid-May to early October, the rest of the year weekends only, tel. 46/40-454504.

four, this rents for between $290 and $392 weekly. A flat in a former railway station house at Fyledalen rents from $258–322 per week and sleeps five. One Malmö agent for long-term rentals is Kullenberg.

Skånes Turistråd, Bredgaten 25, SE 22221 Lund, tel. 46/46-12-43-50, fax 46/46-12-23-72, email: info@skanetourist.com.

Ystads Turistbyrå, St Knuts Torg 20, 27142 Ystad, tel. 46/411-57-76-81, fax 46/411-55-55-85, email: turistinfo@ystad.se.

Malmö Turism, Centralstationen, Skeppsbron, 21120 Malmö, tel. 46/40-34-12-00, fax 46/40-34-12-09, email: info@tourism.malmo.com.

Kullenberg i Malmö Fastighets Förvaltning AB, Amiralsgaten 13 200-22 Malmö, tel. 46/40-306970, fax 46/40-871187, www.kullenberg.com.

NORWAY

Norway, the Land of the Midnight Sun, is also a land of fjords, glaciers, and rugged mountains. Parts of this remote country lie within the Arctic Circle and if skiing is your thing, it's possible to do it here year-round. Despite the large number of summer tourists who hop on and off the little ships that sail right up to the Russian border, this is arguably Scandinavia's least-known country. However, it's good to be aware that prices are even higher here than in Denmark and Sweden, and the summer season only extends from the beginning of June to mid-August. Outside that period, many tourist attractions shut up shop.

It's not really a country for big city pleasures—a mere 4.3 million people live here—and communities tend to be small-scale. Even the capital, Oslo, only numbers half a million citizens. What most vacationers come here for is the scenery of the western fjords. Consider basing yourself in or around Bergen, a largish town (by Norwegian standards) on the outermost edge of Europe.

Norwegian Tourist Board, 655 Third Ave., Suite 1810, New York, NY 10163-4649, 212/885-9700, fax 212/885-9710, email: usa@ntr.no, www.visitnorway.com.

Legalities

Unless you have obtained the required work and residency permits, staying in Norway for longer than three months is difficult for most North Americans. However, those with close relatives in Norway may be granted an extended stay. The country has strong historic links with the United States—between 1825 and 1940, more than one third of Norway's population emigrated to America. For more information contact:

Norwegian Embassy, 2720 34th St. NW, Washington, DC 20008, 202/333-6000, www.norway.org.

Norwegian Embassy, 90 Sparks St., Ottawa, Ontario K1P 5B4, 613/238-6571.

The Language

Norwegian is broken down into two languages. *Bokmal* is the form you're most likely to encounter. *Nynorsk*, a dialect, stems from the Old Norse of the Vikings and is only spoken in remote rural districts. Should you wish to learn Norwegian, contact the adult education organization Friundervisningen for details of local language courses. For example, the Folkeuniversitetet in the western town of Stavanger runs an 80-hour course over 10 weeks, costing $865. Berlitz also has a language school in Oslo.

Friundervisningen, Torggata 7, 0105 Oslo, tel. 47/22-47-60-00, fax 47/22-47-60-01.

Berlitz AS, Akersgarten 16, 0159 Oslo, tel. 47/22-33-10-30, fax 47/22-33-10-03, info@berlitz.no.

Vacation Rentals

Options range from town apartments to countryside chalets and log cabins. Most rural properties (*hytter*) have electricity, heating, and kitchens equipped with hot plates. However, in more remote areas the lighting comes from kerosene lamps, cooking is done by bottled gas, and you fetch your water from a nearby well or stream. Chalets are often clustered around a central building containing a restaurant, grocery shop, and sauna—sometimes even an indoor swimming pool. For a real back-to-nature experience, you could opt for a *Rorbu* hut. Used by fishermen during the winter cod-fishing season, these are often rented to summer vacationers. An excellent website for locating holiday properties on Norway's scenic west coast is www.fjordnorway.no. Or contact a large rental company such as Novasol for brochures.

Many individuals and small businesses are on the Internet. Going to a search engine and typing in "fjord hytter" yields good results, and lots of sites have English pages. Herdla has five properties that are a 45-minute drive from Bergen. Sample price for a five-person cottage is $422 to $514 weekly, depending on season. Further north, 17 properties around the beautiful Geirangerfjord are available through Grande Fjordhytter. Cabins sleeping four rent from $462 to $545, larger properties from $508 to $736 weekly. Rental arrangements are similar to Denmark and Sweden: electricity is usually charged extra and you can rent bed linens for around $9 per set.

The Norwegian Tourist Authority advises those traveling in the high season—approximately mid-June to mid-August—to book accommodations in advance. Information offices in Norway often have a reservation service, and you should first contact the tourist office for listings and contact numbers. It would be impossible to list them all here—there are at least 250 tourist offices!

During the high season, bookings for standard furnished self-catering accommodations outside of cities are usually for a week. However, you will also find chalets (called *hytter* in Norwegian) on campgrounds—I don't know how many chalets there are, but at the last count Norway had over 1,000 campgrounds. In these campground cabins, it's possible to spend just one night there and then move on. The cabins are furnished and are classed 1–5 stars depending on size and standard. Prices range from $33 to $105 per night.

Novasol AS, Rygårde Alle 104, DK 2900 Hellerup, Denmark, tel. 45/73-75-66-11, email: novasol@novasol.com.

A/S Herdla Fjordhytter Laxeneset, C/O Saebo, Arstadveien 17g, 5009 Bergen, tel. 47/55-31-95-54, fax 47/55-31-97-93, email: booking@ hytteutleie.com.

Grande Fjordhytter, 6216 Geiranger, tel. 47/95-10-75-27, fax 47/70-26-19-99.

Long-Term Rentals

Oslo rental flats are often in blocks of low-rise apartment buildings, but throughout the rest of Norway the tendency is towards suburban-style homes. Most Norwegians are homeowners and although the state provides municipal rental housing, waiting lists are lengthy. It's practically impossible for foreigners to rent municipal flats and you'll have to look to the private sector. Rentals are advertised under *Til Leie* sections in newspapers.

Many realtors also handle furnished rentals. NEF, the national organization for licensed real estate agents, can provide details of members. For agents on the Internet, go to www.fredensborg.no. They have over 450 part/fully furnished apartments in Oslo for long-term rent. One-bedroom apartments start at $673 monthly, two bedrooms from $1,040.

Fredensborg AS, Mollerveien 4, 0182 Oslo, tel. 47/23-29-20-00, fax 47/23-29-20-01, email: apartment@fredensborg.no.

NEF Norges Eiendomsmeglerforbund, Inkognitogaten 12, N-0258 Oslo, tel. 47/22-54-20-80, fax 47/22-55-31-06, email: firmapost@nef.no.

LONG-TERM AGREEMENTS

The housing market is strictly regulated. The law stipulates the number of people who may live in an apartment—normally it must not exceed more than two persons per bedroom. Lease contracts usually run for one year initially, then for subsequent terms of five years with a mutual right to give notice. Deposits (3–6 months' rent) are sought, and termination notice is generally three months.

Once You're There

Regarding health concerns, if you need to visit a doctor you can obtain lists of local practitioners from tourist offices as well as the embassy. Fees are in the region of $15–30. Although travelers need health insurance, long-term residents may qualify for free hospital care, reimbursement of doctors' fees, and medicines. Costs are covered by a national health insurance plan. Those residing in Norway for 12 months have to subscribe, regardless of nationality.

Some Costs: 10 eggs $3.15, 250 g (8.75 oz) coffee $2.37, bread $1.50–2.50, 10 kg (22 lb) potatoes $8.56, 1 kg (2.2 lb) mackerel $6.40, 1 kg (2.2 lb) bananas $2.11, 1 kg (2.2 lb) apples $3.40, 1 liter (1.76 pt) milk $1.32, 1 kg (2.2 lb) steak $21.15, 1 kg (2.2 lb) fresh salmon $13.76, 500 g (17.5 oz) rice $2.64.

Banks are generally open 8:15 A.M. to 3:30 P.M. Monday to Friday. There is usually a designated day during the week when business hours are extended, but this varies from bank to bank.

Oslo

Population-wise, Oslo is one of Europe's smallest capitals but its boundaries spread over a vast distance—453 sq km (111,891 sq acres). Like other Scandinavian capitals, it has a thing about cleanliness, efficient public transport, parks, and cycle paths. Although the city center is compact, there's a feeling of being surrounded by space. Oslonians like nothing better than spending good-weather weekends on the island beaches of the Oslofjord or hiking in the forested Nordmarka hills above the city. Floodlit during winter evenings, Oslo's surroundings include 1,500 km (930 m) of cross-country ski trails.

Museums come thick and fast, many focusing on maritime history. The Vikingskipshuset with its Viking dragon ships, and the Kon-Tiki Museum, which contains the crafts on which Thor Heyerdahl crossed the Pacific and Atlantic Oceans are but two. Art buffs won't want to miss *The Scream* and the vampire *Madonna* in the Munch museum or the Vigeland museum—an outdoor sculpture park containing virtually all of Gustav Vigeland's naked human life forms. Another famous son was Henrik Ibsen, whose plays are performed at the National Theater.

Oslo is at its best as a summertime city, but if you do come in winter, pavements are kept snow-free by an underground heating system. For short-term stays in either the center or the suburbs, Oslo Apartments have fully equipped properties ranging in size between one and five rooms. Prices range from $52 to $118 per night, though reductions kick in if you're staying for a month or longer.

Also check the classifieds in the English-language newspaper, the *Norway Post*. Properties are sometimes available for three- and four-month periods. I saw furnished one- and two-bedroom apartments for rents of $630 to $790 monthly, and you can place an "accommodation wanted" advertisement. Oslo real estate agents such as Bjerke, Megler, and Eiendom also handle rentals.

Oslo Apartments AS, St. Edmundsvei 37, 0280 Oslo, tel. 47/22-51-02-50, fax 47/22-51-02-59, email: info@osloapartments.no.

Norway Post, P.O. Boks 25, 1355 Baerum, tel. 47/671-76875, fax 47/671-76851, www.norwaypost.no.

Bjerke Eiendom, Øvre Slottsg 29, 0157 Oslo, tel. 47/22-00-45-80, email: post@bjerke-eiendom.no.

Megler 1AS, Bryggetorget 13/15 0122 Oslo, tel. 47/22-83-37-00, fax 47/22-83-37-01.

Oslo Eiendom AS, Hoffsveien 21/23 Postboks 80 Skøyen, 0212 Oslo, tel. 47/22-51-76-00, fax 47/22-51-76-01, email: firmapost@osloeiendom.no.

Bergen

If you're keen on a diet of scaly, silver creatures, the "capital" of Norway's fjord country may be your idea of heaven. Back in 1890, a traveler called Lillie Leland visited Bergen and wrote: "Everything is fishy. You eat and drink fish and smell fish and breathe fish." More than a hundred years later, the description is as apt as ever.

Renowned for its mountains and fjords as well as its fish, Bergen is a natural starting point for exploring Norway's wild west coast. Unfortunately its geographical setting produces astonishing rainfall levels—up to 80 inches annually. It's understandable why apartment owners place so much emphasis on providing "drying facilities." One old joke tells that Bergen horses will bolt if they see anyone not carrying an umbrella. Another cites the rain-sodden tourists who spend two weeks waiting for the sun to shine. They ask a youngster if it ever stops raining. "I don't know," he replies. "I'm only ten years old."

Home to just 225,000 people, it's hard to believe this maritime town was once Norway's capital, the country's main settlement and religious center in medieval times. Built on seven hills around A.D. 1070, it was to become an important trading post for Hanseatic merchants. Apart from a castle, little of ancient Bergen survives, but the merchant traders' timber dwellings and warehouses can still be seen in the oldest part of town, Bryggen, whose wharfside hugs Vågen harbor. The fish market is in full cry from Mondays to Saturdays; just follow your nose along Torget Bryggen. If you're shopping for mementos, Bergen is troll town central. Edvard Grieg, composer of the *Peer Gynt Suites,* had a home just outside Bergen named Troldhaugen (Hill of the Trolls). Collectors of curious museums will undoubtedly thrill to Bergen's *Lepramuseet*—the Leprosy Museum.

In central Bergen, InCity has one-, two-, and three-room apartments, all with central heating, cable TV, and equipped kitchens. Prices start at $99 per night for studios, rising to $185 nightly for three-room suites. Amunds Apartments are in Bergen's picturesque old quarter of colorful wooden houses and cobbled streets. Studios for two cost $66 nightly, an apartment sleeping six costs $66–132, depending on the number of occupants. If you're seeking a long-term rental, NEF agents here include Activum.

With sea and fjord views, Årvika Rorbu is a classier version of the traditional fisherman's cabin, though even this has an area for gutting fish. A 21-kg (46-lb) monster cod was caught here with rod and line in 1999. Perfect for two families traveling together, the cabin can sleep eight, and a motorboat is available for rent. Available between July and September, the cabin rents for $383 to $924 weekly.

A boat is included in the price of cabins at Fana, 20 km (12.4 m) south of Bergen. The beachside Fanafjorden cabins sleep up to six and rent for between $69 and $105 nightly.

Bykjernen Apartments, Chr. Michelsens Gate 2b, N-5012 Bergen, tel. 47/55-23-16-13, fax 47/55-23-03-28, email: eiend-as@online.no.

Amunds Apartments, Strangehagen 26, N-5011 Bergen, tel. 47/55-23-10-84, fax 47/55-23-33-39, email: amnordla@online.no.

Activum Eiensdomsmegling Bergen AS, Postboks 158 Laguneparken, 5758 Bergen, tel. 47/55-11-21-60, fax 47/55-11-21-61, email: bentzon@activum.no.

Årvika Rorbu, V/Nordsjøfartsmuseet, 5380 Taelavåg, tel. 47/91-17-09-54, fax 47/95-56-93-13, www.aarvika.no.

Fanafjorden Hytteleutleie, Krokeideveien 264, 5244 Fana, tel. 47/55-91-73-01, fax 47/55-91-69-56.

PART VIII

Appendix

Useful Resources

Embassies and Consulates

If you're only in Europe for a holiday visit, it's not really necessary to register your presence with the local U.S. or Canadian embassy. However, just in case there's an emergency back home, registering makes it easier for people to track you down if your plans change once you're in a country. Obviously nobody wants to contemplate being thrown into a foreign jail, but it makes sense to know where these offices are should you run into any difficulties—you might lose your passport or plane ticket or even your money. Although the embassy isn't going to provide you with new wads of cash, at least they'll be able to offer advice and help with contacting your bank or family back home. They also keep lists of English-speaking doctors should you need medical attention.

Depending on your own circumstances, if you're in Europe for a longer stay, you may want to let your local embassy know that you're in town. Bring your passport so details can be noted—should the original be lost or stolen, it will be easier to get a replacement. Consulate sections also assist with passport renewal, voter registration, income tax forms, notary services, and can answer questions regarding veteran and Social Security pensions as well as other federal benefits.

AUSTRIA
U.S. Embassy, Boltzmanngasse16, A-1090 Vienna, tel. 43/1- 31339, www.usembassy-vienna.at.
U.S. Embassy Consular Section, Gartenbaupromenade 2, A-1010 Vienna, tel. 43/1-31339/7532, fax 43/1-512-5835.
Canadian Embassy, Laurenzerberg 2, A-1010 Vienna, tel. 43/1-531-38-3000, fax 43/1-531-38-39-05.

BELGIUM
U.S. Embassy Consular Section, 27 Blvd. du Régent, B-1000 Brussels, tel. 32/0-2-508-21-11, fax 32/0-2-511-27-25.
Canadian Embassy, 2 Tervuren Avenue, B-1040 Brussels, tel. 32/0-2-741-06-11, fax 32/0-2-741-06-43.

DENMARK
U.S. Embassy, Dag Hammarskjölds Alle 24, 2100 Copenhagen, tel. 45/35-55-31-44, fax 45/35-43-02-23.
Canadian Embassy, Kr. Bernikowsgade 1, 1105 Copenhagen, tel. 45/33-48-32-20, fax 45/33-48-32-20.

FRANCE

U.S. Embassy, 2 Avenue Gabriel, 75008 Paris, tel. 33/0-1-43-12-22-22, fax 33/0-1-42-86-82-91.

U.S. Consulate, 2 Rue St. Florentin, 75382 Paris CEDEX 08, tel. 33/0-1-43-12-48-40 (3–6 P.M.), fax 33/0-1-42-61-61-40.

Canadian Embassy, 35 Avenue Montaigne, 75008 Paris, tel. 33/0-1-44-43-29-00.

GERMANY

U.S. Embassy, Neustädtische Kirchstrasse 4-5, 10117 Berlin, tel. 49/0-30-832-9233, fax 49/0-30-8305-1215, www.usembassy.de.

Canadian Embassy, Friedrichstrasse 95, 23rd Fl., 10117 Berlin, tel. 49/0-30-203-120, fax 49/0-30-203-12121, www.kanada-info.de.

GREECE

American Embassy, 91 Vassilissis Sophias Avenue, 10160 Athens, tel. 30/0-1-721-2951.

Canadian Embassy, 4 Ioannou Ghennadiou Street, 11521 Athens, tel. 30/0-1-727-3400, fax 30/0-1-727-3480.

IRELAND

U.S. Embassy, 42 Elgin Rd., Dublin 4, tel. 353/0-1-668-8777.

Canadian Embassy, Canada House, 65/68 St. Stephen's Green, Dublin 2, tel. 353/0-1-478-1988.

ITALY

U.S. Embassy, Via Vittorio Veneto 119A, Rome 00187, tel. 39/06-46741, fax 39/06-4882-672, www.usis.it.

U.S. Consulate, General Lungarno Amerigo Vespucci 38, Firenze (Florence) 50123, tel. 39/055-2398276, fax 39/055-284088.

Canadian Embassy, Via G.B. de Rossi 27, Rome 00161, tel. 39/06-445981.

NETHERLANDS (HOLLAND)

U.S. Embassy, Lange Voorhout 102, Den Haag, tel. 31/70-310-9209.

U.S. Consulate General, Museum Plein 19, Amsterdam, tel. 31/20-575-5309.

Canadian Embassy, Sophialaan 7, Den Haag, tel. 31/70-311-1600.

NORWAY

U.S. Embassy, Drammenveien 18, 0244 Oslo, tel. 47/22-44-85-50, fax 47/22-56-27-51.

Canadian Embassy, Wergelandsveien 7, 0244 Oslo, tel. 47/22-99-53-00, fax 47/22-99-53-01.

PORTUGAL

American Embassy, Av. das Forças Armadas, 1600 Lisbon, tel. 351/21-727-3300, fax 351/21-727-9109, www.american-embassy.pt.

Canadian Embassy, Av. Da Liberdade 144/56-4th Fl., 1200 Lisbon, tel. 351/21-316-4600, fax 351/21-316-4692.

SPAIN
U.S. Embassy, Serrano 75, 28006 Madrid, tel. 34/1-91587-2200, fax 34/1-91587-2303, www.embusa.es.
Canadian Embassy, 35 Nunez de Balboa, 28001 Madrid, tel. 34/1-914-223-250.

SWEDEN
American Embassy, Dag Hammarskjölds Väg 31, SE-11589 Stockholm, tel. 46/0-8-783-53-00, fax 46/0-8-661-1964, www.usemb.se.
Canadian Embassy, Tegelbacken 4, SE-10323 Stockholm, tel. 46/0-8-453-3000, fax 46/0-8-242491.

SWITZERLAND
U.S. Embassy, Jubilaeumstrasse 93, Bern, tel. 41/31-357-7011, www.us-embassy.ch. Consulate offices in Zürich and Geneva.
Canadian Embassy, Kirchenfeldstrasse 88, Bern, tel. 41/31-352-63-81/357-32-00.

UNITED KINGDOM
U.S. Embassy, 24 Grosvenor Square, London W1A 1AE, tel. 44/0-20-7499-9000, www.usembassy.org.uk.
U.S. Consulate, 3 Regent Terrace, Edinburgh EH7 5BW, tel. 44/0-131-556-8315.
Canadian High Commission, Macdonald House, 1 Grosvenor Square, London W1X 0AB, tel. 44/0-207-258-6600, fax 44/0-20-7258-6333.

Emergency Telephone Numbers

Across the European Union, a standard emergency telephone number, 112, is being introduced. However, some countries haven't yet implemented it, and you should always check the emergency numbers for the area you are in.

Austria	Ambulance: 144	Fire: 122	Police: 133
Belgium	Ambulance: 112	Fire: 112	Police: 112
Cyprus	Ambulance: 112	Fire: 112	Police: 112
Denmark	Ambulance: 112	Fire: 112	Police: 112
France	Ambulance: 112	Fire: 112	Police: 112
Germany	Ambulance: 112	Fire: 112	Police: 110
Greece	Ambulance: 112	Fire: 112	Police: 112
Ireland	Ambulance: 112/999	Fire: 112/999	Police: 112/999
Italy	Ambulance: 112	Fire: 112	Police: 112
Malta	Ambulance: 112	Fire: 112	Police: 112
Netherlands	Ambulance: 112	Fire: 112	Police: 112
Norway	Ambulance: 113	Fire: 110	Police: 112
Portugal	Ambulance: 112	Fire: 112	Police: 112
Spain	Ambulance: 112	Fire: 112	Police: 112
Sweden	Ambulance: 112	Fire: 112	Police: 112
Switzerland	Ambulance: 144	Fire: 118	Police: 117
United Kingdom	Ambulance: 112/999	Fire: 112/999	Police: 112/999

A Home Away From Home

*W*hy not consider trying a home-swap? It's not a permanent arrangement—home-swapping means staying rent-free in somebody's home for an agreed period of time while they move into yours. For most house-swappers, the big attraction is that it's a great way of having an inexpensive vacation. Although you'll still need to pay airfare, accommodation will be rent-free. Secondly, a real home, often in a tourist-free residential area, is likely to be much more comfy than the normal holiday rental. Best of all, you won't be just another foreign visitor. Even if it's only for a short time, you'll be able to live just like a local, experience a brand-new lifestyle, and undoubtedly get to know your hosts' neighbors too.

Although the idea of opening up their home to strangers won't suit everyone, it's certainly worth thinking about if you're seeking a holiday with a difference. Take Ireland, for instance. There's more to Irish culture than seeing the sights, downing pints of stout, and tapping your feet to a fiddle player. Wouldn't you like to get your own turf fire roaring? Or use an old-fashioned range cooker to bake soda bread or cook up an authentic Irish stew?

Although home exchange is a relatively recent concept within Europe, numbers are increasing all the time. France and the UK seem to have the most number of potential swappers, but people in every European country are looking to exchange their homes for a North American base for periods of anything from a week to six months. And while many swappers seem to be professional types such as teachers, doctors, and lawyers, home-exchange is open to everybody. Some European couples have a gaggle of kids and are looking to get away during school holidays; other swappers are adventurous retirees and can be a lot more flexible regarding the exchange period.

Regarding homes and locations, not every family wishes to exchange like-for-like. So long as you're honest in describing your property, it doesn't really matter if it's a modest home with no fancy frills. Probably the most important question is will there be enough room to accommodate the exchange family? As for the location factor, many exchangers prefer to avoid well-known tourist areas completely. Of course, if you're lucky enough to live somewhere sunny, that's undoubtedly going to be a major draw for home-swappers from Ireland, Britain, and many other parts of northern Europe.

When it comes to exchanging homes, common sense is going to be the most useful guideline. For instance, a retired couple may feel more comfortable knowing that people of a similar age are enjoying their home. If I'd spent a lifetime collecting fragile antique porcelain, I don't think I'd be very keen on exchanging with a family who had a troop of boisterous toddlers.

But how do you know that a strange family won't wreck your kitchen, eat the budgie, and hold all-night raves in the rose garden? Although it's unlikely to happen, the short answer is that you don't. Unfortunately there are no iron-clad guarantees that the family who seemed so nice and *normal* in their introductory letters won't be the visitors from hell. Remember, though, the exchange family is going to worry about exactly the same things as you. Another thing to bear in mind is that an occupied house is much less likely to be burgled.

Unless you already have European friends to exchange with, probably the best way to make contact is through an agency. A number of international agencies facilitate home exchange, though most charge an annual fee to register with them. What happens is that you give details about your property and yourself, where and when you'd like to go, and your contact address and telephone number. Listings and photos are often only available to other members of the same exchange club and are found either in directories or on the Internet—your personal contact details aren't available to nonmembers. Membership fees range from $65 to $150 annually.

What kind of European homes are available for exchange? And where do people want to go? Well, an Irish couple with two children living in a traditional-style farmhouse in the wilds of rural Cork are looking for a three- to six-week exchange with a family in north Florida. An arty family of potters living on the Greek Cycladean Island of Páros have a four-bedroom home and are looking for home-exchange suggestions. A Mediterranean island? An English couple living on the island of Malta have a small town house built into the 16th-century walls of the Grand Harbor at Valletta. They're looking for a swap with somebody in California's San Diego or Palo Alto areas.

Naturally not everybody wants to give up the bright city lights—a 44-year-old tour manager hopes to exchange his one-bedroom apartment in the Spanish city of Barcelona for a New York address. So does a hockey scout who lives in Austria's capital, Vienna. A 25-year-old Danish student of cultural geography who lives in the Copenhagen suburb of Fredericksberg is looking to home swap "anywhere in North America."

In some cases, more than property is included in the exchange. Arrangements may include the family car—though participants will obviously need to make sure both insurance companies will provide coverage. If both sets of swappers agree, pets sometimes come as part of the package too. It may simply involve feeding an outdoor cat once a day, but some families seem to be operating a small private zoo! If you fancy caring for three cats, one guinea pig, one hamster, and two budgies, another Irish exchanger in county Wicklow is open to suggestions from other pet-lovers around the world.

Be prepared to spend a fair bit of time writing letters or telephoning before making a final commitment. Are there shops within walking distance? Is the garden safe for kids? Does the other family have a greenhouse filled with plants to water? Is your own home a smoke-free zone? If home-swapping does sound appealing, ensure all the nitty-gritty questions have been asked and answered well before Exchange Day.

Utility bills? In general, owners pay for gas, fuel, and electricity; guests pay for their own telephone calls. However, if it's a six-month exchange over the winter, you may prefer to come to another arrangement. And remember that unlike a normal holiday, arrangements can't be left until the last minute. So make plans *months* in advance rather than weeks.

You can contact Europeans looking for North American exchanges through these international agencies.

Home Exchange COM, P.O. Box 30085, Santa Barbara, CA 93130, 800/877-8723, fax 805/898-9199, www.HomeExchange.com, email: cs@HomeExchange.com.

Intervac USA, Lori Horne & Paula Jaffe, 30 Corte San Fernando, Tiburon, CA 94920, 800/756-4663, www.intervacus.com, email: info@intervacus.com.

Intervac Canada, Suzanne Cassin, 606 Alexander Crescent NW, Calgary, Alberta T2M 4T3, 403/284-3747, fax 403/284-3747, email: sc@intervac.ca.

HomeLink International, Karl Costabel, P.O. Box 650, Key West, FL 33041, 800/638-3841, fax 813/910-8144, www.swapnow.com, email: usa@homelink.org.

Green Theme International Home Exchange, Lower Milltown, Nr Lostwithiel, Cornwall PL22 0JL, England, tel. 44/0-1208-873123, www.gti-home-exchange.com.

Home Base Holidays, 7 Park Avenue, London N13 5PG, England, tel. 44/0-208-886-8752, www.homebase-hols.com.

The International Home Exchange Network, 118 Flamingo Avenue, Daytona Beach, FL 32118, tel. 386/238-3633, email: linda@ihen.com.

Metric Conversion Table

WEIGHT

	IMPERIAL METRIC
1 oz (ounce)	28.3 grams
1 lb (pound)	454.0 grams
3.5 oz	100.0 grams
2.2 pounds	1.0 kilo
1 stone (14 pounds)	6.36 kilos

LENGTH

1 inch	25.4 millimeters (mm)
1 foot	30.5 centimeters (cm)
1 yard	0.914 meters (m)
1 mile (1,760 yards)	1.61 kilometers (km)
0.39 inches	1.0 centimeter
3.28 feet	1.0 meter
0.62 miles	1.0 kilometer

VOLUME

1 pint	568 milliliters
1 gallon	4.55 liters
1.76 pints	1.0 liter

(An Imperial gallon is larger than the U.S. gallon of 3.79 liters)

AREA

1 square foot	929 square cms
1 square yard	0.836 square meters
1 acre	0.405 hectares
1 square mile	259 hectares
10.8 square feet	1.0 square meter
2.47 acres	1.0 hectare
247 acres	1 square kilometer

SPEED

1 mph	1.61 km/h
0.621 mph	1.00 km/h

TEMPERATURE

Centigrade to Fahrenheit: multiply by 1.8 then add 32.
Fahrenheit to Centigrade: subtract 32 then multiply by 5/9.

Clothing and Shoe Sizes

Clothing and shoe sizes may initially seem a bit confusing. My advice is try before you buy. Although size labels on clothes throughout mainland Europe are obviously different, Irish/UK sizes are a trap for the unwary. Women's sizes are larger than in the United States, so don't buy straight from the rack—you may find the kids can use your new dress as a tent on outdoor camping expeditions!

WOMEN'S CLOTHING

American	8	10	12	14	16	18	20
Irish/UK	10	12	14	16	18	20	22
European	36	38	40	42	44	46	48

MEN'S SUITS AND JACKETS

American	34	36	38	40	42	44	46
Irish/UK	34	36	38	40	42	44	46
European	44	46	48	50	52	54	56

SHIRT COLLAR SIZES

American	14	14.5	15	15.5	16	16.5	17
Irish/UK	14	14.5	15	15.5	16	16.6	17
European	36	37	38	39	40	41	42

WOMEN'S SHOES

American	6	6.5	7	7.5	8	8.5	9
Irish/UK	4.5	5	5.5	6	6.5	7	7.5
European	36	37	38	38	38	39	40

MEN'S SHOES

American	6.5	7.5	8.5	9.5	10.5	11.5	12.5
Irish/UK	6	7	8	9	10	11	12
European	40	41	42	43	44	45	46

Index

A

accommodations: Cyprus, 184-185;
Malta, 186-187. *see also* home
exchange; long-term rentals; vacation
rentals.
advance bookings, 10
advantages of renting, 6-8
agriturismo properties, 161
Algarve, 222-225
Alsace, 77-79
amber, 247
Amsterdam, 87-90
Andalucia, 200-202
Århus, 240-241
arriving at the rental, 11
arrondissements, 70-71
Athens, 176-177
Austria, 127-139: banks, 132; embassies,
128; grocery costs, 132; health care,
131-132; Kitzbuhel, 138; language,
128-129; legalities, 128; long-term
rentals, 131; rental agreements, 131;
residency permits, 128; Salzburg,
134-135; Seefeld, 138; tourist offices,
128; transportation costs, 132; Tyrol,
136-139; vacation rentals, 129-131;
Vienna, 132-134; visas, 128;
Vorarlberg, 136-139

B

Balearic Islands, 208-210
banks/banking hours: Austria, 132; Belgium, 98; Denmark, 236; France, 68;
Germany, 112; Great Britain, 25;
Greece, 175; Ireland, 45; Italy, 157;
Netherlands, 87; Norway, 250; Portugal, 216-217; Spain, 196; Sweden, 244;
Switzerland, 143
Barcelona, 202-204
Bavaria, 115-118
Belgium, 93-104: banks, 98; Bruges,
102-104; Brussels, 99-102; embassies,
94; grocery costs, 98; health care, 98;
language, 94-95; legalities, 93-94;
long-term rentals, 96-98; residency
permits, 93-94; tourist offices, 93;

transportation costs, 98; vacation
rentals, 95-96
Bergen, 252-253
Berlin, 112-115
Bokmal language: *see* Norwegian
language schools.
Britain: See Great Britain.
Bruges, 102-104
Brussels, 99-102

C

Cambridge, 32-35
Canadian embassies, 256-258
car rental, 12-13
Cascais, 221-222
Catalonia, 202-205
children, 15-16
classes, 34
Clerkenwell, 28
clothing sizes, 263
consulates, 256-258. *see also* embassies;
specific country.
contracts and agreements: *see* long-term
agreements; rental agreements; vacation rental agreements.
Copenhagen, 236-240
Cork (city and county), 48-50
Costa Brava, 204-205
Costa Del Sol, 198-200
Costa Verde (Portugal), 225-227
cost of living: See grocery costs;
transportation costs; utility costs.
Crete, 181-182
currencies, 14-15
Cyclades Islands, 177-181
Cyprus, 183-185: embassies, 184; legalities, 184; tourist offices, 184; visas, 184

D

Danish language schools, 233
definitions of foreign terms: France, 64;
Germany, 109; Greece, 171; Italy, 153;
Netherlands/Belgium, 83; Portugal,
213; Scandinavia, 233; Spain, 194
Den Haag: See The Hague.
Denmark, 232-241: Århus, 240-241;
banks, 236; Copenhagen, 236-240;

About the Author

Steenie Harvey lives in county Roscommon in the west of Ireland. Born in the United Kingdom of Latvian and English parents, she moved to Ireland in 1988 with her Scottish husband Michael and their daughter Magdalen. After renting a house for a year, Steenie and her family decided to buy their own Irish property—a hilltop cottage overlooking the magical waters of Lough Key.

A freelance writer, Steenie writes about travel, folklore, and real estate for publications both at home and abroad. Her U.S. magazine credits include *The World of Hibernia, The World & I,* and *International Living;* she was IL's "Travel Writer of the Year" in 1997. Recent travels have taken her to the Greek islands, the jungles of Malaysian Borneo, and eastern Germany.

Along with delving into Ireland's Celtic heritage, Steenie also enjoys opera, organic gardening, and countryside hikes.

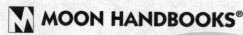

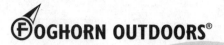

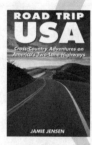